Fodor's
Chicago

Fodor's Travel Publications, Inc.
New York and London

1-1991 ed.

Fodor's Chicago

Editor: Jillian Magalaner
Editorial Contributors: Bob Blake, Paul A. Camp, Elizabeth Gardner, Dominic A. Pacyga, Carolyn Price, Linda K. Schmidt, Barbara Shortt, Doris L. Taub
Art Director: Fabrizio La Rocca
Cartographer: David Lindroth
Illustrators: Joseph Sipri, Karl Tanner
Cover Photograph: Brooks/Masterfile

Design: Vignelli Associates

Special Sales

Contents

Foreword

The Chicago most visitors see first is the commercial and cultural heart of the city, the Downtown and Near North areas that contain the world-famous architecture, the impressive skyline, the department stores, major hotels, and fine restaurants that together define a great American city. This Chicago is the primary focus of the present guide, which takes an entirely new look at the town, gives extensive new information on places to stay, and provides new reviews of more than 120 recommended places to eat throughout the city.

Yet there is another, equally interesting Chicago, a vibrant Chicago of the neighborhoods and their distinctive populations, and this guide takes the reader into some of those neighborhoods and shows how the tides of immigration have led to change, development, and curious ethnic juxtapositions. Quite a few of the restaurants recommended here are located in those neighborhoods, too.

Fodor's Chicago 1991, through its walking tours and essays, examines the two Chicagos—the downtown and the neighborhoods—and tries to suggest the greater political and human entity that is the foremost city of the American Middle West.

While every care has been taken to assure the accuracy of the information in this guide, the passage of time will always bring change, and consequently the publisher cannot accept responsibility for errors that may occur.

All prices and opening times quoted here are based on information supplied to us at press time. Hours and admission fees may change, however, and the prudent traveler will avoid inconvenience by calling ahead.

Fodor's wants to hear about your travel experiences, both pleasant and unpleasant. When a hotel or restaurant fails to live up to its billing, let us know and we will investigate the complaint and revise our entries where the facts warrant it.

Send your letters to the editors of Fodor's Travel Publications, 201 East 50th Street, New York, NY 10022.

Highlights '91 and Fodor's Choice

Highlights '91

Chicago's hotel-building spree, which added more than 2,000 rooms to the city's supply during the '80s, has not abated in the '90s. Two all-suite hotels, Guest Quarters and Hyatt Regency Suites, were due to open during 1990, adding almost 700 rooms to the Michigan Avenue area. The 600-room Stouffer Riviera Hotel is slated to open later this year in the north Loop at Wacker Drive and State Street, and the 1,200-room Sheraton Chicago is on the board for a 1992 opening at Columbus Drive and the Chicago River.

A 322-suite Embassy Suites Hotel is expected to open late this year at State and Ohio streets, continuing the rejuvenation of a formerly neglected corridor, consisting largely of parking lots, between Michigan Avenue and Clark Street, north of the Chicago River. The shiny new headquarters of the American Medical Association at Wabash Avenue and Grand Avenue, completed in 1990, helped spark a renaissance of the area, and it's likely to see much skyscraper construction in the coming years.

Chicago faces a mayoral race in 1991, though at this writing Mayor Richard M. Daley seems like a safe bet for reelection. He won an interim election in 1989 over acting mayor Eugene Sawyer, who took office in the aftermath of Harold Washington's untimely death in 1987. Washington was the city's first black mayor, and Sawyer was the second. The city's voters often polarize along color lines first, with an almost 50–50 split between black and white. Black voters were unable to unite behind a candidate in 1989, and Daley swept into office partly because of that dissension, though being the son of another long-time Chicago mayor, Richard J. Daley, didn't hurt. He was previously state's attorney. Mayor Daley's term has been relatively placid, and he seems to have left behind the nickname "Richie."

In sports, the 1991 White Sox are due to play their first game in a brand-new stadium built across the street from Comiskey Park, the oldest ballpark in the major leagues. Many baseball fans are shedding belated tears over the scheduled razing of the old park (though few stepped up to defend it during the debate over building the new one) and several proposals have been made to preserve the facade.

The Chicago Bears are angling for a new stadium to replace the gusty and occasionally foggy Soldier Field, a graceful, pillared structure on the lakefront, north of McCormick Place. One proposal—dubbed "McDome"—would incorporate a domed arena into the expansion of that already enormous convention center. The new construction would displace a venerable Chicago institution, the R.R. Don-

nelley printing plant, as well as many smaller businesses. At this writing, the proposal has been shelved by
the legislature in the wake of a debate over who will pay for
the $1.3 billion project. Another proposal would put much
of the burden on tourists, with extra taxes on hotels, restaurants, and rental cars. Like other big-ticket Chicago
items, McDome has awakened the resentment of the rest of
Illinois, which is largely rural and resents footing the bill
for urban problems.

The fate of Navy Pier, another such item, remains up in the
air as well. An elegant but decrepit structure jutting almost a mile into Lake Michigan, the pier is now used largely
as a recreation area. It needs more than $100 million in re-
pairs just to keep it safe, and that probably means the pier
will have to produce more income than it does now from a
handful of special events. The Metropolitan Pier and Exposition Authority has studied several proposals to make it an
entertainment/shopping complex, but no action has been
taken. At this writing, a stop-gap $40 million allocation for
repairs has been rejected in Springfield.

Competition is heated over where to build a proposed third
airport for the Chicago area, to ease the congestion at
O'Hare and Midway. The $3 billion facility, wherever it is,
would probably not be operational much before the year
2,000, but it's an economic plum worth billions of dollars
and thousands of jobs to the winning location. A joint
Illinois-Indiana committee has proposed either expansion
of Gary, Indiana, Regional Airport or a brand-new facility
south of Chicago, near the Indiana border. At this writing,
Mayor Daley favors a site on Lake Calumet, on the southeast side, that would displace the residents of a stable blue-
collar neighborhood, but would keep the airport within the
city limits.

The Chicago Symphony Orchestra is facing a change as 22-
year maestro Sir Georg Solti passes the baton to Daniel
Barenboim at the beginning of the 1991–92 season. Barenboim conducts frequently during the 1990–91 season as
well, giving Chicago music lovers a chance to see how a new
leader will influence one of the world's great orchestras. In-
itial opposition by some local critics to Barenboim's appointment seems to have died down.

After several years of negotiation, the Steppenwolf Theater Company is due to transplant its brooding and sometimes brutal American brand of acting to a glossy new
theater at North Avenue and Halsted Street, abandoning a
cramped storefront farther north. The company was hon-
ored in 1990 with a Tony award for its New York production
of John Steinbeck's *The Grapes of Wrath*.

Fodor's Choice

No two people will agree on what makes a perfect vacation, but it's fun and helpful to know what others think. We hope you'll have a chance to experience some of Fodor's Choices yourself while visiting Chicago. For detailed information about each entry, refer to the appropriate chapters in this guidebook.

Activities

Watching the animals in a "thunderstorm" in the rain forest at the Brookfield Zoo

Singing "Take Me Out to the Ballgame" during the seventh-inning stretch at Wrigley Field

Exploring the tomb of Unis-ankh in "Inside Ancient Egypt," the new permanent exhibit at the Field Museum of Natural History

Turn-of-the-Century Architecture

Fisher Building

Robie House

The Rookery

Modern Architecture

Northwestern Atrium Center

State of Illinois Center

333 North Wacker Drive

Moments

Feeding time at the coral reef of the John G. Shedd Aquarium

The winter orchid show at the Chicago Botanic Garden

The skylit sculpture court at the Art Institute

Sights

Chicago skyline from the Halsted Street Bridge

Chicago skyline from Olive Park

Chicago skyline from South Lake Shore Drive

The panoramic view of the city from the top of the John Hancock Building

Hotels

The Drake (*Very Expensive*)

Chicago Hilton and Towers (*Expensive–Very Expensive*)

The Raphael (*Moderate–Expensive*)

Restaurants

The Everest Room (French, *Very Expensive*)

La Tour (French, *Very Expensive*)

Le Francais (French, *Very Expensive*)

Charlie Trotter's (American, *Expensive–Very Expensive*)

Hatsuhana (Japanese, *Moderate–Expensive*)

House of Hunan (Chinese, *Moderate–Expensive*)

Arun's (Thai, *Moderate*)

Frontera Grill (Mexican, *Moderate*)

Ed Debevic's (American 1950s, *Inexpensive*)

Gin Go Gae (Korean, *Inexpensive*)

Northeastern Illinois

WISCONSIN

0   10 miles
0   15 km

Channel Lake   *Loon Lake*

Grass Lake

Zion

Old Mill Creek   Wadsworth

Pistakee Lake

Lake Villa

Fox Lake   Druce Lake

Waukegan

McHenry   Gurnee

North Chicago

Lake Michigan

Volo

Ivanhoe   Lake Bluff

Wauconda   Libertyville   Lake Forest

Mundelein   Highwood

Lake Zurich   Highland Park

Barrington Hills   Buffalo Grove   Deerfield   Glencoe

Carpentersville   Northbrook   Winnetka

Dundee   Arlington Heights   Kenilworth   Wilmette

Schaumburg   Mount Prospect   Glenview

Elgin   Des Plaines   Evanston

Morton Grove   Skokie

Chicago-O'Hare International Airport   Park Ridge

Franklin Park

CHICAGO

West Chicago   Villa Park   River Forest

Wheaton   Lombard   Elmhurst   Oak Park

Glen Ellyn

Warrenville   Berwyn   Cicero

Aurora   Downers Grove   Chicago Midway Airport

Darien   Bedford Park

Burbank   Evergreen Park

Orland Park   Riverdale

Plainfield   Lockport   Calumet City

Marley   Homewood   Lansing

Joliet   Chicago Heights

Park Forest

N

INDIANA

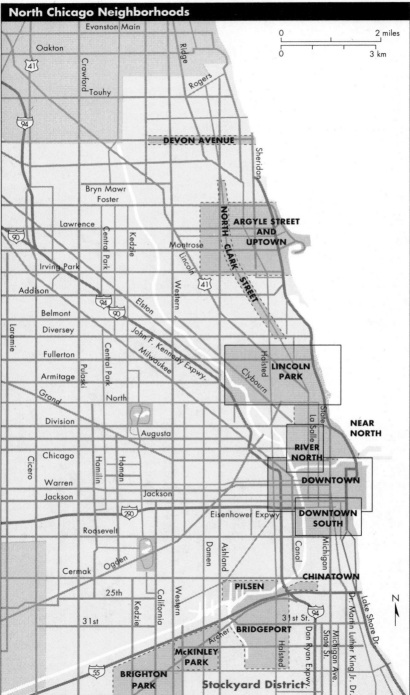

North Chicago Neighborhoods

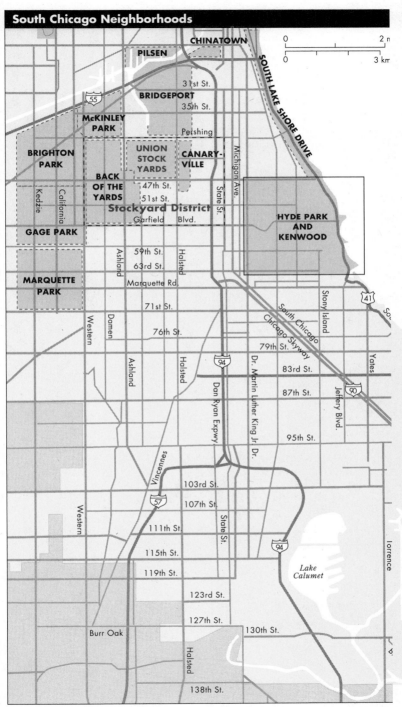

South Chicago Neighborhoods

CHINATOWN

PILSEN

BRIDGEPORT

31st St.

35th St.

McKINLEY PARK

Pershing

BRIGHTON PARK

UNION STOCK YARDS

CANARY-VILLE

BACK OF THE YARDS

Michigan Ave.

State St.

47th St.

51st St.

Kedzie

California

Stockyard District

Garfield Blvd.

GAGE PARK

HYDE PARK AND KENWOOD

Ashland

59th St.

63rd St.

Halsted

MARQUETTE PARK

Marquette Rd.

71st St.

Stony Island

Damen

76th St.

US 41

Western

79th St.

South Chicago Skyway

Yates

I-94

83rd St.

Dr. Martin Luther King Jr. Dr.

87th St.

Jeffery Blvd.

I-90

Ashland

Halsted

Dan Ryan Expwy

95th St.

Vincennes

103rd St.

I-57

107th St.

111th St.

Western

State St.

115th St.

I-94

119th St.

Lake Calumet

Torrence

123rd St.

127th St.

Burr Oak

130th St.

Halsted

138th St.

0   2 n

0   3 km

SOUTH LAKE SHORE DRIVE

I-55

World Time Zones

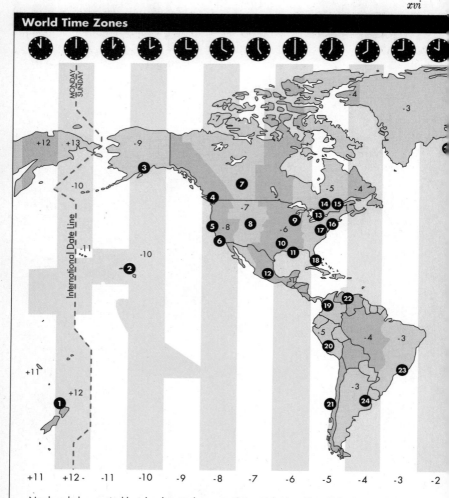

+12 +13 -9 -10 -11 -10

International Date Line

MONDAY
SUNDAY

-4 -3

-7 -5 -4

-5 -4

-7 -8 -6

-6

+11

+12

-5

-4 -3

-5

-3

-3

| +11 | +12 - | -11 | -10 | -9 | -8 | -7 | -6 | -5 | -4 | -3 | -2 |

Numbers below vertical bands relate each zone to Greenwich Mean Time (0 hrs.).
Local times frequently differ from these general indications,
as indicated by light-face numbers on map.

Algiers, **29**
Anchorage, **3**
Athens, **41**
Auckland, **1**
Baghdad, **46**
Bangkok, **50**
Beijing, **54**

Berlin, **34**
Bogotá, **19**
Budapest, **37**
Buenos Aires, **24**
Caracas, **22**
Chicago, **9**
Copenhagen, **33**
Dallas, **10**

Delhi, **48**
Denver, **8**
Djakarta, **53**
Dublin, **26**
Edmonton, **7**
Hong Kong, **56**
Honolulu, **2**

Istanbul, **40**
Jerusalem, **42**
Johannesburg, **44**
Lima, **20**
Lisbon, **28**
London (Greenwich), **27**
Los Angeles, **6**
Madrid, **38**
Manila, **57**

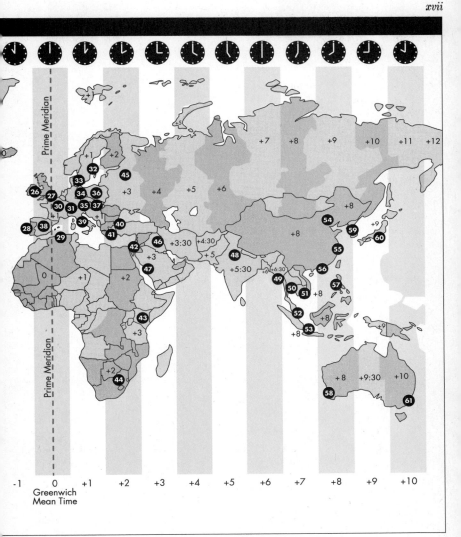

Mecca, **47**
Mexico City, **12**
Miami, **18**
Montreal, **15**
Moscow, **45**
Nairobi, **43**
New Orleans, **11**
New York City, **16**

Ottawa, **14**
Paris, **30**
Perth, **58**
Reykjavík, **25**
Rio de Janeiro, **23**
Rome, **39**
Saigon, **51**

San Francisco, **5**
Santiago, **21**
Seoul, **59**
Shanghai, **55**
Singapore, **52**
Stockholm, **32**
Sydney, **61**
Tokyo, **60**

Toronto, **13**
Vancouver, **4**
Vienna, **35**
Warsaw, **36**
Washington, DC, **17**
Yangon, **49**
Zürich, **31**

Introduction

by Studs Terkel

A writer, a broadcaster, and of late a film actor, Studs Terkel has come to be a virtual symbol of Chicago. His newest collection of oral histories is The Great Divide: Second Thoughts on the American Dream.

Janus, the two-faced god, has both blessed and cursed the city-state Chicago. Though his graven image is not visible to the naked eye, his ambiguous spirit soars atop Sears, Big Stan, and Big John. (Our city is street-wise and alley-hip of the casually familiar. Thus the Standard Oil Building and the John Hancock are, with tavern gaminess, referred to as Big Stan and Big John. Sears is simply that; never mind Roebuck. Ours is a one-syllable town. Its character has been molded by the muscle rather than the word.)

Our double-vision, double-standard, double-value, and double-cross have been patent ever since—at least, ever since the earliest of our city fathers took the Pottawattomies for all they had. Poetically, these dispossessed natives dubbed this piece of turf *Chikagou*. Some say it is Indian lingo for "City of the Wild Onion"; some say it really means "City of the Big Smell." "Big" is certainly the operative word around these parts.

Nelson Algren's classic *Chicago: City on the Make* is the late poet's single-hearted vision of his town's doubleness. "Chicago . . . forever keeps two faces, one for winners and one for losers; one for hustlers and one for squares . . . One face for Go-Getters and one for Go-Get-It-Yourselfers. One for poets and one for promoters. . . . One for early risers, one for evening hiders."

It is the city of Jane Addams, settlement worker, and Al Capone, entrepreneur; of Clarence Darrow, lawyer, and Julius Hoffman, judge; of Louis Sullivan, architect, and Sam Insull, magnate; of John Altgeld, governor, and Paddy Bauler, alderman. (Paddy's the one who some years ago observed, "Chicago ain't ready for reform." It is echoed in our day by another, less paunchy alderman, Fast Eddie.)

Now, with a new kind of mayor, whose blackness is but one variant of the Chicago norm, and a machine—which like the old gray mare ain't what it used to be—creaking its expected way, all bets are off. Race, though the dominant theme, is but one factor.

It is still the arena of those who dream of the City of Man and those who envision a City of Things. The battle appears to be forever joined. The armies, ignorant and enlightened, clash by day as well as night. Chicago is America's dream, writ large. And flamboyantly.

This essay is drawn from Studs Terkel's Chicago, *which was originally published in 1986, when the late Harold Washington was mayor of Chicago.*

It has—as they used to whisper of the town's fast woman—a reputation.

Elsewhere in the world, anywhere, name the city, name the country, Chicago evokes one image above all others. Sure, architects and those interested in such matters mention Louis Sullivan, Frank Lloyd Wright, and Mies van der Rohe. Hardly anyone in his right mind questions this city as the architectural Athens. Others, literary critics among them, mention Dreiser, Norris, Lardner, Algren, Farrell, Bellow, and the other Wright, Richard. Sure, Mencken did say something to the effect that there is no American literature worth mentioning that didn't come out of the palatinate that is Chicago. Of course, a special kind of jazz and a blues, acoustic rural and electrified urban, have been called Chicago style. All this is indubitably true.

Still others, for whom history has stood still since the Democratic convention of 1968, murmur: Mayor Daley. (As our most perceptive chronicler, Mike Royko, has pointed out, the name has become the eponym for city chieftain; thus, it is often one word, "Maredaley.") The tone, in distant quarters as well as here, is usually one of awe; you may interpret it any way you please.

An English Midlander, bearing a remarkable resemblance to Nigel Bruce, encounters me under London's Marble Arch: "Your mayor is my kind of chap. He should have bashed the heads of those young ruffians, though he did rather well, I thought." I tell him that Richard J. Daley died several years ago and that our incumbent mayor is black. He finds this news somewhat startling.

"Really?" He recovers quickly: "Nonetheless, I do like your city. I was there some thirty-odd years ago. Black, is he?"

Yeah, I tell him, much of the city is.

He is somewhat Spenglerian as he reflects on the decline of Western values. "Thank heavens, I'll not be around when they take over, eh?"

I nod. I'm easy to get along with. "You sound like Saul Bellow," I say.

"Who?"

"Our Nobel laureate. Do you realize that our University of Chicago has produced more Nobel Prize winners than any other in the world?"

"Really?"

"Yeah."

He returns to what appears to be his favorite subject: gumption. "Your mayor had it. I'm delighted to say that our lady prime minister has it, too."

I am suddenly weary. Too much Bells Reserve, I'm afraid. "So long, sir. I'll see you in Chicago."

"Not likely; not bloody likely."

In Munich, a student of the sixties, now somewhat portly and balding, ventures an opinion. Not that I asked him. Chicago does that to strangers as well as natives.

"Your Mayor Daley vas bwutal to those young pwotesters, vasn't he?"

Again I nod. Vat could I say?

But it isn't Daley whose name is the Chicago hallmark. Nor Darrow. Nor Wright. Nor is it either of the Janes, Addams or Byrne. It's Al Capone, of course.

In a Brescian trattoria, to Italy's north, a wisp of an old woman, black shawl and all, hears where I'm from. Though she has some difficulty with English (far less than I have with Italian), she thrusts both hands forward, index fingers pointed at me: *Boom, boom,* she goes. I hold up my hands. We both laugh. It appears that Jimmy Cagney, Edward G. Robinson, and Warner Brothers have done a real job in image making.

Not that Al and his colleagues didn't have palmy days during what, to others, were parlous times. Roaring Twenties or Terrible Thirties, the goose always hung high for the Boys. I once asked a casual acquaintance, the late Doc Graham, for a résumé. Doc was, as he modestly put it, a dedicated heist man. His speech was a composite of Micawber and Runyon:

"The unsophisticated either belonged to the Bugs Moran mob or the Capone mob. The fellas with talent didn't belong to either one. We robbed both."

Wasn't that a bit on the risky side?

"Indeed. There ain't hardly a one of us survived the Biblical threescore and ten. You see this fellow liquidated, that fellow—shall we say, disposed of? Red McLaughlin was the toughest guy in Chicago. But when you seen Red run out of the drainage canal, you realized Red's *modus operandi* was unavailing. His associates was Clifford and Adams. They were set in Al's doorway in his hotel in Cicero. That was unavailing."

Was it a baseball bat Al used?

"You are doubtless referring to Anselmi and Scalisi. They offended Al. This was rare. Al Capone usually sublet the matter. Since I'm Irish, I had a working affiliate with Bugs Moran. Did you know that Red and his partners once stole the Checker Cab Company? They took machine guns, went up, and had an election. I assisted in that operation."

What role did the forces of law and order play?

"With a bill, you wasn't bothered. If you had a speaking acquaintance with Mayor Thompson, you could do no wrong. Al spoke loud to him." . . .

Chicago is not the most corrupt of cities. The state of New Jersey has a couple. Need we mention Nevada? Chicago, though, is the Big Daddy. Not more corrupt, just more theatrical, more colorful in its shadiness.

It's an attribute of which many of our Respectables are, I suspect, secretly proud. Something to chat about in languorous moments. Perhaps something to distract from whatever tangential business might have engaged them.

Consider Marshall Field the First. The merchant prince. In 1886, the fight for the eight-hour day had begun, here in Chicago. Anarchists, largely German immigrants, were in the middle of it for one reason or another.

There was a mass meeting; a bomb was thrown; to this day, nobody knows who did it. There was a trial. The Haymarket Eight were in the dock. With hysteria pervasive— newspaper headlines wild enough to make Rupert Murdoch blush—the verdict was in. Guilty.

Before four of them were executed, there was a campaign, worldwide, for a touch of mercy. Even the judge, passionate though he was in his loathing of the defendants, was amenable. A number of Chicago's most respected industrialists felt the same way. Hold off the hooded hangman. Give 'em life, what the hell. It was Marshall Field I who saw to it that they swung. Hang the bastards. Johnny Da Pow had nothing on him when it came to power.

Lucy Parsons, the youngest widow of the most celebrated of the hangees, Albert—an ex-soldier of the Confederacy —lived to be an old, old woman. When she died in the forties and was buried at Waldheim Cemetery, my old colleague Win Stracke sang at the services. Though Parsons sang "Annie Laurie" on his way to the gallows, Win sounded off with "Joe Hill." It was a song, he said, that Lucy liked. When I shake hands with Win, I shake hands with history. That's what I call continuity.

The Janus-like aspect of Chicago appeared in the being of John Peter Altgeld. One of his first acts as governor of Illinois in 1893 was an 18,000-word message, citing chapter and verse, declaring the trial a frame-up. He pardoned the three survivors. The fourth had swallowed a dynamite cap while in the pokey.

Though it ended his political life. Altgeld did add a touch of class to our city's history. He was remembered by Vachel Lindsay as Eagle Forgotten. Some kid, majoring in something other than business administration or computer programming, might come across this poem in some anthology. Who knows? He might learn something about eagles.

Eagles are a diminished species today, here as well as elsewhere. On occasion, they are spotted in unexpected air pockets. Hawks, of course, abound, here as well as elsewhere. Some say this is their glory time. So Dow-Jones tells us. Observe the boys and girls in commodities. Ever ride the La Salle Street bus? Bright and morning faces; *Wall Street Journals* neatly folded. The New Gatsbys, Bob Tamarkin calls them. Gracelessness under pressure.

Sparrows, as always, are the most abundant of our city birds. It is never glory time for them. As always, they do the best they can. Which isn't very much. They forever peck away and, in some cock-eyed fashion, survive the day. Others—well, who said life was fair? They hope, as the old spiritual goes, that His eye is on all the sparrows and that He watches over them. And you. And me . . .

On a hot summer day, the lake behaves, the beach is busy, and thousands find cool delight. All within sight of places where ads are created telling you Wendy's is better than Burger King, where computers compute like crazy, and where billions of pages are Xeroxed for one purpose or another, or for no purpose at all. All within one neighborhood. It's crazy and phenomenal. No other city in the world has a neighborhood like this. Visitors, no matter how weary-of-it-all and jaded, are always overawed. You feel pretty good; and, like a spoiled débutante, you wave a limp hand and murmur: It *is* rather impressive, isn't it? . . .

But those damn bridges. Though I haven't searched out any statistics, I'll bet Chicago has more bridges than Paris. When up they go and all traffic stops, you lean against the railing and watch the boats: pulp paper from Canada for the *Trib* and *Sun-Times*, and ore from where?—the Mesabi iron range?—and all sorts of tugs easing all sorts of lake vessels, bearing all sorts of heavy stuff, big-shouldered stuff. You may not feel particularly chesty, yet there's a slight stirring, a feeling of Chicago's connection with elsewhere.

However—and what an infuriating however—when a lone sailboat comes through with two beautiful people sporting Acapulco or Palm Beach tan, she in a bikini and he in Calvin Klein shorts, and the two, with the casualness and vast carelessness of a Tom and Daisy Buchanan, wave at the held-up secretaries, file clerks, and me, I look around for a rock to throw, only to realize I'm not Walter Johnson, and I settle for a mumbled *sonofabitch* and I'm late for lunch. *Sonofabitch.*

There's no other city like this, I tell you.

And taxi drivers.

When, in eighth-grade geography, Miss O'Brien, her wig slightly askew, quizzed you ferociously on populations of the world's great cities, you had to, with equal ferocity, look them up in the atlas. Thanks to Third World hackies, you can save an enormous amount of time and energy.

You peek up front toward the driver and you see the name Ahmed Eqbal. Naturally, you ask him what's the population of Karachi and he tells you. With great enthusiasm. If his surname is Kim, you'll find out that Seoul is close to seven million. If the man driving at an interesting speed is Marcus Olatunji, you might casually offer that Ibadan is bigger than Lagos, isn't it? If his name has as many syllables as a Welsh town's, you simply ask if Bangkok has changed much; has its population really experienced an exponential growth?

Of course, all short cuts to knowledge have their shortcomings. Sometimes he'll whirl around, astonished, and in very, very precise British English ask, "How do you *know* that?" A brief cultural exchange ensues as suddenly you cry out, Watch out! We missed an articulated bus with a good one-tenth of an inch to spare. If it's a newspaper circulation truck, God help the two of us.

Chicago's traffic problem is hardly any problem at all—if you forget about storms, light rains, accidents, and road construction—when compared with other great cities. In contrast to New York's cacophony of honks and curses, ours is the song of the open road. Mexico City is not to be believed. Ever been to Paris where the driver snaps his fingers, frustrated, as you successfully hop back onto the curb? Need we mention the Angeleno freeway? . . .

So we're reminiscing about one thing or another, Verne and I. Vernon Jarrett knocks out a *Sun-Times* column: reflections of black life in Chicago and elsewhere. I can't get that Jubilee Night, '38, out of my mind. He tells me of that same celebratory moment in Paris, Tennessee, along the IC tracks. Hallelujah and hope. We see our reflections in the mirror behind the bar and neither of us looks too hopeful. Hallelujah for what?

"The ghetto used to have something going for it," he says. "It had a beat, it had a certain rhythm and it was all hope. I don't care how rough things were. They used to say, If you can't make it in Chicago, you can't make it anywhere. You may be down today; you're gonna be back up tomorrow."

The lyric of an old blues song is rolling around in my head like a loose cannonball:

I'm troubled in mind, baby, I'm so blue,
But I won't be blue always
You know the sun, the sun gonna shine
In my back door someday.

"You had the packinghouses going, you had the steel mills going, you had secondary employment to help you 'get over.'"

Oh, there's still a Back of the Yards, all right, but where are the yards? And Steeltown. Ever visit South Chicago these days? Smokestacks with hardly an intimation of smoke. A town as silent, as dead as the Legionnaires' fortress in *Beau Geste*. Where the executioner's ax fell upon Jefferson and Johnson as upon Stasiak, Romano, and Polowski.

"Now it's a drag," says Verne. "There are thousands of people who have written off their lives. They're serving out their sentences as though there were some supreme judge who said, 'You're sentenced to life imprisonment on earth and this is your cell here.' What do you do if you've got a live sentence? You play jailhouse politics. You hustle, you sell dope, you browbeat other people, you abuse other cellmates, you turn men into weaklings, and girls you overcome.

"If I'm feeling good and want to have my morale lowered, all I have to do is drive out Madison Street on a bright, beautiful day and look at the throng of unemployed young guys in the weird dress, trying to hang on to some individuality. Can't read or write; look mean at each other. You see kids hating themselves as much as they hate others. This is one thing that's contributed to the ease with which gangs kill each other. Another nigger ain't nothin'."

Is it possible that ol' Hightower, the pub-crawling buddy of Dude and me during those Jubilee hours on a June night so long ago, has a signifying grandson among the wretched and lost on some nonsignified corner somewhere on the West Side?

From the year one we've heard Lord Acton cited: Power corrupts and absolute power corrupts absolutely. You're only half right, Your Lordship, if that. In a town like Chicago, Johnny Da Pow and a merchant prince and, in our day, a Croatian Sammy Glick run much of the turf because of another kind of corruption: the one Verne Jarrett observed. Powerlessness corrupts and absolute powerlessness corrupts absolutely. You see, Lord A knew nothing of Cabrini-Green. Or—*memento mori*—47th and South Parkway, with exquisite irony renamed Martin Luther King, Jr., Drive. Mine eyes haven't seen much glory lately.

However—there's always a however in the city Janus watches over . . .

Somethin's happenin' out there not covered by the six-o'clock news or a Murdoch headline. There is a percolating and bubbling in certain neighborhoods that may presage unexpected somethings for the up-againsters. A strange something called self-esteem, springing from an even stranger something called sense of community.

Ask Nancy Jefferson. It happened at the Midwest Community Council on the West Side. She's director of this grass-roots organization. "This morning I had a young man. He had taken some money from us. I didn't think I'd see him again. I spread the warning: 'Watch out; he's a bad egg.' Today, out of the clear blue sky, he walked into my office. He says, 'I want to pay back my debt at fifty dollars a month. I've gotten a job. I didn't want to see you until I got a job.' I didn't know what made him come back. Was it the spirit of the community?"

In South Chicago, a bit to the southeast, Fast Eddie is finding out about UNO. That's the United Neighborhood Organization. While the alderman was busy giving Harold a hard time, his Hispanic constituents in the Tenth Ward were busy giving Waste Management, Inc., a hard time. The multinational toxic dumper was about to dump some of the vile stuff in the neighborhood. Hold off, big boy, said Mary Ellen Montez, a twenty-six-year-old housewife. So far, she and her neighbors are doing a far better job than Horatio ever did at the bridge.

UNO's grassroots power is being felt in Pilsen, too, where rehabs are springing up without the dubious touch of gentrification. The community folk are there because they're there and that's where they intend to stay. No shoving out in these parts. And no yuppies need apply.

Farther west, the South Austin Community Council, when not challenging joblessness and street crime, has sent housewives and suddenly redundant steelworkers to Springfield as well as to City Hall to lobby for the Affordable Budget, so that gas and electric bills don't destroy those whom God has only slightly blessed with means. They're not waiting for the hacks to fight for it; they're do-it-yourselfers.

Talk about fighting redundancy, the Metro Seniors are among the most militant. Never mind the wheelchairs, crutches, tea, and sympathy. They bang away everywhere, with or without canes and walkers: Keep your grubby hands off Medicare and Social Security. Ever hear of the time they marched into official sanctums with a cake: Cut the cake but not the COLA (cost-of-living adjustment)? The hacks ate that cake more slowly and thoughtfully than ever. There are 7,500 such scrappers in town, the youngest sixty-five. They may not have heard "Me and Bobby McGee," but they sure know the lyric: "Freedom's just another word for nothin' left to lose."

All sorts of new people from Central America and Southeast Asia, together with the more settled have-nots, are at it in Uptown with ONE (Organization of the North East). Tenants' rights, lousy housing, ethnic identity—name it; if it's an elementary right, they're battling for it.

And let's not forget all those nimble neighborhood organizers coming out of Heather Booth's Midwest Academy. Their style is sixties hipness, Saul Alinsky's Actions (political jujitsu, he called it), and eighties hard-earned awareness. They're all over town, astirring.

This is house-to-house, block-by-block, pavement-pounding, church-meeting, all-kinds-of-discussion stuff that may, as we wake up some great gettin'-up morning, reveal a new kind of Chicago. Nick Von Hoffman, who for a time was Alinsky's right arm, said it: "You who thought of yourself, up to that moment, as simply being a number, suddenly spring to life. You have that intoxicating feeling that you can make your own history, that you really count."

Call it a back-yard revolution if you want to. It will sure as hell confute the Johnny Da Pows of our day, the merchant princes and the Fast Eddies. And, incidentally, lay the ghost of Lord Acton: less powerlessness that corrupts and more power than may ennoble.

Perhaps mine eyes may yet see the glory.

1 Essential Information

Before You Go

Visitor Information

For information on the city, contact the **Chicago Tourism Council** (806 N. Michigan Ave., Water Tower in the Park, Chicago, IL 60611, tel. 312/280–5740).

If you plan on traveling outside Chicago, contact the **Illinois Office of Tourism** (310 S. Michigan Ave., Chicago, IL 60604, tel. 312/793–2094) for a free packet of brochures on travel in the state of Illinois.

Foreign travelers may wish to contact the **International Visitors Center** (520 N. Michigan Ave., Chicago, IL 60611, tel. 312/645–1836).

Tips for British Travelers

Passports You will need a valid 10-year passport. You do not need a visa if you are staying for less than 90 days, have a return ticket, and are flying with a participating airline. There are some exceptions, so check with your travel agent or with the **United States Embassy** (Visa and Immigration Department, 5 Upper Grosvenor St., London W1A 2JB, 071/499–3443).

No vaccinations are required for entry into the United States.

Customs Returning to Britain, you may bring home (1) 200 cigarettes or 100 cigarillos or 50 cigars or 250 grams of tobacco; (2) 2 liters of table wine and, in addition, (a) 1 liter of alcohol over 22% by volume (most spirits) or (b) 2 liters of alcohol under 22% by volume (fortified or sparkling wine); (3) 60 milliliters of perfume and ¼ liter of toilet water; and (4) other goods up to a value of £32.

Insurance We heartily recommend that you insure yourself to cover health and motoring mishaps with **Europe Assistance** (252 High St., Croydon CR0 1NF, tel. 081/680–1234). Their excellent service is all the more valuable when you consider the possible costs of health care in the United States.

Airfares We suggest that you explore the current scene for budget flight possibilities, including Virgin Atlantic Airways. Be warned, however, that these cut-rate flights are fiendishly hard to come by, so be sure to book well in advance. Check, also, on APEX and other money-saving fares, because, quite frankly, only business travelers who don't have to watch the price of their tickets fly full price these days—and find themselves sitting right beside an APEX passenger!

Tour Operators Among the many tour operators who offer packages to Chicago, you may like to consider some of these as you plan your trip:

American Airplan (Airplan House, Churchfield Rd., Walton-on-Thames, Surrey KT12 2TZ tel. 0932/246166).
North American Vacations (Acorn House, 172/174 Albert Rd., Jarrow, Tyne, & Wear NE32 5JA, tel. 091/483–6226).
Trek America (Trek House, The Bullring, Deddington, Oxford OX5 4TT, tel. 0869/38777).

Information Contact **United States Travel and Tourism Administration** (22 Sackville St., London W1X 2EA, tel. 071/439–7433).

When to Go

Chicago promises activities and attractions to keep any visitor busy at any time of year. Travelers whose principal concern is to have comfortable weather for touring the city may prefer spring or fall, when moderate temperatures can make it a pleasure to be out and about, and the city's cultural institutions are well into their seasons. Late fall has a special dividend for children of all ages in the lavish Christmas decorations in the stores of the Magnificent Mile and the State Street Mall.

Summertime brings many opportunities for outdoor recreation. Yet the temperatures will climb to the 90s in hot spells, and the humidity can be uncomfortably high. In more normal times the presence of Lake Michigan has a moderating effect on the city's weather, keeping it several degrees cooler in summer, a bit warmer in winter.

Those winters can see very raw weather and occasionally the news-making blizzard, and temperatures in the teens are to be expected; wintertime visitors should come prepared for the cold. Yet mild winters, with temperatures in the 30s, are common, too. There are January sales to reward those who venture out, and many indoor venues let one look out on the cold in warm comfort.

Climate What follows are the average daily maximum and minimum temperatures for Chicago.

Jan.	32F	0C	May	65F	18C	Sept.	73F	23C
	18	− 8		50	10		58	14
Feb.	34F	1C	June	75F	24C	Oct.	61F	16C
	20	− 7		60	16		47	8
Mar.	43F	6C	July	81F	27C	Nov.	47F	8C
	29	− 2		66	19		34	1
Apr.	55F	13C	Aug.	79F	26C	Dec.	36F	2C
	40	4		65	18		23	− 5

Updated hourly weather information in 750 cities around the world—450 of them in the United States—is only a phone call away. Dialing WeatherTrak, at tel. 900/370–8728, will connect you to a computer, with which you can communicate by touch tone—at a cost of 75¢ for the first minute and 50¢ a minute thereafter. A taped message will tell you to dial the three-digit access code to any of the 235 destinations. The code is either the area code (in the USA) or the first three letters of the foreign city. For a list of all access codes, send a stamped, self-addressed envelope to Cities, Box 7000, Dallas, TX 75209. For further information, call 214/869–3035 or 800/247–3282.

Festivals and Seasonal Events

Chicagoans love celebrations. They find occasions for them in anniversaries and events, and when those don't come up often enough, they will hold a celebration for no particular reason at all. Spring and summer are the festival seasons. The **International Theatre Festival** arrives in April during even-numbered years and stays for a month, presenting selections by talented writers and theater groups from around the world. Summer brings a multitude of art fairs, including the outstanding juried

Hyde Park Art Fair during the first weekend in June. Parades and neighborhood ethnic, cultural, and food fairs are almost weekly occurrences, capped by the granddaddy of them all, **A Taste of Chicago,** during the week of July 4. Columbus Drive between Jackson and Randolph is closed to traffic for the duration, and half a million people or more each day flock to sample the culinary offerings of scores of local purveyors. The 4th of July weekend is also the occasion for a splendid coordinated celebration by the Grant Park Symphony Orchestra and the City of Chicago: The city sets off an awesome fireworks display on the lakefront, providing the cannon sound effects for the Symphony's rendition of Tchaikovsky's *1812 Overture.*

The **James C. Petrillo Bandshell,** in Grant Park, is the site of outdoor music all summer, beginning with the **Blues and Gospel festivals** in mid-June, continuing with four performances weekly by the **Grant Park Symphony Orchestra and Chorus** in late June through the end of August, and ending with a week-long **Jazz festival.** Labor Day brings the *Chicago Tribune's* **Ribfest,** with some 500 avid barbecuers and their families and friends pitching grills, nursing briquettes, marinating slabs in secret concoctions, and generating a dense, aromatic cloud of hickory smoke seasoned with beer that hovers over the central city and the marchers in the **Labor Day parade.** Fall brings **Oktoberfest** to the Berghoff Restaurant downtown and to neighborhood watering holes around the city, providing a delightful way to end an evening spent at the **Chicago International Film Festival,** a three-week showing at the Music Box and Biograph theaters of distinguished new American and foreign films.

Celebrations move indoors for the winter. The Museum of Science and Industry mounts a **Christmas Around the World** show that displays trees decorated in the traditional styles of more than 40 countries. February chills are dispelled by the warmth of celebrations honoring **Black History Month,** with special exhibitions and music and dance performances at the Museum of Science and Industry, the DuSable Museum, the Chicago Cultural Center, and other institutions.

The following is a small sampling of the many events that Chicagoans and visitors alike enjoy each year. For precise dates and details, contact the Chicago Tourism Council (Historic Water Tower-in-the-Park, 806 N. Michigan Ave., Chicago, IL 60611, tel. 312/280–5740) or consult one of these excellent calendars of events for the weekend and the upcoming week: *The Reader,* a free weekly newspaper distributed on Thursdays in many stores in Hyde Park, the Loop, and the North Side; the Friday section of the Friday *Chicago Tribune;* and the "Weekender" section of the Friday *Chicago Sun-Times.*

Month of Feb. Black History Month celebrations at the Museum of Science and Industry (57th St. and Lake Shore Dr., tel. 312/684–1414), the DuSable Museum (740 E. 56th Pl., tel. 312/947–0600), the Chicago Cultural Center (78 E. Washington St., tel. 312/346–3278), the Field Museum (Roosevelt Rd. at Lake Shore Dr., tel. 312/332–8854), the Art Institute of Chicago (Michigan Ave. at Adams St., tel. 312/443–3600) and other Chicago cultural institutions include arts and crafts exhibitions and theater, music, and dance performances.

Mid-Feb.–Early Mar. Azalea and Camellia Show at Lincoln Park Conservatory (2400 N. Stockton Dr., tel. 312/294–4770).

Mid-Feb. Chicago International Auto Show previews the complement of next year's domestic and imported models (McCormick Pl., 2300 S. Lake Shore Dr., tel. 312/698–6630).

Late Feb.–mid-Mar. Medinah Shrine Circus at Medinah Temple (600 N. Wabash Ave., tel. 312/266–5000).

Mar. 17. The Chicago River is dyed green, and the center stripe of Dearborn Street is painted the color of the Irish for a **St. Patrick's Day parade** from Wacker Drive to Van Buren Street.

Late Mar.–early Apr. Spring and Easter Flower Show blooms at the Lincoln Park Conservatory.

Mid-May. International Art Exposition at Navy Pier (600 E. Grand Ave., tel. 312/787–6858).

Mid-May. See masterpieces by Frank Lloyd Wright and other Prairie School architects on the **Wright Plus House Walk,** Oak Park (tel. 708/848–1978).

Late May, Festival of Illinois Film and Video Artists, a two-day visual arts display, has events at various theaters (tel. 312/663–1600).

Memorial Day. Buckingham Fountain, in Grant Park, is turned on. Shows daily; colored lights nightly, 9–10, through Labor Day.

Early June. Viva Chicago!, a festival of Latino culture, takes place in Grant Park (tel. 312/744–3315).

Early June. Body Politic Street Festival takes over the 2200 North block of Lincoln Avenue with food and theatrics (tel. 312/348–7901).

Early June. 57th Street Art Fair (Ray School yard, 57th St., and Kimbark Ave.), one of the major juried art fairs in the Midwest, selects exhibitors from applicants from all over the country. Offerings include both the decorative and the utilitarian: paintings, sculpture, jewelry, ceramics and other crafts, and clothing and textiles (tel. 312/744–3315).

Mid-June. Chicago International Boat Show is held at Navy Pier (600 E. Grand Ave., tel. 312/787–6858).

Mid-June. Printer's Row Book Fair, a two-day multimedia event that takes place in the historic Printer's Row District, is built around books and the printer's and binder's arts. Clowns, jugglers, and food vendors weave their way through displays from major and specialty booksellers and craftspeople demonstrating book-related arts (Dearborn St. between Harrison and Polk, tel. 312/663–1595).

Mid-June. Chicago Blues Festival in Grant Park, a three-day, three-stage event featuring blues greats from Chicago and around the country.

Late June. Grant Park Symphony Orchestra and Chorus give four concerts weekly through mid-August (tel. 312/819–0614).

Late June—early Sept. Ravinia Festival, Highland Park, hosts a variety of classical and popular musical artists in a pastoral setting north of the city (tel. 312/728–4642).

All summer. Noontime music and dance performances are held outdoors weekdays at the Daley Plaza Civic Center (Washington St. between Dearborn and Clark Sts.) and at the First National Bank of Chicago Plaza (Dearborn St. at Madison St.).

July 4. Evening fireworks along the lakefront; bring a blanket and a portable radio to listen to the *1812 Overture* from Grant Park.

Early July. Taste of Chicago (Columbus Dr. between Jackson and Randolph) feeds 4 million hungry visitors with specialties from scores of restaurants in the Chicago area.

Late July. Air and water show along the Near North lakefront at

North Avenue features precision flying teams and displays of antique and high-tech aircraft going through their paces.

Late July. Chicago to Mackinac Island Boat Race originates at Belmont Harbor under the auspices of the Chicago Yacht Club (Monroe St. Harbor, tel. 312/861–7777).

Mid-Aug. Chicago International Sky Nights features two nights of fireworks and boats festooned with lights (Monroe St. Harbor, Grant Park, tel. 312/744–3315).

Late Aug. Chicago Triathlon participants plunge in at Oak Street Beach for a one-mile swim, followed by a 10-kilometer run and a 25-mile bike race on Lake Shore Drive.

Labor Day. *Chicago Tribune* **Ribfest** in Grant Park (tel. 312/222 –3232). **Chicago Federation of Labor Parade** on Dearborn Street, from Wacker Drive to Congress Street.

Labor Day weekend. Chicago Jazz Festival, Grant Park.

Late Sept.–early Oct. Oktoberfest brings out the best in beer and German specialties at the Berghoff Restaurant (17 W. Adams St., tel. 312/427–3170) and Chicago area pubs.

Columbus Day. Columbus Day Parade on Dearborn Street from Wacker Drive to Congress Street.

Mid-Oct. International Antiques Show, Navy Pier (tel. 312/787–6858).

Late Oct. Chicago Marathon starts at Daley Bicentennial Plaza (337 E. Randolph St.) and follows a course through the city (tel. 312/951–0660).

Late Oct.–early Nov. Chicago International Film Festival brings outstanding new American and foreign films to the Music Box and Biograph theaters. Some Music Box intermissions feature a live organist performing in restored 1920s movie palace grandeur (tel. 312/644–3400).

Thanksgiving Weekend. Friday marks the illumination of **Chicago's Christmas tree** in the Daley Center Plaza (Washington St. between Dearborn and Clark Sts.). The **Christmas parade,** with balloons, floats, and Santa bringing up the rear, travels down Michigan Avenue on Saturday.

Late Nov–Dec. Christmas Around the World display at the Museum of Science and Industry (57th St. and Lake Shore Dr., tel. 312/684–1414) features trees decorated in the traditional styles of more than 40 countries.

Early Dec. The Goodman Theatre (200 S. Columbus Dr., tel. 1312/443–3800) presents *A Christmas Carol,* and *The Nutcracker* is performed at the Arie Crown Theatre at McCormick Place (2300 S. Lake Shore Dr., tel. 312/791–6000).

Late Dec.–early Jan. Christmas Flower Show at Lincoln Park Conservatory.

What to Pack

Pack light, because porters and luggage carts are hard to find. Luggage allowances on domestic flights vary slightly from airline to airline. Most allow three checked pieces and one carry-on. Some give you the option of two checked and two carry-on. In all cases, check-in luggage cannot weigh more than 70 pounds per piece or be larger than 62 inches (length + width + height). Carry-on luggage cannot be larger than 45 inches (length + width + height) and must fit under the seat or in the overhead luggage compartment.

Be prepared for cold, snowy weather in the winter and hot, sticky weather in the summer. Jeans (shorts in summer and T-

shirts or sweaters and slacks are fine for sightseeing and informal dining. Men will need jackets and ties, women dresses, for
expensive restaurants. In the winter take boots or a sturdy
pair of shoes with nonslip soles for icy sidewalks, and a hat to
protect your ears from the numbing winds that buffet Michigan
Avenue. In the summer, bring a swimsuit for Lake Michigan
swimming or sunning.

Cash Machines

Virtually all U.S. banks belong to a network of ATMs (Auto-
matic Teller Machines), which gobble up bank cards and spit
out cash 24 hours a day in cities throughout the country. There
are some eight major networks in the United States, the largest
of which are Cirrus, owned by MasterCard, and Plus, affiliated
with Visa. Some banks belong to more than one network. These
cards are not automatically issued; you have to ask for them. If
your bank doesn't belong to at least one network, you should
consider moving funds, for ATMs are becoming as essential as
check cashing. Cards issued by Visa and MasterCard may also
be used in the ATMs, but the fees are usually higher than the
fees on bank cards, and there is a daily interest charge on the
"loan," even if monthly bills are paid on time. Each network has
a toll-free number you can call to locate machines in a given
city. The Cirrus number is tel. 800/4–CIRRUS; the Plus number is 800/THE–PLUS. Check with your bank for fees and for
the amount of cash you can withdraw on any given day.

Traveling with Film

If your camera is new, shoot and develop a few rolls of film before leaving home. Pack some lens tissue and an extra battery
for your built-in light meter. Invest about $10 in a skylight fil-
ter and screw it onto the front of your lens. It will protect the
lens and also reduce haze.

Film doesn't like hot weather. If you're driving in summer,
don't store film in the glove compartment or on the shelf under
the rear window. Put it behind the front seat on the floor, on
the side opposite the exhaust pipe.

On a plane trip, never pack unprocessed film in check-in luggage; if your bags get X-rayed, say good-bye to your pictures.
Always carry undeveloped film with you through security and
ask to have it inspected by hand. (It helps to isolate your film in
a plastic bag, ready for quick inspection.) Inspectors at American airports are required by law to honor requests for hand inspection; abroad, you'll have to depend on the kindness of
strangers.

The old airport scanning machines—still in use in some Third
World countries—use heavy doses of radiation that can turn a
family portrait into an early morning fog. The newer models—
used in all U.S. airports—are safe for anything from five to 500
scans, depending on the speed of your film. The effects are cu-
mulative; you can put the same roll of film through several scans
without worry. After five scans, though, you're asking for
trouble.

If your film gets fogged and you want an explanation, send it to
the **National Association of Photographic Manufacturers** (550

Mamaroneck Ave., Harrison, NY 10528). They will try to determine what went wrong. The service is free.

Traveling with Children

Publications *Family Travel Times,* an eight- to twelve-page newsletter published 10 times a year by TWYCH (Travel with Your Children, 80 8th Ave., New York, NY 10011, tel. 212/206–0688). Subscription includes access to back issues and twice-weekly opportunities to call in for specific advice.
Great Vacations with Your Kids: The Complete Guide to Family Vacations in the U.S., by Dorothy Ann Jordon and Marjorie Adoff Cohen (E.P. Dutton, 2 Park Ave., New York, NY 10016; $12.95), details everything from city vacations to adventure vacations to child-care resources.
Chicago: A Child's Kind of Town (Dept. of Child Psychiatry, The Children's Memorial Hospital, 2300 Children's Plaza, Chicago, IL 60614; $4.50).
Chicago Parent News Magazine (141 S. Oak Park Ave., Oak Park, IL 60302, tel. 708/386–5555) is a monthly publication with events and resource listings available free at locations throughout the city. You can call and ask for an issue to be sent before your trip. There is a $1 charge for postage and handling.

Hotels The Ritz-Carlton (160 E. Pearson St., Chicago, IL 60611, tel. 312/266–1000 or 800/621–6906) provides many children's services, from complimentary strollers to a children's menu, and kids stay free in their parents' room. The Drake (140 E. Walton Place, Chicago, IL 60611, tel. 312/787–2200) allows kids under 18 to stay in their parents' room at no extra charge and provides a children's menu in the restaurant. Most Days Inn hotels (tel. 800/325–2525) charge only a nominal fee for children under 18 and allow kids 12 and under to eat free (many offer efficiency-type apartments, too). Many other Chicago hotels offer family plans in which kids stay free or at nominal cost in their parents' room (*see* Chapter 7).

Home Exchange Exchanging homes is a surprisingly low-cost way to enjoy a vacation in another part of the country. **Vacation Exchange Club, Inc.** (Box 820, Haleiwa, HI 96712, tel. 800/638–3841), specializes in domestic home exchanges. The club publishes one directory in February, one in April, and another in September. Membership is $50 per year, for which you receive one listing. Loan-a-Home (2 Park La., Mount Vernon, NY 10552, tel. 914/664–7640) is popular with academics on sabbatical and businesspeople on temporary assignment. There's no annual membership fee or charge for listing your home; however, one directory and a supplement costs $30.

Getting There On domestic flights, children under two not occupying a seat travel free. Various discounts apply to children two to 12 years of age. Regulations about infant travel on airplanes are in the process of changing. Until they do, however, if you want to be sure your infant is secured in his/her own safety seat, you must buy a separate ticket and bring your own infant car seat. (Check with the airline in advance; certain seats aren't allowed. Or write for the booklet "Child/Infant Safety Seats Acceptable for Use in Aircraft," from the **Federal Aviation Administration,** APA–200, 800 Independence Ave., SW, Washington, DC 20591, tel. 202/267–3479.) Some airlines allow babies to travel in their own safety seats at no charge if there's a spare seat on the plane available; otherwise, safety seats will be stored and the child will have to be held by a parent. If you opt to hold your baby on your lap, do so with the infant outside the seatbelt, so he or she won't be crushed in case of a sudden stop.

Also inquire about special children's meals or snacks. See the February 1990 issue of *Family Travel Times* for "TWYCH's Airline Guide," which contains a rundown of the children's services offered by 46 airlines.

Baby-sitting Services Make child-care arrangements with the hotel concierge or housekeeper or through **American Registry for Nurses and Sitters** (3921 N. Lincoln Ave., Chicago, IL 60613, tel. 312/248–8100) and **Art Resource Studio** (551 W. Diversey Pkwy., Chicago, IL 60614, tel. 312/975–1671), with weekday craft workshops and drop-off care on weekends.

Hints for Disabled Travelers

The Information Center for Individuals with Disabilities (Fort Point Pl., 1st floor, 27–43 Wormwood St., Boston, MA 02210–1606, tel. 617/727–5540) offers useful problem-solving assistance, including lists of travel agents that specialize in tours for the disabled.
Moss Rehabilitation Hospital Travel Information Service (12th St. and Tabor Rd., Philadelphia, PA 19141, tel. 215/329–5715) provides information for a small fee on tourist sights, transportation, and accommodations in destinations around the world.
Mobility International (Box 3551, Eugene, OR 97403, tel. 503/343–1284) has information on accommodations, organized study, etc., around the world.
The Society for the Advancement of Travel for the Handicapped (26 Court St., Brooklyn, NY 11242, tel. 718/858–5483) offers access information. Annual membership costs $40, or $25 for senior travelers and students. Send a stamped, self-addressed envelope.
The Itinerary (Box 2012, Bayonne, NJ 07002, tel. 201/858–3400) is a bimonthly travel magazine for the disabled.
Access to the World: A Travel Guide for the Handicapped, by Louise Weiss is available from Henry Holt & Co. for $12.95 plus $2 shipping (tel. 800/247–3912; the order number is 0805001417).
Greyhound/Trailways (consult local directory for number) will carry a disabled person and companion for the price of a single fare. **Amtrak** (tel. 800/USA–RAIL) requests 24-hour notice to provide redcap service, special seats, and a 25% discount.
Access Living (310 S. Peoria, Suite 201, Chicago, IL 60607, offers personal-attendant referrals for disabled travelers.
Travel Industry and Disabled Exchange (TIDE, 5435 Donna Ave., Tarzana, CA 91356, tel. 818/368–5648) is an industry-based organization with a $15 per person annual membership fee. Members receive a quarterly newsletter and information on travel agencies and tours.

Hints for Older Travelers

The American Association of Retired Persons (AARP, 1909 K St. NW, Washington, DC 20049, tel. 202/662–4850) has two programs for independent travelers: (1) The Purchase Privilege Program, which offers discounts on hotels, airfare, car rentals, and sightseeing; and (2) the AARP Motoring Plan, which offers emergency aid and trip routing information for an annual fee of $33.95 per couple. The AARP also arranges group tours through **American Express Vacations** (Box 5014, Atlanta, GA 30302, tel. 800/241–1700 or, in Georgia, tel. 800/637–6200). AARP members must be 50 or older. Annual dues are $5 per person or per couple.

When using an AARP or other identification card, ask for a reduced hotel rate at the time you make your reservation, not when you check out. At restaurants, show your card to the maitre d' before you're seated, since discounts may be limited to certain set menus, days, or hours. When renting a car, remember that economy cars, priced at promotional rates, may cost less than cars that are available with your ID card.

Elderhostel (80 Boylston St., Suite 400, Boston, MA 02116, tel. 617/426–7788) is an innovative 16-year-old program for people 60 and older. Participants live in dorms on some 1,200 campuses around the world. Mornings are devoted to lectures and seminars; afternoons, to sightseeing and field trips. The all-inclusive fee for two- to three-week trips, including room, board, tuition, and round-trip transportation, is $1,700–$3,200.

National Council of Senior Citizens (925 15th St. NW, Washington, DC 20005, tel. 202/347–8800) is a nonprofit advocacy group with some 5,000 local clubs across the country. Annual membership is $12 per person or per couple. Members receive a monthly newspaper with travel information and an ID card for reduced-rate hotels and car rentals.

Mature Outlook (6001 N. Clark St., Chicago, IL 60660, tel. 800/336–6330), a subsidiary of Sears Roebuck & Co., is a travel club for people over 50, with hotel and motel discounts and a bimonthly newsletter. Annual membership is $9.95 per couple. Instant membership is available at participating Holiday Inns.

Golden Age Passport is a free lifetime pass to all parks, monuments, and recreation areas run by the federal government. People over 62 should pick them up in person at any national park that charges admission. A driver's license or other proof of age is required.

Further Reading

In *Fabulous Chicago* Emmett Dedmon provides an interesting look at the city. Studs Terkel's *Division Street* contains interviews with people in and around Chicago.

Saul Bellow's novel *The Adventures of Augie March* follows the life of the son of Russian Jewish immigrants. Andrew M. Greeley's *Lord of the Dance* is a drama about an Irish Catholic family.

Other Chicago titles include *Maud Martha*, by Gwendolyn Brooks, *Studs Lonigan*, by James T. Farrell, *Dandelion Wine*, by Ray Bradbury, and Richard Wright's explosive story of black ghetto life, *Native Son*.

A librarian in Chicago recommends *The Gorilla of Chicago*, by Mary Parker, *The Story of Eva*, by Will Paine, *The Second Generation*, by James Linn, *Purple Peeks*, by John Driver, and Susan Glaspell's *The Glory of the Conquered*.

Arriving and Departing

By Plane

Every national airline, most international airlines, and a number of regional carriers fly into Chicago. The city has two national airports and one regional airport. **O'Hare International Airport,** one of the world's busiest, is some 20 miles from downtown, in the far northwestern corner of the city.

Midway Airport, on Chicago's Southwest Side, about 7 miles from downtown, is distinguished by its relative lack of crowds and confusion and its smaller scale. Meigs Field, on the lakefront just south of Downtown, serves commuter airlines with flights to downstate Illinois and Wisconsin.

Smoking Smoking is banned on all scheduled routes within the 48 contiguous states; within the states of Hawaii and Alaska; to and from the U.S. Virgin Islands and Puerto Rico; and on flights of less than six hours to and from Hawaii and Alaska. The rule applies to the domestic legs of all foreign routes, but does not affect international flights.

On a flight on which smoking is permitted, you can request a nonsmoking seat during check-in or when you book your ticket. If the airline tells you there are no seats available in the nonsmoking section, insist on one: Department of Transportation regulations require U.S. carriers to find seats for all nonsmokers, provided they meet check-in time restrictions.

Carry-on Luggage New rules have been in effect since January 1, 1988, on U.S. airlines with regard to carry-on luggage. The model for the new rules was agreed to by the airlines in December 1987 and then circulated by the Air Transport Association with the understanding that each airline would present its own version.

Under the model, passengers are limited to two carry-on bags. For a bag you wish to store under the seat, the maximum dimensions are 9″ × 14″ × 22″, for a total of 45″. For bags that can be hung in a closet or on a luggage rack, the maximum dimensions are 4″ × 23″ × 45″, for a total of 72″. For bags you wish to store in an overhead bin, the maximum dimensions are 10″ × 14″ × 36″, for a total of 60″. Your two carry-ons must each fit one of these sets of dimensions, and any item that exceeds the specified dimensions will generally be rejected as a carry-on and handled as checked baggage. Keep in mind that an airline can adapt these rules to circumstances; don't be surprised when you are allowed only one carry-on bag on an especially crowded flight.

The rules list eight items that may be carried aboard in addition to the two carry-ons: a handbag (pocketbook or purse), an overcoat or wrap, an umbrella, a camera, a reasonable amount of reading material, and crutches, a cane, braces, or other prosthetic device upon which the passenger is dependent. Infant/child safety seats may also be brought aboard if parents have purchased a ticket for the child or if there is space in the cabin. (Rules on safety seats are in the process of changing, so check with your airline before leaving.)

Note that these regulations are for U.S. airlines only. Foreign airlines generally allow one piece of carry-on luggage in tourist class, in addition to handbags and bags filled with duty-free goods. Passengers in first and business class are also allowed to carry on one garment bag. It is best to check with your airline in advance to learn its rules regarding carry-on luggage.

Checked Luggage U.S. airlines allow passengers to check two suitcases whose total dimensions (length + width + height) do not exceed 62″ and whose weight per piece does not exceed 70 pounds.

Rules governing foreign airlines vary from airline to airline, so check with your travel agent or the airline itself before you go. All airlines allow passengers to check two bags. In general, expect the weight restriction on the two bags to be not more than 70 pounds each, and the size restriction to be 62″ total dimensions on each bag.

Lost Luggage Airlines are responsible for lost or damaged property only up to $1,250 per passenger on domestic flights; $9.07 per pound (or $20 per kilo) for checked baggage on international flights; and up to $400 per passenger for unchecked baggage on international flights. When you carry valuables, either take them with you on the airplane or purchase additional insurance for lost luggage. Some airlines will issue additional luggage insurance when you check in, but many do not. American Airlines is one that does. Its additional insurance is only for domestic flights or flights to Canada; rates are $1 for every $100 valuation, with a maximum of $25,000 valuation per passenger. Hand luggage is not included.

Insurance for lost, damaged, or stolen luggage is available through travel agents or from various insurance companies. Two that issue luggage insurance are Tele-Trip, a subsidiary of Mutual of Omaha, and The Travelers Insurance Co.

Tele-Trip (tel. 800/228–9792) operates sales booths at airports and issues insurance through travel agents. Tele-Trip will insure checked luggage for up to 180 days and for $500 to $3,000 valuation. For one to three days, the rate for a $500 valuation is $8.25; for 180 days, $100.

The Travelers Insurance Co. (Ticket and Travel Dept., 1 Tower Sq., Hartford, CT 06183, tel. 203/277–0111 or 800/243–3174) will insure checked or hand luggage for $500 to $2,000 valuation per person, for a maximum of 180 days. For one to five days, the rate for a $500 valuation is $10; for 180 days, $85.

The two companies offer the same rates on both domestic and international flights. Consult the travel pages of your Sunday newspaper for the names of other companies that insure luggage. Before you travel, itemize the contents of each bag in case you need to file an insurance claim. Be certain to put your home address on each piece of luggage, including carry-on bags. If your luggage is stolen and later recovered, the airline must deliver the luggage to your home free of charge.

From the Airport to Downtown Chicago *By Public Transit* You can reach the Chicago Transit Authority's rapid transit station at O'Hare Airport from the baggage claim level without going outdoors. When you're heading to the North Side or Downtown and you don't have much luggage, this is the cheapest ($1.25) way to get from the airport to the city. Travel time is 40–60 minutes. The first stop in the Loop (downtown) is Washington and Dearborn streets. From here you can take a taxi to your hotel or change to other rapid transit lines. There is no convenient public transportation downtown from Midway Airport.

By Bus **Continental Air Transport** (tel. 312/454–7799) coaches provide express service from both airports to major Downtown and Near North hotels; the coaches leave every half hour. The trip downtown from O'Hare takes an hour or longer, depending on traffic conditions and your point of debarkation; the fare is $12. (When taking the coach to O'Hare to catch a departing flight, be sure to allow at least 1½ hours.) The trip downtown from Midway takes about half an hour; the fare is $9.

CW Limo (tel. 312/493–2700) offers moderately priced express van service from both airports to locations in Hyde Park and the South Side. Vans leave O'Hare about every 45 minutes, and the travel time to Hyde Park is about an hour (more when traffic is heavy); the fare is $9.75. CW serves Midway with five vans daily, at Midway's traffic peaks; the fare is $8.50.

By Taxi Metered taxicab service is available at both O'Hare and Midway airports. Expect to pay about $28–$32 plus tip from O'Hare to Near North and Downtown locations, about $14 plus tip from Midway. Some cabs participate in a share-a-ride program that combines two or three individuals going from the airport to Downtown; the cost per person is substantially lower than the full rate.

By Rental Car On leaving the airport, follow the signs to I–90 east to Chicago. This is the Kennedy Expressway, which merges with I–94, the Edens Expressway. Take the eastbound exit at Ohio Street for Near North locations, the Washington or Madison Street exits for Downtown. After you exit, continuing east about a mile will take you to Michigan Avenue.

By Car

Travelers coming from the east can pick up the Indiana Toll Road (I–80/90) westbound for about 30 miles to the Chicago Skyway (also a toll road), which runs into the Dan Ryan Expressway (I–90/94). Take the Dan Ryan north (westbound) just past the turnoff for I–290 to any of the Downtown eastbound exits (Monroe, Madison, Washington, Randolph, Lake) and drive east about a mile to reach Michigan Avenue. If you are heading to the Near North, take the Ohio Street exit eastbound and continue straight through local streets for about a mile to reach Michigan Avenue.

Travelers coming from the south should take I–57 northbound to the Dan Ryan Expressway.

Travelers from the west may follow I–80 eastbound across Illinois to I–55, which is the major artery from the southwest. Continue east on I–55 to Lake Shore Drive. Those coming from areas due west of Chicago may prefer to pick up I–290 eastbound, which forks as it nears the city, heading to O'Hare in one direction (where it meets I–90) and to downtown Chicago in the other (where it ends).

Travelers from the north will need to be on I–90 eastbound, which merges with I–94 south (eastbound) to form the Kennedy Expressway (I–90/94) about 10 miles north of Downtown. (I–90/94 is called the Kennedy Expressway north of I–290 and the Dan Ryan Expressway south of I–290).

Car Rentals

Chicago's extensive network of buses and rapid transit rail, as well as the availability of taxis and limousine services (often priced competitively with metered cabs) make having a car in Chicago unnecessary, particularly for those whose visit is confined to the Loop, Near North, and Lakefront neighborhoods. If your business or interests take you to the suburbs, you may want to rent a car for that part of your trip. Like most major cities today, Chicago traffic is often heavy, on-street parking is nearly impossible to find, parking lots are expensive, congestion creates frustrating delays, and other drivers may be impatient with those who are unfamiliar with the city and its roads. During the 1990s, extensive repair work is planned for several of the city's major arteries, including Lake Shore Drive and the Kennedy Expressway (I–90/94). Similar work on the Dan Ryan Expressway in 1988–1989 caused a nightmare of snarled traffic during rush hours. In these circumstances, the visitor to Chicago may find a car to be a liability rather than an asset.

If business or pleasure obliges you to rent a car, however, you will have no trouble finding vendors to serve you. National companies, most with airport, as well as downtown, locations, include **Alamo Rent-A-Car** (tel. 800/327–9633), **Amerex Rent-A-Car** (tel. 800/843–1143), **Avis** (tel. 800/331–1212), **Budget** (tel. 800/527–0700), **Dollar** (tel. 800/421–6868), **Hertz** (tel. 800/654–3131), **National** (tel. 800/328–4567), and **Sears** (tel. 800/527–0770). Budget and Sears also have numerous suburban locations. Local and lower-cost companies include **Airways** (tel. 312/678–2300). **American International** (tel. 800/527–0202), **Fender Benders** (tel. 312/569–2678), and **Rent-a-Wreck** (tel. 800/421–7253).

Make your car arrangements before you leave home, and do some comparison shopping before making a reservation. Costs vary greatly among companies, depending on the number of days you expect to need the car, whether you need it for weekend or weekday use, and whether you expect to do a lot of driving or a little, and car rental advertisements can be misleading. Be sure to ask about add-on charges for insurance coverage (collision, personal injury), gasoline (some companies include gas in their daily rate, others in their mileage fees, others make a separate charge for gas, and still others leave the gas up to you), and drop-off at a location other than the one where you picked up the car (subcharges here can be substantial).

Find out what the collision damage waiver (usually an $8–$12 daily surcharge) covers and whether your corporate or personal insurance already covers damage to a rental car (if so, bring along a photocopy of the benefits section). Companies are holding renters responsible for theft and vandalism if they don't buy the CDW. In response, some credit card and insurance companies are extending their coverage to rental cars. They include Dreyfuss Bank Gold and Silver MasterCards (tel. 800/847–9700), Chase Manhattan Bank Visa cards (tel. 800/645–7352), and Access America (tel. 800/851–2800). When you've decided on the company and reserved a car, *be sure to get a reservation number*. Remember, if the company doesn't have the car you reserved when you arrive to pick it up, the company must provide a comparable or better car at the price you reserved.

By Train

Amtrak (800/USA–RAIL) offers nationwide service to Chicago's Union Station (Jackson and Canal Sts., tel. 312/558–1075). Some trains travel overnight, and you can sleep in your seat or book a roomette at additional cost. Most trains have attractive diner cars with acceptable food, but you may prefer to bring your own. Excursion fares, when available, may save you nearly half the round-trip fare.

By Bus

Greyhound/Trailways (630 W. Harrison St., tel. 312/408–5971) has nationwide service to its main terminal in the Loop and to its neighborhood bus stations: on the South Side at the 95th Street and Dan Ryan Expressway CTA station; on the northwest side at the Cumberland CTA station, 5800 North Cumberland Avenue, near O'Hare Airport.

Indian Trails, Inc. (tel. 312/928–8606 or 408–5971), serves Chicago from Indiana and Michigan, sharing Greyhound's terminal facilities at 630 W. Harrison Street and at 95th Street and the Dan Ryan Expressway.

Staying in Chicago

Important Addresses and Numbers

Tourist Information The main **Tourist Information Center** is housed in the Historic Water Tower, in the middle of the Magnificent Mile (806 N. Michigan Ave., tel. 312/280–5740).
The **Mayor's Office of Special Events General Information and Activities** (121 N. La Salle St., tel. 312/744–3315) will tell you about city-sponsored events of interest.
The **State of Illinois Office of Tourism** (310 S. Michigan Ave., tel. 312/793–2094) maintains a **Tourism Hotline** (tel. 800/252–8987).

Emergencies **Police, fire, ambulance** (tel. 911).

Hospitals In the Near North or north, **Northwestern Memorial Hospital** (Superior St. at Fairbanks Ct., tel. 312/908–2000). In the Loop, **Rush Presbyterian St. Luke's** (1753 W. Congress Pkwy., tel. 312/942–5000). In Hyde Park and the South Side, **Michael Reese Hospital** (Lake Shore Dr. at 31st St., tel. 312/791–2000), or the **Bernard Mitchell Hospital at the University of Chicago** (5841 S. Maryland Ave., tel. 312/702–1000). Michael Reese and other hospitals sponsor storefront clinics for fast treatment of minor emergencies. Call the hospitals for information, or check the Chicago Consumer Yellow Pages under "Clinics."

Dentists The **Chicago Dental Society Emergency Service** (tel. 312/726–4321) makes referrals at all hours.

24-Hour Pharmacies **Walgreen's** (757 N. Michigan Ave., at Chicago Ave., tel. 312/664–8686).

Opening and Closing Times

Banks are generally open 8:30–3; some banks open for a half day on Saturday and close on Wednesday.

The main **U.S. Post Office** (433 W. Van Buren St., tel. 312/765–3210) is open weekdays 24 hours, Saturday until 5, closed Sunday. The post office at O'Hare International Airport is open daily 24 hours.

The **Kluczynski** and **Dirksen federal buildings** (230 S. Dearborn St., 219 S. Dearborn St.) are open weekdays 8–4, closed on federal holidays.

The **State of Illinois Building** (100 W. Randolph St., tel. 312/793–3500), is open weekdays, closed on state holidays.

Chicago City Hall (121 N. La Salle St., tel. 312/744–6873) is open weekdays, closed on city holidays.

Stores Most department stores, except those in Water Tower Place, are open Monday–Saturday 9:45–5:30 or 9:45–6, Thursday until 7. Sunday hours at Magnificent Mile department stores are usually noon–5. Loop department stores are closed Sunday except once a month (designated Super Sunday); the newspapers announce the specific day. Lord & Taylor and Marshall Field at the Water Tower are open Monday–Saturday 10–8 and Sunday noon–6.

Getting Around

Chicago's planners followed a grid pattern in laying out the city's streets. Madison Street is the baseline for streets and avenues that run north/south; Michigan Avenue (for example) is North Michigan Avenue above Madison Street, South Michigan Avenue below it. House numbers start at 1 at the baseline and climb in each direction, generally by 100 a block. Thus the Fine Arts Building at 410 South Michigan Avenue is four blocks south of Madison Street. Even-numbered addresses are on the west side of the street, odd numbers on the east side.

For streets that run east–west, State Street is the baseline; 18th Street (for example) is East 18th Street east of State Street and West 18th Street west of State Street. House numbers start at 1 at the baseline and rise in each direction, east and west. Even-numbered addresses are on the north side of the street, odd numbers on the south side.

The **Chicago Consumer Yellow Pages** has a complete guide to Chicago street locations and zip codes in the white pages in the center of the book.

By Train and Bus Chicago's extensive public transportation network includes buses and rapid transit trains, both subway and elevated. The **Chicago Transit Authority (CTA)** publishes an excellent map of the transit system, available on request from the CTA, Merchandise Mart, Chicago, IL 60654. The **RTA Travel Information Center** (tel. 312/836–7000) will provide information on how to get about on city rapid transit and bus lines, suburban bus lines, and commuter trains.

In 1990 the CTA restructured its fares to make a 25¢ fare increase more palatable to Chicagoans, but the result is likely to confuse the uninitiated. The basic fare is $1.25 for rapid transit trains; this fare also applies to buses during morning and after-noon rush hours (at other times, the bus fare is $1). Tokens (which can be used for full fare on either buses or rapid transit trains) offer a substantial discount over the regular fare: a roll of 10 tokens costs $9. Tokens can be bought at currency ex-changes, some rapid transit stations, and Jewel and Dominick's supermarkets. Transfers, which must be bought when you board the bus or train, cost an extra 25¢; they can be used twice within a two-hour time period but not twice on the same route. Children ages 7–11, senior citizens, and disabled passengers travel for less than half fare (40¢ at this writing). Children un-der 7 travel free. Several different weekly and monthly passes are available, but tokens are still probably the most economical option for those staying in the city for only a short time.

Most, but not all, rapid transit lines operate 24 hours; some sta-tions are closed at night. (In general, late-night CTA travel is not recommended.) To transfer between Loop's elevated ("el") lines and subway lines, or between rapid transit and bus serv-ice, you must use a transfer; be sure to *buy the transfer when you board the first conveyance.* Buses generally stop on every other corner northbound and southbound (on State Street they stop at every corner). Eastbound and westbound buses gener-ally stop on every corner. The Loop is a terminus for most north–south buses that serve it: Buses generally run either south from the Loop or north from the Loop. Principal transfer points are on Michigan Avenue at the north side of Randolph Street for northbound buses, Adams and Wabash for west-bound buses and the el, and State and Lake streets for south-bound buses.

By Taxi Chicago taxis are metered, with fares beginning at $1 for the first ⅛ mile and 10¢ for each addition ⅒ mile (or each minute of waiting time). A charge of 50¢ is made for each additional pas-senger between the ages of 12 and 65. A charge of 25¢ per bag may be levied when luggage is bulky. Expect to pay $28–$30, including tip, between O'Hare Airport and downtown and about half that amount for a trip to or from Midway Airport. Taxi drivers expect a 15% tip. The principal taxi companies are **American United Cab Co.** (tel. 312/248–7600), **Yellow Cab Co.** (tel. 312/829–4222), and **Checker Cab Co.** (tel. 312/829–4222).

Guided Tours

Every city has its sightseeing buses and walking tours, but how many have sightseeing boats on a river that twists and turns its way through the busiest areas of the city? You can see Chicago by land, lake, or river.

Orientation Tours The **Sunday Culture Bus** of the Chicago Transit Authority may
By Land be the best guided-tour bargain in the city. There are three narrated tours: **The West tour** takes you through many of Chicago's ethnic neighborhoods, including Mexican Pilsen, Greektown, and the Ukrainian and Polish communities. En route, the bus stops at the Museum of Holography, the Mexican Fine Arts Center, and the Museum of Broadcast Communica-tions. **The North tour** takes you through the upscale Lincoln Park area and the Lincoln Park Zoo, stopping at the Museum of Contemporary Art and the Chicago Historical Society. **The South tour** takes you to the Field Museum, the Planetarium,

the Aquarium, and the mansions of Hyde Park and Kenwood, with stops at the Museum of Science and Industry, the DuSable Museum of Afro-American History, the Oriental Institute, and Chinatown. The narrated portion of a tour lasts two to three hours, but you can leave a tour at any stop and pick up a later bus to continue the tour. *From the first Sunday in May through the last Sunday in September buses leave from the Art Institute of Chicago, Michigan Ave., and Adams St., every 30 minutes, 10:30–5. Tel. 312/664–7200. Cost: $2.50 adults, $1.25 children 7–11 and senior citizens.*

Chicago Motor Coach Co. Double-decker buses take visitors on narrated tours of Chicago landmarks. *Tel. 312/922–8919. Tours leave Sears Tower, Franklin and Adams St., daily 10–4. Cost: $2–$22, depending on duration. One-, two-, and three-hour tours are available.*

Gray Line has sightseeing tours of downtown, Lincoln Park, Chinatown, and Hyde Park, lasting two to seven hours. Pickups are available from downtown hotels with prior reservation. All Gray Line tours include a stop of at least 30 minutes at the Museum of Science and Industry in Hyde Park and may include stops at the Lincoln Park Zoo and the Sears Tower observation deck and a tour of the Chicago River on a Wendella boat cruise. (730 W. Lake St., tel. 312/454–0322). *Tours leave from the Palmer House, 33 E. Monroe, throughout the day. Call for times. Tours operate daily Memorial Day–Labor Day, weekends other times. Cost: $14–$19, depending on length of tour.*

American Sightseeing. The North tour along State Street and North Michigan Avenue includes the John Hancock Center, Water Tower Place, and the Lincoln Park Conservatory. The South tour covers the financial district, Grant Park, the University of Chicago, the Museum of Science and Industry, and Jackson Park. Tours leave from the Congress Hotel (530 S. Michigan Ave.), or you can arrange to be picked up at your hotel. *Tel. 312/427–3100. Cost: $13 adults, $6.50 children 5–14. Two-hour tours leave daily 9:30, 11:30, 1:30, and 3:30 during the summer, 10 and noon in winter.*

By Boat Touring Chicago by boat offers a different kind of sightseeing and travel experience. Schedules vary by season; be sure to call for exact times and fares.

Wendella Sightseeing Boats (400 N. Michigan Ave., tel. 312/337–1446). Guided tours traverse the Chicago River to south of the Sears Tower and through the locks; on Lake Michigan, they travel between the Adler Planetarium on the south and Oak Street Beach on the north. Available May–September. Ninety-minute tours at 10, 11:30, 1:15, and 3; cost: $8 adults, $4 children 11 and under. Two-hour evening tours at 7:30; cost: $10 adults, $5 children 11 and under. Wendella also offers an unscheduled, but fairly frequent, one-hour tour on Lake Michigan only; cost: $6 adults, $3 children. All Wendella tours leave from lower Michigan Avenue at the foot of the Wrigley Building on the north side of the river.

Mercury Skyline Cruises (tel. 312/332–1353). A 90-minute river and lake cruise departs at 10, 11:30, 1:15, 3:15, and 7:30; cost: $8 adults, $4 children under 12. A two-hour sunset cruise costs $9 adults, $4.50 children under 12. Tickets can be obtained one hour before departure time. One-hour lakefront cruises, not prescheduled, are available evenings: daily 5–9 PM and weekends at 9:30, 10, and 11 PM. A one-hour Chicago River cruise begins at noon, weekends only, June–August; cost: $6 adults, $3 children under 12. All Mercury cruises leave from Wacker Drive at Michigan Avenue (the south side of the Michigan Avenue bridge).

Shoreline Marine (tel. 708/673–3399). Half-hour boat trips on Lake Michigan are offered daily between Memorial Day and Labor Day. Tours leave from the Adler Planetarium (1800 S. Lake Shore Dr.) at quarter past the hour daily, 12:15–9:15; from the Shedd Aquarium 11:15–5:15; and in the evening from Buckingham Fountain, 6:15–11:15. Cost: $4 adults, $1.50 children.

Interlude Enterprises (tel. 312/641–1210). Lunchtime cruises with an architectural narrative leave from the southeast corner of Wabash Avenue and Wacker Drive, lower level, by the Wabash Avenue bridge, daily at 11:30 AM. Tours run from mid-May to early October, depending on the weather. Reservations can be made from two weeks in advance to 10 AM the day of the tour. The boat travels on the Chicago River through the Loop and the locks, and into Lake Michigan and Monroe Harbor. The cost of $18 includes the boat trip and lunch.

Special-Interest Tours

Pumping Station (806 N. Michigan Ave., tel. 312/467–7114). Tour the facility at the historic Water Tower and see a multimedia show about the city, *Here's Chicago!* Shows begin every half hour Monday–Thursday 10–5:30, Friday and Saturday 10 –6:30. Cost: $3.75 adults, $2 children.

Merchandise Mart (tel. 312/661–1440). This massive monument to commerce on the Chicago River displays the latest in wholesale furniture, fixtures, clothing, gifts, and Christmas wares to the trade. Though normally closed to the public, these showrooms can be visited during a 90-minute tour on Tuesday and Thursday. Tours assemble at 10 AM at the main desk on the first floor of the Mart between Wells and Orleans streets. Cost: $4.75. No cameras are allowed on the tour.

O'Hare International Airport. The nation's busiest airport offers free 90-minute tours of its taxiways and terminals, baggage-handling facilities, and fire station. Groups of 15–40, are eight and older. Groups should make reservations six to eight weeks in advance. Call the Chicago Department of Aviation at O'Hare (tel. 312/686–2300 for reservations and information).

Newspaper Tours. The *Chicago Tribune* offers free weekday tours of its new Freedom Center production facility (777 W. Chicago Ave., tel. 312/222–2116) to individuals and groups of up to 30, age 10 and older. Reservations must be made in advance of your visit.

Chicago Mercantile Exchange (30 S. Wacker Dr., tel. 312/930–8249). The visitors' gallery, which offers a view of the often frenetic trading floor, is open 7:30–3:15. Tours are given to groups of 15 or more by advance reservation on weekday mornings. Individuals can join prereserved groups when space is available.

Walking Tours

The **Chicago Architecture Foundation** gives core tours, such as a walking tour of Loop architecture and tours of historic houses, on a regular daily or weekly schedule, depending on the season. It also offers an astonishing number of tours on an occasional, seasonal, or prescheduled basis. They include tours of Beverly, the far south side Chicago community known for its beautiful Victorian-era homes; the Pullman neighborhood, a planned residential community for workers at the adjacent Pullman Motor Coach Co.; Graceland Cemetery; Frank Lloyd Wright's Oak Park buildings; and bicycle tours of Lincoln Park and Oak Park. Tour departure times vary; prices run about $5–$10 per person. For information, write or call the foundation at Glessner House (1800 S. Prairie Ave., tel. 312/326–1393), where the house tours begin, or at the Archicenter (330 S. Dearborn St., tel. 312/782–1776), where most other tours originate.

2 Portraits of Chicago

Neighborhoods of the Southwest Side

Pacyga

*An urban
historian who
teaches at
Columbia College
in Chicago,
Dominic A.
Pacyga is the
coauthor of*
Chicago: City of
Neighborhoods.

Chicago is proud of its ethnic neighborhoods. The "City of the Big Shoulders" is also the city of the blues and the polka, the jig and the tarantella. Tacos, kielbasa, Irish meat pies, and soul food are the sustenance of Chicago beyond the Loop and the high-rise towers of the lakefront. On Chicago streets newspapers in Polish, Lithuanian, Arabic, Spanish, German, and Greek are sold alongside the better-known English-language dailies, and a black newspaper, the *Chicago Defender*, makes its voice heard throughout the city. Many of the churches whose spires dot the cityscape can trace their origins to the arrival in Chicago of a particular national group. Schools, hospitals, museums, monuments, even street names (Emerald Avenue, King Drive, Lituanica Street, Pulaski Road) speak to the influence of ethnic groups on the city's history and political life.

As the city grew along with the Industrial Revolution of the 19th century, its neighborhoods became mazes of railroads, mills, factories, and packinghouses that reached across the Illinois prairie. The huge industrial complexes attracted workers from all over the United States, Europe, and Asia. Every major wave of migration that affected the United States after 1825 had a part in transforming Chicago. In recent years Arab, Vietnamese, Mexican, and Chinese immigrants have joined the descendants of the Germans, Irish, Swedes, Poles, Jews, Italians, and black Americans who made earlier journeys in search of peace and prosperity. And each group has left its mark on the city: Hispanic and Vietnamese cultural centers and museums have now joined the long-established Polish Museum on the Northwest Side, the Balzekas Museum of Lithuanian Culture on the Southwest Side, and the DuSable Museum of African American Culture on the South Side.

Chicago's communities have not always lived in harmony. Clashes between white ethnic groups have marked the history of the city, and relationships between whites and blacks exploded in a calamitous race riot in 1919. Although much has changed over the last 30 years, Chicago is still known as the nation's most segregated city. Yet its pluralism remains intact and healthy. Polish, Hmong, Greek,

The areas of the communities described in this essay are shown in the Chicago Neighborhoods map. A note following the essay gives directions and suggestions for visiting these neighborhoods, which are not covered in the tours of the Exploring Chicago chapter.

Arabic, and other languages mix freely with English, and summer in Chicago is a time when ethnic and community street fairs attract crowds.

The neighborhoods that lie like a fan to the southwest of the meeting of State Street and Archer Avenue have seen a succession of working-class ethnic populations. Archer Avenue, which runs roughly parallel to the South Branch of the Chicago River and the Chicago Sanitary and Ship Canal, is part of a huge transportation corridor that includes rail lines and the Stevenson Expressway (I–55). On this corridor much of the industrial history of the city took place.

Father Jacques Marquette and the explorer Louis Jolliet, who first arrived in the area in 1673, suggested the construction of a canal to connect Lake Michigan with the Illinois River. Begun in 1836, the monumental task took 12 years to complete. The Illinois–Michigan Canal gave Chicago commercial transportation to the hinterlands, and the canal and the river soon teemed with barges, docks, and factories. The activity quickly brought the railroads as well to the Archer Avenue corridor. By the turn of the century, the larger Chicago Sanitary and Ship Canal had also been constructed.

Irish workers made up a large portion of those who came to dig the Illinois–Michigan Canal, many of them having worked on the Erie Canal. The "canal" Irish tended to settle along the river in the area known originally as Hardscrabble or Lee's Farm; the building of the canal brought a change in name to Bridgeport. This working-class community anchored the northern end of Archer Avenue. St. Bridget's Church at Archer Avenue and Arch Street stands as a reminder of the canal workers who flocked to Chicago before the Civil War. The present structure of 1906 resembles a cathedral built by Irish monks in Novara, Italy, in 1170; its survival in the face of the construction of the Stevenson Expressway in 1964 is a tribute to the efforts of its pastor and to Bridgeport's political clout. (Planners swung the expressway directly behind St. Bridget's and its Shrine of Our Lady of the Highway.)

The river and the canal soon attracted Chicago's most famous industry: Meat packing plants opened along the South Branch and fouled the river with pollution. The packinghouses in turn attracted skilled German and Bohemian butchers and brought more Irish to Bridgeport. On Christmas Day, 1865, the Union Stock Yard opened west of Halsted Street, between Pershing Road (39th Street) and 47th Street, just to the south of Bridgeport. The huge livestock market became the center of the nation's meat packing industry. In time, an immigrant city grew up around the more than 400 acres of livestock pens, chutes, and railroad yards. Bridgeport's Irish, Germans, and Bohemians found themselves surrounded by Poles, Lithuanians, Slovaks, Italians, French Canadians, black Americans, and others; this was the beginning of the ethnic mélange of the South Side.

In 1905 the Chicago stockyards were rocked by the publication of Upton Sinclair's muckraking novel *The Jungle*. Sinclair portrayed the life of a Lithuanian immigrant family that lived in Back of the Yards, just to the southwest of the stockyards and Bridgeport. The Chicago stockyards soon had an international reputation for unwholesome practices, and it was not the last time the area was looked upon unfavorably in literature or in the press.

In fact the area contains four of the most written about, most famous neighborhoods in the history of urban America. Bridgeport, McKinley Park, Back of the Yards, and Canaryville surround the old Union Stock Yard. Bridgeport, the oldest settlement, predates the founding of the stockyards; much of its fame rests on its working-class ethnicity and its peculiar brand of politics. Richard J. Daley, its best-known political son, was only one of four Chicago mayors born and raised in Bridgeport, who together ran the city from the death of Anton Cermak in 1933 until the election of Jane Byrne in 1979. For many people, the name Bridgeport still means politics, especially Irish machine politics.

Bridgeport today has more than a dozen resident ethnic groups, some of them the overflow from neighboring communities. Pilsen, to the north, across the Chicago River, was once the center of Chicago's lumber industry; by 1900 it had become the largest Bohemian community outside Chicago; today it is the home of the city's principal concentration of Mexicans. Chinatown, to the northeast, its heart at the intersection of Cermak Road and Wentworth Avenue, was once occupied by Germans and Irish; Italians followed them before the Chinese arrived after 1900. The Chinatown community today is a growing and prosperous one, with a good deal of cohesion, and new immigrants have helped to solidify the Asian presence in the inner city.

Canaryville, to the south of Bridgeport, between Pershing Road and 49th Street, Halsted and the old New York Central Railroad yards, is a largely Irish-American neighborhood with many Mexicans and Appalachian whites. Here, at the corner of 45th Street and Lowe Avenue, is St. Gabriel's, perhaps the most famous church in the Stock Yard District. One of John Root's finest designs, the Romanesque structure was built in 1887–1888 with financial help from the packinghouse owners who were close friends of Fr. Maurice Dorney, the founder of the parish in 1880.

The neighborhoods that once surrounded the stockyards have more than 30 Roman Catholic churches and many Protestant houses of worship. Each is a monument to the faith and community-building spirit of an ethnic group that settled in the area. Polish packinghouse workers, who came to the area in large numbers between 1880 and 1920, alone built six of the structures. Today many of the old national parishes are of mixed ethnicity; many have services in the language of their founders, as well as in English and Spanish. Worshipers enter and Throop, across the street from Sherman Park, are greeted by the flags of Poland, Mexico, the United States, and the Vatican.

The Stock Yard District, once known as Town of Lake, a suburb of Chicago until it was annexed in 1889, behaved in some ways like a city in itself. As its residents moved to the south and west after World War I, out of the core neighborhoods of wooden two-flats and cottages in close proximity to the stockyards and the packinghouses, they created suburbs in the new neighborhoods of the Southwest Side, principally along Archer Avenue. These areas are part of Chicago's "bungalow belt."

During the 1920s bungalows appeared throughout the Southwest, Northwest, and Southeast sides. The single-family dwellings, with their small front and backyards, were the pre-Depression equivalent of suburban sprawl. Today they comprise much of Chicago's second tier of ethnic neighborhoods: Brighton Park, Gage Park, and Marquette Park all owe their existence to the movement away from the stockyard communities of Bridgeport, McKinley Park, Back of the Yards, and Canaryville. And the movements of ethnic groups can be traced across the Southwest Side in the churches and other institutions they left behind.

The Lithuanian community, for example, organized its first church, St. George's, in 1892 in Bridgeport. (The present structure was dedicated in 1902.) A second Lithuanian parish, Providence of God, was founded in 1900, north of St. George's in the Pilsen community. Three more Lithuanian parishes opened in 1904, including Holy Cross in Back of the Yards. Ten years later the Lithuanian community was supporting 10 Roman Catholic parishes, a consequence of the large East European emigration to America that took place before 1914. These arrivals became part of Chicago's first tier of ethnic neighborhoods.

As Lithuanians settled into better jobs following World War I, many of them decided to move away from the old industrial districts, and they looked to the bungalow belt for newer, more spacious housing. In the 1920s the Marquette Park area near the intersection of Marquette Road and California Avenue attracted Lithuanian Americans. A Lithuanian order of religious sisters had laid the foundation for the community in 1911 by opening the Academy of St. Casimir (later Maria High School). In 1928 ground was broken for a Lithuanian parish, Nativity B.V.M., at 68th Street and Washtenaw, and the parish quickly became a central institution in the Lithuanian community. In the same year the

Sisters of St. Casimir opened Holy Cross Hospital near the church and the high school.

The large institutional base drew more Lithuanians to the neighborhood throughout the interwar period. After World War II, another major emigration from Eastern Europe rejuvenated the Lithuanian community, and Marquette Park became its new center. The present Nativity Church, designed by John Mulokas and dedicated on May 12, 1957, is a striking example of Lithuanian architecture. Its dedication to Our Lady of Siluva celebrates the site of a famous Shrine to the Blessed Virgin in Lithuania.

The movement of Lithuanians away from the inner city has been typical of that of ethnic groups that originally settled in the area. By 1988 many of the Marquette Park Lithuanians were relocating in the southwest suburbs near Lemont. Yet the neighborhood they left behind continues to nourish the community; many people and cultural institutions choose to stay in Chicago, and Marquette Park remains the Lithuanian "gold coast."

The Union Stock Yard closed its gates on August 1, 1971, after 105 years of active livestock trading. In reality the meat packing business had begun to leave the city nearly 20 years earlier, when Wilson and Company announced the closing of its huge Chicago plant. By the early 1960s the big packers had left the city, and Chicago was facing its first post-industrial crisis. The area west of the Union Stock Yard, formerly the center of one of the nation's great industries, now resembled a ghost town.

Recent years have seen a partially successful attempt to redevelop some of the land the stockyards and packing--houses had occupied. A visit to the Old Stone Gate at Exchange and Peoria, which marks the entrance to the area, will show you industrial buildings mixed with open prairie and abandoned packinghouse buildings. Yet the new industries, important as they are to the city's economic base, employ only a fraction of the number of workers formerly employed by Chicago's most infamous industry. Meanwhile, new immigrants from Poland, Mexico, and elsewhere continue to come to the district in search of employment.

The economic future of Chicago's Southwest Side looked bleak just a few years ago. Now a resurgent Midway Airport at 55th Street and Cicero and a new rapid transit line that is scheduled to open by 1993 have infused the local economy with optimism. Bridgeport, in part because of its proximity to downtown and an excellent public transportation system that will improve when the Southwest Rapid Transit opens, is already witnessing economic rebirth. Areas a little farther down Archer Avenue should see new development as Midway Airport increases its capacity and the rapid transit line reaches them. The entire area along the canal and the river is now part of the Illinois–Michigan Canal National Heritage Corridor, and there are plans for riverfront parks and other amenities. In the shadow of great economic, cultural, and social change, Chicago's ethnic communities continue to maintain their heritage in the old and the new neighborhoods.

Visiting the Southwest Side

The Southwest Side is easily accessible by public or private transportation. The Archer Avenue (No. 62) bus, which can be boarded on State Street, makes its way southwest through the corridor. The Dan Ryan Rapid Transit Line will take you to Chinatown (Cermak Avenue) or to Comiskey Park (35th Street), the home of the Chicago White Sox. By automobile, you can take Archer and turn down Halsted Street (800 W), Ashland Avenue (1600 W), Western Avenue (2400 W), or another major street and follow it until you find an interesting side street or attraction to explore. If you continue west on Archer past Kedzie Avenue, stop at the Dom Podhalan or Polish Highlanders Hall at 4808 South Archer Avenue; it is as authentic a Polish mountain chalet as you are likely to see this side of the Odra River. A visit to the Balzekas Museum of Lithuanian Culture at 6500 South Pulaski Road would be worthwhile (*see* Museums and Galleries in Sightseeing Checklists, below). Wonderful and inexpensive Lithuanian restaurants line 71st Street from Western to California avenues (2600 W). Some of the best Middle Eastern restaurants in Chicago are located along 63rd Street between Western and Central Park avenues (3600 W). While the Northwest Side, along Milwaukee Avenue, is famous for Polish cuisine, the South Side holds its own: Tatra Inn serves a satisfying smorgasboard at 6038 South Pulaski. Mexican restaurants abound in Back of the Yards near the intersection of Ashland Avenue and 47th Street and in Pilsen along 18th Street and on Blue Island Avenue. Mi Pueblo, at 2908 West 59th Street, resembles a Mexican hacienda. The Southwest Side Italian community is well represented with restaurants along Oakley Avenue (2300 W), Western just north of 26th Street, and on 63rd Street, where Palermo's at 3715 West 63rd Street and Little Joe's at 63rd Street and Richmond are noteworthy. Many of the churches hereabouts have beautiful interiors, and Sunday is the best time to visit them, when services are scheduled. At other times of the week, you may find the church you want to see closed unless you call in advance of your visit.

The Builders of Chicago

by Barbara
Shortt

A practicing
architect and an
architectural
historian,
Barbara Shortt
writes frequently
on architecture
and travel.

When Mrs. O'Leary's cow kicked over the lantern and started the Great Chicago Fire of 1871, she set the scene for the birth of a Modern Architecture that would influence the entire globe. If Chicago today is a world capital of modern architecture landmarks—a city whose buildings embody contemporary architectural history from its beginnings in the 1880s—it is thanks to this cataclysmic fire and a unique set of cultural circumstances that were fueled by the new wealth of the thriving port city. In 1871 Chicago was isolated from European and East Coast opinion. At the same time, it was not uncivilized frontier, nor had it been traumatized by the Civil War. And it was strongly conscious of being the metropolis of the American heartland. Yet it had absolutely no existing architectural tradition; physically and aesthetically, it was wide open.

Because Chicago had been built mainly of wood, it was wiped out by the fire. Virtually the only building left standing downtown, where it still dominates the intersection of North Michigan and Chicago avenues, was the bizarre yellow stone Water Tower of 1869. Oscar Wilde, that infamous aesthete, called it a "monstrosity" when he visited Chicago in 1882. Today, with its fake battlements, crenellations, and turrets, it looks like a transplant from Disneyland rather than a real part of a vibrant and serious city. It serves now as a tourist information center, and even amid the amazingly varied architecture of central Chicago it appears to be an anachronism.

In the years following the fire, many remarkable people flocked to the building opportunity in the city that sprawled for miles along the western shore of Lake Michigan and inland along the branches of the Chicago River. A brilliant engineer named William LeBaron Jenney and a young Bostonian trained at MIT and Paris named Louis Sullivan, who would become a great architect, philosopher, writer, and teacher, were joined by a group of ingenious architects and engineers from diverse parts of America and Europe: Dankmar Adler (from Denmark), William Holabird (from New York), John Wellborn Root, Frank Lloyd Wright (from Wisconsin), Henry Hobson Richardson (from Louisiana via Boston and Paris), Daniel H. Burnham, and Martin Roche, among others. During the 1880s and 1890s in Chicago, these men did nothing less than create the foundations of modern architecture and construction.

The skyscraper was born here. The "curtain-wall," a largely glass exterior surface that does not act as a "wall" supporting the building but is supported on the floors from within, originated here. Modern metal-frame, multi-story construction was created here. The Chicago Window, a popular window design used in buildings all over America (until air-conditioning made it obsolete), consisting of a large fixed glass panel in the center, with a narrow operable sash on each side, was developed here. Chicago builders also discovered how to fireproof the metal structures that supported their buildings, which would otherwise melt in fires and bring total collapse: They covered the iron columns and beams with terra-cotta tiles that insulated the structural metal from heat.

Philosophically, the Chicago architects believed they were creating a democratic architecture to express the soul of American civilization, an architecture pragmatic, honest, healthy, and unashamed of wealth and commerce. Louis Sullivan, a philosopher, a romantic, and a prolific writer (his most famous book on architecture, *Kindergarten Chats*, is a Socratic dialogue), originated and propagated the ideas that "form follows function" and "a building is an act." For Sullivan, social purpose and structure had to be integrated to create an architecture of human satisfaction.

Technologically, the Chicago School, as they became known, were aware of the latest developments in European iron structures, such as the great railroad stations. Jenney had his engineering degree from Paris in 1856—he was older than the others, many of whom worked for him—yet he, Richardson, and John Root were the only conventionally well educated men of the group. At the same time, they had in Chicago a daring and innovative local engineering tradition. Jenney, a strict rationalist, incarnated this no-nonsense tradition and gave romantics like Sullivan and, later on, Sullivan's disciple Wright the tools with which to express their architectural philosophy.

The term *Chicago School of Architecture* refers to the work of these men, whose offices served as their true school: Jenney and Mundie, Root and Burgee, Adler and Sullivan, Holabird and Roche, Burnham and Root, H. H. Richardson, and Frank Lloyd Wright. In many instances it requires a scholarly effort to figure out precisely who did what, as they worked for and with one another, living in each other's pockets, shifting partnerships, arguing the meaning of what they did as well as how best to do it. Jenney and Adler were essentially engineers uninterested in decoration; with the exception of Richardson's Romanesque motifs, Sullivan's amazing ornament, and Wright's spatial and ornamental forms, these builders did not have distinct, easily discernible "styles." It becomes an academic exercise to try to identify their individual efforts.

The Chicago School's greatest clients were wealthy businessmen and their wives. The same lack of inhibition that led Mrs. Potter Palmer and Mrs. Havemeyer to snap up Impressionist paintings that had been rejected by French academic opinion (and today are the core of the Art Institute collection) led sausage magnates to hire young, inventive, local talent to build their mansions and countinghouses. Chicagoans may have been naive, but history has vindicated their taste.

Although they started building in the 1870s, nothing of note remains from before 1885. The oldest important structure is H. H. Richardson's massive granite Italian Romanesque-inspired Glessner House, with its decorative interiors derived from the innovative English Arts and Crafts movement. The only Richardson building left in Chicago, the Glessner House is considered by some his highest creation; Wright was influenced by its flowing interior space. At the corner of 18th Street and the Prairie Avenue Historic District, it now houses the offices of the Chicago Architecture Foundation.

Downtown, Richardson designed a Wholesale Building for Marshall Field that was later demolished. An addition to the Field store in the same architectural vocabulary, done by Burnham in 1893 and now part of the Marshall Field block, stands at the corner of Wabash and Washington streets. Burnham completed the block in 1902–1907, but in the airy, open, metal-frame, Chicago Window style.

In 1883 William LeBaron Jenney invented the first "skyscraper construction" building, in which a metal structural skeleton supports an exterior wall on metal shelves. (The metal frame or skeleton, a sort of three-dimensional boxlike grid, is still used today.) His earliest surviving metal-skeleton structure, the Second Leiter Building of 1891, is now Sears, Roebuck and Company, at the southeast corner of State and Van Buren streets in the Loop. The granite-face facade is extremely light and open, suggesting the metal frame behind. The building looks so modern that it comes as a shock to realize it is nearly a century old.

At 209 South La Salle Street, the Rookery Building of 1886, a highly decorated, structurally transitional building by Burnham and Root, employs masonry bearing walls (brick, terra-cotta, and stone) on the two major street facades and lots of iron structure (both cast-iron columns and wrought-iron beams) elsewhere. Here the decoration emphasizes the structural elements—pointing out, for example, the floor lines. Note also how specially shaped bricks are used at the edges of the window openings and to make pilasters. The plan, a freestanding square "donut," was unusual at the time. A magnificent iron and glass skylight covers the lower two stories of the interior courtyard, which was renovated in 1905 by Frank Lloyd Wright, who designed light fixtures and other decorative additions.

The nearby Marquette Building of 1894 at 140 South Dearborn Street, by Holabird and Roche, is almost a prototype for the modern office building, with its skeleton metal frame covered by decorative terra-cotta and its open, cellular facade with Chicago Windows. The marble lobby rotunda has Tiffany mosaic portraits of Indian chieftains and Père Marquette, a hymn to local history.

The most advanced structure from this period, one in which the exterior wall surface is freed of all performance of support, is Burnham's Reliance Building of 1895 at 36 North State Street. Here the proportion of glass to solid is very high, and the solid members are immensely slender for the era. Today the white terra-cotta cladding needs cleaning, and the building's seedy condition mars its beauty; the casual observer would be surprised to learn that most critics consider it the masterpiece of the Chicago School's office buildings.

To appreciate fully the giant leap taken by the architects of the Reliance, look at Burnham and Root's Monadnock Building of 1889–1892, at 53 West Jackson Boulevard. Its 16 stories are supported by conventional load-bearing walls, which grow to six feet thick at the base! While elegant in its stark simplicity (the result of a cheap-minded entrepreneur who had all the decoration removed from the plans while Root was traveling), its ponderousness contrasts sharply with the delicate structure and appearance of the Reliance Building. The Monadnock Building may have been the swan song of conventional building structure in Chicago, yet its verticality expressed the aspirations of the city.

Jenney's Manhattan Building of 1890, at 431 South Dearborn Street, with its variously shaped bay windows, was the first tall building (16 stories) to use metal-skeleton structure throughout; it is admired more for its structure than for its appearance. Both it and the equally tall Monadnock would never have come into being without Elisha Otis's elevator invention, which was already in use in New York City in buildings of nine or 10 stories at most.

The impetus toward verticality was an essential feature of Chicago commercial architecture. Verticality seemed to embody commercial possibility, as in "the sky's the limit!" Even the essential horizontality of the 12-story, block-long Carson Pirie Scott store is offset by the rounded corner tower at the main entrance.

The Chicago School created new decorative forms to apply to their powerful structures, and they derived them largely from American vegetation rather than from classical motifs. The apogee of this lush ornament was probably reached by Sullivan in his Carson Pirie Scott and Company store of 1899–1904 at State and Madison streets. The cast-iron swirls of rich vegetation and geometry surround the ground-floor show windows and the entrance, and they grow to the second story as well, with the architect's initials, LHS, worked into the design. (A decorative cornice that was originally at the top was removed.) The facade of the intermediate floors is extremely simple, with wide Chicago Windows surrounded by a thin line of delicate ornament; narrow vertical and horizontal bands, all of white terra-cotta, cover the iron structure behind.

Terra-cotta plaques of complex and original decoration cover the horizontal spandrel beams (the beams that cover the outer edges of the floors, between the vertical columns of the facades) of many buildings of this era, including the Reliance and the Marquette. Even modest residential and commercial structures in Chicago began to use decorative terra-cotta, which became a typical local construction motif through the 1930s.

Adler and Sullivan's Auditorium Building of 1887–1889 was a daring megastructure sheathed in massive granite, the same material Richardson used, and its style derives from his Romanesque forms. Here the shades of stone color and the rough and polished finishes provide contrasts. Built for profit as a civic center at South Michigan Avenue and Congress Street, facing Lake Michigan, the Auditorium Building incorporated a theater, a hotel, and an office building; complex engineering solutions allowed it to carry heavy and widely varying loads. Adler, the engineer, devised a hydraulic stage lift and an early air-conditioning system for the magnificent theater. Sullivan freely decorated the interiors with his distinctive flowing ornamental shapes.

In the spirit of democracy and populism, Adler wanted the Auditorium to be a "people's theater," one with lots of cheap seats and few boxes. It is still in use today as the Auditorium Theater, Adler's belief in the common man having been upheld when thousands of ordinary Chicagoans subscribed to the restoration fund in 1968. The rest of the building is now Roosevelt University.

Frank Lloyd Wright, who had worked for a year on the Auditorium Building in Adler and Sullivan's office, remained in their employ and in 1892 designed a house for them in a wealthy area of the Near North Side of town. The Charnley House, 1365 North Astor Street, built of long, thin, yellowish Roman brick and stone, has a projecting central balcony and shows a glimmer of Wright's extraordinary later freedom with volumes and spaces. The Charnley House, with its exquisite interior woodwork and the exterior frieze under the roof, has now been completely restored. Soon after the Charnley House project, Wright left Adler and Sullivan to work on his own.

Wright's ability to break apart and recompose space and volume, even asymmetrically, was given full range in the many houses he built in and around Chicago. What became typical of American domestic "open plan" interiors (as opposed to an arrangement of closed, boxlike rooms) derived from Wright's creation, but they could never have been practical without the American development of central heating, which eliminated the need for a fire in each room.

Wright was the founder of what became known as the Prairie School, whose work consisted largely of residences rather than buildings intended for commerce. Its principal characteristic was a horizontality evocative of the breadth of the prairies that contrasted with the lofty vertical shafts of the business towers. Like his teacher Sullivan, Wright also delighted in original decorative motifs of geometric and vegetable design.

The opening of the Lake Street el railway west to the new suburb of Oak Park gave Wright an enormous opportunity to build. In 1889 he went to live there at 951 Chicago Avenue, where he created a studio and a home over the next 22 years. Dozens of houses in Oak Park, of wood, stucco, brick, and stone, with beautiful leaded- and stained-glass windows and carved woodwork, were designed or renovated by him. He was almost obsessional in his involvement with his houses, wanting to design and control the placement of furniture and returning even after his clients had moved in. For Wright a house was a living thing, both in its relationship to the land and in its evolution through use.

Yet Wright's masterpiece in Oak Park is not a house but the Unitarian Unity Temple of 1906, at Kenilworth Avenue and Lake Street, a short walk from the Oak Park Avenue el stop. Because of intense budget limitations, he built it of the daring and generally abhorred material, poured concrete, and with only the simplest details of applied wood stripping. Nevertheless, Wright's serene creation of volume and light endures to this day. It is lit by high windows from above and has operable colored-glass skylights inserted into the "coffers" of the Roman-style "egg-crate" ceiling, intended for ventilation as well as light. The design of the windows and skylights echoes the designs applied to the walls, the door grilles, the hinges, the light fixtures; everything is integrated visually, no detail having been too small to consider.

Unity Temple was built on what became known as an H plan, which consisted of two functionally separate blocks connected by an entry hall. The Unity Temple plan has influenced the planning of public buildings to the present day. Recently restored to its original interior greens and ochers, Unity Temple is definitely worth a pilgrimage.

On the South Side of Chicago is the most famous of all Wright's houses, the Robie House of 1909, now on the University of Chicago campus, at 5757 South Woodlawn Avenue. Its great horizontal overhanging roof lines are echoed by the long limestone sills that cap its low brick walls. Wright designed everything for the house, including the furniture. Wright's stock has soared of late: A single lamp from the Robie House sold at auction recently for three-quarters of a million dollars!

The World's Columbian Exposition of 1893 was held at Midway Park in South Chicago. For complex political reasons, the planning was turned over mainly to eastern architects, who brought the influence of the international Beaux-Arts style to Chicago. A furious Louis Sullivan prophesied that "the damage wrought to this country by the Chicago World's Fair will last half a century." He wasn't entirely wrong in his prediction; the classicist style vied sharply over the next decades with the native creations of the Chicago and Prairie schools, all the while incorporating their technical advances. But the city fathers succumbed to the "culture versus commerce" point of view; thus most of the museums and public buildings constructed before World War II in Chicago were built in classical Greek or Renaissance styles.

Many of these public buildings are fine works in their own right, but they do not contribute to the development of 20th-century architecture. The most notable of them, the Public Library of 1897, at 78 East Washington Street, by Shepley, Rutan and Coolidge, has gorgeous interiors of white and green marble and glass.

Many of Chicago's museums are situated in Grant Park and along Lake Shore Drive, magnificent points from which to view the city skyline. The park and the drive were built on landfill in the 1910s and 1920s after the tracks of the Illinois Central Railroad along the old lakefront had been bridged over. Lake Shore Drive, with its parks and beaches, seems such an integral part of today's city that it is hard to imagine a Chicago without it. Daniel Burnham called for this development in his "Chicago Plan" of 1909.

In 1922 an important international competition offered a prize of $100,000 for the design of a Tribune Building that would dominate the Chicago River just north of the Loop. Numerous modernist plans were submitted, including one by Walter Gropius, of the Bauhaus. Raymond Hood's Gothic design—some called it Woolworth Gothic—was chosen. The graceful and picturesque silhouette of the Tribune Tower was for many years the symbol of Chicago, not to be overshadowed until general construction resumed, following World War II. More important, the Tribune Building moved the center of gravity of downtown Chicago north and east, causing the Michigan Avenue bridge to be built and opening the Near North Side to commercial development along Michigan Avenue.

The postwar Chicago School was dominated by a single personality who influenced modern architecture around the world: Ludwig Mies van der Rohe. The son of a stonemason, Mies was director of the Bauhaus in Dessau, Germany, the world's leading modern design center, from 1930 until Nazi pressure made him leave in 1937. On a trip to the United States he met John Holabird, son of William, who invited him to head the School of Architecture at the Armour Institute, later the Illinois Institute of Technology. Mies accepted—and redesigned the entire campus as part of the deal. Over the next 20 years he created a School of Architecture that disseminated his thinking into architecture offices everywhere.

Whatever Mies owed to Frank Lloyd Wright, such as Mies's own open-plan houses, his philosophy was very much in the tradition of Chicago, and the roots of Bauhaus architecture can be traced to the Chicago School. Mies's attitudes were profoundly pragmatic, based on solid building techniques, technology, and an appreciation of the nature of the materials used. He created a philosophy, a set of ethical values based on a purist approach; his great aphorisms were "Less is more" and "God is in the details." He eschewed applied ornament, however, and in that sense he was nothing like Wright. All Mies's "decoration" is generated by fine-tuned structural detail. His buildings are sober, sometimes somber, highly orderly, and serene; their aesthetic is based on the almost religious expression of structure.

The campus of IIT was built in 1942–1958 along South State Street, between 31st and 35th streets. Mies used few materials in the two dozen buildings he planned here: light cream colored brick, black steel, and glass. Quadrangles are only suggested, space is never rigidly defined. There is a direct line of descent from Crown Hall (1956), made of black steel and clear glass, with its long-span roof trusses exposed above the level of the roof, to the great convention center of 1970 on South Lake Shore Drive at 23rd Street, McCormick Center by C. F. Murphy, with its great exposed black steel space-frame roof and its glass walls.

Age requirements forced Mies to retire from IIT in 1958, but his office went on to do major projects in downtown Chicago, along Lake Shore Drive, and elsewhere. He had impressed the world in 1952 with his black steel and clear glass twin apartment towers, set at right angles to one another, almost kissing at the corner, at 860–880 North Lake Shore Drive. Later he added another, darker pair just to the north, 900–910.

In 1968 Heinrich and Schipporeit, inspired by "860" and by Mies's Berlin drawings of 1921 for a free-form glass skyscraper, built Lake Point Tower. This dark bronze metal and glass trefoil shaft, near the Navy Pier at East Grand Avenue, is a graceful and dramatic joy of the Chicago skyline. It is one of the few Chicago buildings, along with Bertram Goldberg's Marina City of 1964—twin round concrete towers on the river between State and Dearborn streets—to break with strict rectilinear geometry.

Downtown, Mies's Federal Center is a group of black buildings around a plaza, set off by a bright red steel Alexander Calder stabile sculpture, on Dearborn Street between Jackson Boulevard and Adams Street. The Dirksen Building, with its courthouse, on the east side of Dearborn, was built in 1964; the Kluczynski office building at the south side of the plaza and the single-story Post Office to the west were added through 1975. The north side of the large Federal Plaza is enclosed by the Marquette Building of 1894, thereby integrating the past with the present.

The IBM Building of 1971, the last office building designed by Mies, is a dark presence north of the river, between Wabash and State streets.

Perhaps the most important spinoff of Miesian thinking was the young firm of Skidmore, Owings & Merrill, which bloomed after the war. Their gem of the postwar period was the Inland Steel Building of 1957, at 30 West Monroe Street, in the Loop. The bright stainless-steel and pale green glass structure, only 18 stories high, with exposed columns on the long facade and a clear span in the short dimension, has uninterrupted interior floor space. It is considered a classic.

SOM became the largest architecture firm in America, with offices in all major cities. In Chicago the firm built, among other works, the immensely tall, tapering brown Hancock Tower of 1965–1970, with its innovative exterior criss-cross wind-bracing, and the even taller Sears Tower (1970–1975), with two of its nine shafts reaching to 1450 feet, now the tallest structure in the world. SOM may have achieved the epitome of the vertical commercial thrust of the Chicago School.

Meanwhile, Mies's Federal Plaza started a Chicago tradition, that of the outdoor plaza with a focus of monumental art. These plazas are real, usable, and used; they are large-scale city gathering places, not the mingy setbacks of New York office megaliths, and they shape the architectural and spatial character of downtown Chicago.

A string of plazas, featuring sculptures by Picasso and Dubuffet and mosaic murals by Chagall, leads one up Dearborn and Clark streets, to the Chicago River. At the river one finds more outdoor space. The south bank quays, one level down from the street, are a series of imaginatively landscaped gardens. Here one can contemplate the ever-changing light on the river and the 19th-century riveted-iron drawbridges, which prefigure Calder's work. Other monumental outdoor sculpture downtown includes Joan Miró's *Chicago* and Claes Oldenburg's *Batcolumn*.

The Jean Dubuffet sculpture stands before the State of Illinois Building of 1985 at the corner of Randolph and Clark streets. Here there are really two plazas: one outdoors, the other inside the stepped-back, mirrored-glass and pink-paneled irregular donut of a building. This wild fantasy is the work of Helmut Jahn, a German who came to Chicago in the 1960s to study at IIT. His colorful, lighthearted, mirrored Chicago buildings provide a definite counterpoint to the somber Mies buildings of the 1950s and 1960s, and they appear everywhere, influencing the design and choice of materials of the architecture of the 1980s.

Jahn's first important contribution to the Chicago scene was a sensitive addition to the Board of Trade in 1980. The Board of Trade was housed in an architectural landmark at 141 West Jackson Boulevard, at the foot of La Salle Street, a jewel of Art Deco design by the old Chicago firm of Holabird and Root in 1930. Murphy/Jahn's glittering addition echoed numerous features of the original structure. Both parts of the building have sumptuous interior atrium spaces. Marble, nickel, and glass motifs from the earlier edifice are evoked and reinterpreted—but not copied—in the high-tech addition. Within the new atrium, framed by highly polished chromium-plated trusses and turquoise panels, hangs a large Art Deco painting that was found in the older building during renovation. This complex captures the spirit of Chicago architecture: Devoted to commerce, it embraces the present without denying the past.

Next came Jahn's sleek, curving Xerox Center of white metal and reflective glass, at Monroe and Dearborn streets (1980). Mirrored glass, introduced by Jahn, has become one of the favorite materials in new Chicago commerical buildings. It is successful as a foil to the dark Miesian buildings, especially along the river, where it seems to take on a watery quality on an overcast day. His latest accomplishment is the elegant but playful high-tech United Airlines Terminal 1 at O'Hare (1987). The terminal has been praised as a soaring technological celebration of travel, in the same splendid tradition as the 19th-century European iron and glass railroad stations that Jenney had studied.

Two disparate threads of architectural creation are weaving the modern tissue of Chicago, providing aesthetic tension and dynamism, much as in the period following the World's Columbian Exposition of 1893. The solid, muscular past provides an armature that can support diversity and even fantasy without cracking apart. Yet Chicago is a down-to-earth place whose greatest creations have been products of a no-nonsense approach. "The business of Chicago is business"; when Chicago becomes self-consciously "cultural," it fares less well.

Chicago is a city with a sense of continuity, where the traditions of design are strong. Money and technology have long provided a firm support for free and original intellectual thought, with a strong populist local bias. Chicagoans talk of having a "second city" mentality, yet at the same time they have a strong sense of self; perhaps being "second" has indeed freed them to be themselves.

3 Exploring Chicago

Orientation

Ask anyone who has never visited Chicago what images the city's name calls to mind, and you'll hear of gangsters and tommy guns; stockyards and packinghouses; and the Windy City—a grimy, smelly, industrial town whose climate is severe and whose denizens are rough-and-ready workingmen. Few non-Chicagoans know that the city's motto is *Urbs in Horto,* "City in a Garden," and first-time visitors are often astonished to find the elegant and sophisticated shops of Tiffany, Burberry, Neiman Marcus, I. Magnin, Saks Fifth Avenue, Gucci, and Bloomingdale's along Michigan Avenue's Magnificent Mile; the beauty of Grant Park's acres of blooms, sailboats gliding through the sparkling waters of Lake Michigan, and the lush green parkland along the lakefront; and the handsome and impressive buildings, old and new, designed by world-class architects.

This gracious and attractive city is the city most visitors see. The stockyards and packinghouses have been gone for 20 years; the International Amphitheatre, long the sole remaining structure memorializing the stockyards era and the home to such visitors as the circus, tennis tours, and rock stars, now stands an abandoned hulk whose future is uncertain. The sites of storied gangland raids and slayings are now parking lots or piles of bricks and rubble in ghetto neighborhoods. The steel mills, with their soot and stench—"the smell of money" to East Side residents—have closed, leaving a generation of skilled workers unemployed. Comiskey Park, home of the White Sox for 75 years, is slated for demolition.

State Street, once "that great street," the heart of the downtown area known as the Loop (because of the elevated train that circumscribes it), has become the site of risque lingerie shops, sleazy discount stores, and tape and video shops that announce their wares at top volume to passersby; itinerant preachers daily set up sidewalk sound systems to declaim the imminent demise of sinners. Those marvels of 20th-century merchandising, Marshall Field and Carson Pirie Scott, still stand, but Sears, Goldblatt's, and others are gone. The famed Field's toy department that once covered an entire city block—where 8-foot-tall stuffed animals filled the aisles and children ogled dollhouses not much smaller than a Chicago bungalow—is gone, replaced by sports equipment, crafts paraphernalia, and model trains. Upscale shoppers have left State Street for the Magnificent Mile.

Even the Windy City appellation has more to do with the volubility of Chicago's residents than it does with nature's offerings.

While packinghouses, factories, and steel mills have gone, many corporate greats, including Quaker Oats, Helene Curtis, and Johnson Publishing, remain. The Merchandise Mart is the furniture hub of the Midwest. La Salle Street, the financial district, home of the Chicago Board of Trade, the Chicago Board Options Exchange, the Midwest Stock Exchange, and international banking houses, bustles. The business of Chicago continues to be business.

The skyline has changed. In the last two decades the Sears tower, the Amoco Building, the John Hancock Building, The

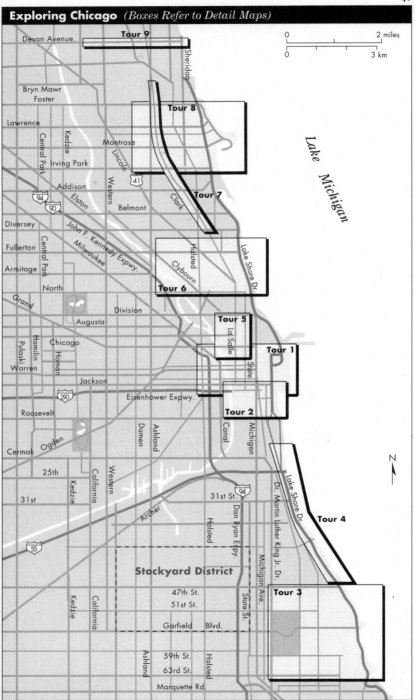

Exploring Chicago *(Boxes Refer to Detail Maps)*

Tour 9

Devon Avenue.

Bryn Mawr
Foster

Lawrence

Central Park
Irving Park

Addison

Diversey

Fullerton

Armitage

North

Grand

Augusta

Chicago

Warren

Jackson

Roosevelt

Cermak   Ogden

25th

31st

Kedzie

Central Park

Kedzie

Western

Pulaski
Homan
Hamlin

Damen
Ashland

California

Archer

Elston

Milwaukee

John F. Kennedy Expwy.

Western

Belmont

Lincoln

Clark

Halsted

Clybourn

Division

La Salle

State

Canal

Michigan

Eisenhower Expwy.

Sheridan

Montrose

Tour 8

Tour 7

Tour 6

Tour 5

Tour 1

Tour 2

Lake Michigan

Lake Shore Dr.

Lake Shore Dr.

Dr. Martin Luther King Jr. Dr.

Tour 4

31st St.

Stockyard District

47th St.
51st St.

Garfield   Blvd.

59th St.
63rd St.

Marquette Rd.

Halsted

Dan Ryan Expwy.

Michigan Ave.

State St.

Ashland

Halsted

Kedzie

California

Tour 3

0   2 miles
0   3 km

N

Associates Center, the NBC Building, Illinois Center, 333 West Wacker, the CNA Building, Lake Point Towers, and other structures have made the Chicago skyline one of the most exciting in the world.

Cultural life flourishes. The Schubert, Blackstone, and Goodman theaters, the Chicago bases for Broadway-scale shows, have been joined by more than 40 little theaters based in the neighborhoods, where young actors polish their skills. Long a city where fine dining meant steak, Chicago is now home to talented chefs who work on the culinary frontiers of New American and pan-Asian cuisine. The art galleries of Ontario and Superior streets are alive and well, augmented by a large new neighborhood of galleries in resurgent River North. The Lyric Opera has extended its season into January, offering nine productions annually that play to houses averaging 95% full; Chicago Opera Theatre augments the Lyric's offerings with a spring season of smaller works. Chicago Symphony subscriptions are a sellout; the Ravinia Festival and the Grant Park Concerts pack people in. Music lovers hungry for more turn to smaller performing groups: the Orchestra of Illinois, Music of the Baroque, the Chicago Brass Ensemble, City Musick, and dozens more.

Leave downtown and the lakefront, however, and you soon encounter a city of neighborhoods: bungalows, two-flats, three-flats, and six-flats, churches and shopping strips with signs in Polish, Spanish, Chinese, Arabic, Hebrew, or Korean, and an ethnic community life that remains vibrant.

The early immigrants came from Ireland, Germany, Lithuania, and Czechoslovakia to settle along Archer and Milwaukee avenues. In time, they or their descendants moved outward—southwest on Archer, northwest on Milwaukee—as new groups arrived in the central city. The Irish settled originally in Bridgeport, a neighborhood that spawned a line of political leaders culminating with the late Mayor Richard J. Daley (still spoken of as "Da Maire") and his protégée, Jane Byrne, and broken only by the ascension of the city's first black mayor, the late Harold Washington. The Mexicans settled in Pilsen, to the north and west of Bridgeport, the Chinese in Chinatown to the northeast. Today, the Bridgeport Irish community, which long resisted opening its borders to "outsiders," is being squeezed by the expansion of Pilsen, as Mexican immigrants continue to arrive, and by the vigorous growth of Chinatown, fueled by the immigration of affluent Hong Kong Chinese.

On the North Side, Polish, German, and Scandinavian groups have moved westward and further north, making way for the tremendous influx of Orthodox Jews from Russia; Middle Easterners and Arabs from Lebanon, Syria, Libya, and other countries; South Asians from India and Pakistan; and Southeast Asians (Koreans, Cambodians, Thai, Vietnamese, and Hmong) fleeing uncertain political conditions in their homelands. In Chicago you'll find delicatessens where kosher salamis and hot dogs in display cases nestle side by side with egg rolls, onion pancakes, and kimchee.

On the South and West sides, Jews from Germany and Eastern Europe who once populated these areas have moved to Hyde Park, northward along the lakefront, and into the northern suburbs, to be replaced by blacks fleeing urban decay. The great Roman Catholic churches of the central city, such as Holy Family, have fallen on hard times; some are slated for demolition because populations too poor or too Protestant to support them have supplanted the Eastern, Central, and Southern Europeans who labored to build them and filled their pews. In their place have come the storefront Iglesias de Dios and African Methodist Episcopal churches that minister to the new populations.

The neighborhoods are the part of Chicago that a visitor rarely sees. Yet it is in the neighborhoods that one can encounter the life of ordinary people, enjoy a great ethnic feast for a pittance, and visit the museums and churches that house cultural artifacts reflecting the soul and spirit of the community. The Chicago of the neighborhoods is the underpinning of the world-class city, and both must be experienced to understand the real Chicago.

In the tours that follow, we explore in depth the many faces of Chicago. We'll begin **Downtown,** in the heart of the world-class city, visiting handsome old landmark buildings and shimmering new ones, the centers of business and trade and the mainstays of culture, new residential areas and renewed older districts. Our visit to **Downtown South** shows how old forms take on new functions that merge with the life of the central city.

Then we'll head south to **Hyde Park and Kenwood,** home of the University of Chicago. We'll see turn-of-the-century mansions and workingmen's cottages, we'll look at the process of urban renewal and the changes it has wrought in the neighborhood, and we'll ramble through museums, churches, and bookstores. We'll head north again via **South Lake Shore Drive,** viewing Chicago's splendid skyline along the way.

On the North Side, we'll visit **River North** to see how the rehabilitation process has transformed an area of factories and warehouses into a neighborhood of upscale shopping strips and more than 50 art galleries.

In **Lincoln Park**—like Hyde Park, one of the city's oldest residential neighborhoods—we'll follow the process of gentrification in Sheffield/De Paul, see some beautiful mid-19th-century houses, and visit the campuses of the old McCormick Seminary and De Paul University. Then we'll head up North Lincoln Avenue for a stop at the historic Biograph Theatre and a look at the shops. Finally, we'll explore the Old Town Triangle, visiting one of the oldest streets in Chicago and one of the most expensive and contrasting the religious expressions found in St. Michael's Church with those at the Midwest Buddhist Temple.

We'll take a bus or a car the length of **North Clark Street** to see how the continuing waves of immigration leave their mark on the face of the city.

Further north, we'll visit **Argyle Street and Uptown** for a brief look at how the immigrant Vietnamese have created a very American economic miracle in one of Chicago's most depressed neighborhoods.

We'll visit **Devon Avenue** on the city's far north side to see how immigrants from the Indian subcontinent live virtually side by side with Orthodox Jews newly arrived from Russia. Here we'll find different customs and cultures in juxtaposition, and we'll sample their ethnic cuisines.

Finally, we'll detour to the suburbs for a look at Oak Park, a community with one of the largest concentrations of the works of Prairie School architect Frank Lloyd Wright and his followers.

Highlights for First-time Visitors

Art Institute (Tour 1: Downtown)
Field Museum of Natural History (Tour 4: South Lake Shore Drive)
Shedd Aquarium (Tour 4: South Lake Shore Drive)
Chicago Historical Society (Tour 6: Lincoln Park)
River North Concourse (Tour 5: River North)
Museum of Science and Industry (Tour 3: Hyde Park and Kenwood)
Grant Park and Buckingham Fountain (Tour 2: Downtown South)
Picasso sculpture in Daley Center (Tour 1: Downtown)
Door of Carson Pirie Scott building (Tour 1: Downtown)
Lobbies of The Rookery and the Board of Trade (Tour 1: Downtown)

Tour 1: Downtown

Numbers in the margin correspond with points of interest on the Tour 1: Downtown map.

Downtown Chicago is a city lover's delight. Here are the buildings by famous architects, the great American cultural institutions, and the canyons of commerce and finance that drive the pulse of the city. Downtown comprises the area south of the Chicago River, west of Lake Michigan, and north of the Congress Parkway/Eisenhower Expressway. Downtown Chicago's western boundary used to be the Chicago River, but the boundary continues to push westward even as this book is written. Handsome new skyscrapers line every foot of South Wacker Drive east and west of the river, and investors have sent construction crews across the bridges in search of more land to fuel the expansion.

We begin our tour on North Michigan Avenue at South Water Street. You can reach it from the north via the No. 2, 3, 11, 145, 146, 147, 151, or 157 bus; get off before the bridge, cross it, and walk the short block to South Water. Coming from the south, you can take the No. 3, 6, 56, 141, 145, 146, 147, 151, or 157 bus; get off at Lake Street and walk one block north to South Water. If you arrive by car, you'll want to park it, for this tour is best done on foot.

On the southwest corner of the intersection stands the elegant Art Deco **Carbide and Carbon Building** (233 N. Michigan). Designed by the Burnham Brothers in 1929, its sleek gold and black exterior is accented by curving, almost lacy brasswork at the entrance. Inside, the lobby is splendid, with more burnished brass, glass ornamentation, and marble.

Tour 1: Downtown

Amoco Building, **5**
Art Institute of Chicago, **23**
Associates Center, **4**
AT&T Building, **17**
Auditorium Theatre, **39**
Berghoff Restaurant, **28**

Buckingham Fountain, **40**
Carbide and Carbon Building, **1**
Carson Pirie Scott, **22**
Chicago Board of Trade, **33**
Chicago City Hall-Cook County Building, **10**
Chicago Mercantile Exchange, **18**

Chicago Public Library Cultural Center, **6**
Chicago Temple, **8**
Civic Opera House, **13**
CNA Building, **36**
Daley Center, **9**
Dawn Shadows, **19**
Federal Center and Plaza, **29**

Fine Arts Building, **38**
First National Bank Plaza, **20**
Fisher Building, **35**
Main Post Office, **43**
Marquette Building, **27**
Marshall Field, **7**
Metropolitan Detention Center, **41**
Monadnock Building, **34**

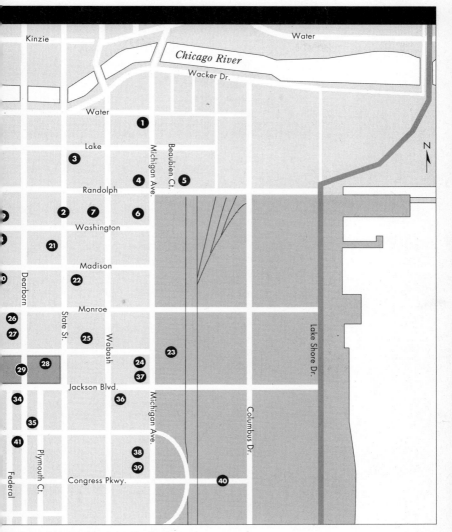

② Walk south on Michigan, turn right on Lake, and continue to State Street and the north end of the **State Street Mall.** Built a decade ago with federal funds, the mall was intended to revive the faltering State Street shopping strip by providing trees, sculptures, and outdoor cafés to encourage shoppers to visit the area and patronize the stores. Because of restrictions on the federal grant, however, the street could not be made a true pedestrian mall; closed to private vehicles, it remained open to police cars, emergency vehicles, and buses. The mall has been a spectacular failure. The improvements and amenities were minimal: The new hexagonal gray concrete bricks are no more appealing than the original sidewalk, the few pieces of sculpture are undistinguished, and the outdoor cafés fail to thrive amid the exhaust fumes of the buses. The exodus of better stores to North Michigan Avenue and elsewhere has continued.

Turn left onto this urban paradise and walk half a block to the **Chicago Theatre** (175 N. State). Threatened with demolition a few years ago, the 70-year-old theater was saved through the efforts of a civic-minded consortium that bought the building and oversaw a multimillion-dollar restoration. It has had several different managers who have been unable to make the theater a financial success. At press time, it is closed while the city
③ searches for a new management company. Next door, the **Page Brothers Building** is one of only two buildings in Chicago known to have a cast-iron front wall. Notice the delicate detail work on the horizontal and vertical bands between the windows. The building behind the facade, now being renovated, will become part of a new Chicago Theatre complex. Notice also the very handsome building, directly across State, that houses WLS-TV.

Continue south, turn left on Randolph Street, and walk to
④ Michigan. On the northwest corner, the **Associates Center** (150 N. Michigan Ave.), the office building with the distinctive diamond-shaped, angled face visible for miles, is the first building in Chicago to be wired for computer use (outlets in every office eliminate the need for costly cabling). An amusing sculpture sits in its small plaza.

⑤ Two blocks east, the **Amoco Building** (200 E. Randolph), formerly the Standard Oil Building, is the largest marble-clad building in the world. Some of the marble cladding has fallen off recently, necessitating an investigation into how to preserve or replace the exterior of this coolly graceful skyscraper. The building sits on a handsome but rather sterile plaza. Harry Bertoia's wind chime sculpture in the reflecting pool makes interesting sounds when the wind blows. The building itself is better appreciated when seen against Chicago's skyline than in its massive presence up close. Next door is the **Prudential Building**, replaced as Chicago's tallest building in the late '60s by the John Hancock. Behind it rises a postmodern spire added in 1990.

⑥ Return west on Randolph to Michigan, walk south a block, and turn right on East Washington Street, to the **Chicago Public Library Cultural Center** (78 E. Washington, tel. 312/269–2900). When you've stepped inside the Romanesque-style entrance, notice the marble and the mosaic work before you climb the curving stairway to the third floor. There you will see a splendid back-lit Tiffany dome, restored during the 1977 renovation

of the building. This is Preston Bradley Hall, used for public
events. Other parts of the building were reputedly modeled on
Venetian and ancient Greek elements. If you love Tiffany
domes, you will find another one on the second floor. More than
an architectural marvel, the Cultural Center offers concerts,
permanent collections, and changing exhibitions. A foreign-
language reading room stocks newspapers and periodicals
from around the world. Civil War buffs will enjoy the artifacts
on display in the Grand Army of the Republic room.

7 Turn right on leaving the Cultural Center from the Washington
Street side, walk to Wabash Avenue, and enter. **Marshall Field
& Co.** (111 N. State) This mammoth store, now undergoing a
massive renovation, boasts some 500 departments, and it's a
great place for a snack (the Crystal Palace ice cream parlor) or
a meal (the grand Walnut Room or Hinky Dink Kenna's in the
basement). Another spectacular Tiffany dome can be found on
Field's southwest corner, near State and Washington.

8 Further west on Washington, we come to the **Chicago Temple**
(77 W. Washington), whose beautiful spire can be seen only at
some distance (the bridge across the river at Dearborn Street
is a good spot for viewing it). In the plaza is Joan Miró's sculpture *Chicago* (1982).

9 Directly opposite is the **Daley Center,** named for the late Mayor
Richard J. Daley, where the Cook County court system is head-
quartered. The building is constructed of a steel known as
Cor-ten, which was developed as a medium that would weather naturally and attractively (and weathering has certainly
improved its appearance). In the plaza is a sculpture by Picasso
that is made of the same material. Known simply as "the Picasso," it provoked an outcry when it was installed in 1967. Specu-
lation about what it is meant to represent (knowledgeable
observers say it is the head of a woman; others have suggested
it is a pregnant cow) has diminished but not ended. In the plaza,
as well, is an eternal flame dedicated to the memory of the
American soldiers who died in Korea and Vietnam. In summertime the plaza hosts concerts, dance presentations, and a weekly farmer's market.

10 Directly across Clark Street from the Daley Center is the
Chicago City Hall–Cook County Building, a handsome neoclassical structure designed by Holabird and Roche in 1911
whose appearance is generally ignored by the citizens who
rush in and out to do business with the City. Inside are spacious
halls, high ceilings, plenty of marble, and lots of hot air, for this
is where the Chicago City Council holds its infamous meetings.

11 Head north on Clark for a block and you'll reach the notorious
State of Illinois Center (100 W. Randolph). Governor James
Thompson, who personally selected the Helmut Jahn design
for the building, hailed it in his dedication speech in 1985 as
"the first building of the twenty-first century." Those who
work there, and many ordinary Chicagoans as well, have
groaned in response, "I hope not." It is difficult to say more
about the design of the building than to point out that it presents multiple shapes and faces. Narrow alternating vertical
strips of mirrored and plain glass give the impression of taffeta
streamers flying from a giant maypole. Some people love it and
some do not; the structure's sky blue, white, and red exterior
colors have elicited such adjectives as "garish" and "tacky"

from viewers. Its enormous interior atrium embraces a volume of 8 million cubic feet. The dramatically patterned circular floor at its base and the soaring vistas, with handsome exposed elevators and a sky-lit glass dome, are impressive.

Yet the very features that evoke awe seem designed to foil the creation of a stable interior environment. The huge central area and the vast expanses of glass around the exterior would cause daunting climate-control problems in the best of settings, and this has not been the best of settings. For the first years after the building opened, the state-of-the-art heating and cooling system simply did not work. In summertime office workers equipped themselves with large fans and parasols to ward off the baking rays that shone relentlessly through the glass. Business dress gave way to beachwear as the interior temperatures soared toward 100 degrees. In wintertime coats and mittens were required for sedentary workers. Ongoing repairs, each round said to have "licked the problem," have mitigated some of the worst extremes, but an enormous and expensive retrofitting will be needed before the problems are fully resolved. Meanwhile, the elevators, handsome as they are, often break down. Once an award ceremony took place in an elevator stalled between floors; the presentation of the plaque, complete with choral tribute, was easily accomplished during the two hours the award recipient and the choir spent together.

On the northwest corner of Randolph and Clark stands *Monument to a Standing Beast,* a sculpture by Jean Dubuffet. Its curved shapes, in white with black traceries, set against the curving red, white, and blue of the center, merely add to the visual cacophony. In another setting it might be a pleasing and enjoyable work.

Now let's look at a building roughly contemporary to the State of Illinois Center that has had a very different public reception. Head west on Randolph, turn right on La Salle Street, left on Lake, and walk two blocks to Franklin Street. The building at **333 West Wacker Drive,** designed by Kohn, Pedersen, Fox in 1983 and constructed on a triangular plot, is a softly curving building with forest green marble columns, a spacious plaza, and a shimmering green glass skin. Its unpromisingly irregular shape, dictated by the parcel on which it sits, is particularly lovely seen at sunset from the bridge over the Chicago River at Orleans Street, when the river and surrounding buildings are mirrored in the glass.

A two-block walk south on Wacker will take you to the **Civic Theatre** and, a bit farther on, the **Civic Opera House** (20 N. Wacker, tel. 312/346–0270), where Chicago's Lyric Opera gives its performances. Built by the utilities magnate and manipulator Samuel Insull, the handsome Art Deco building is also an elegant older office building. The Civic Opera House is very grand indeed, with marble floors and pillars in the main hall, crystal chandeliers, and a marvelous sweeping staircase to the second floor. Lyric Opera performances are oversubscribed (subscriptions are willed to succeeding generations), so you can't expect simply to drop in on one of the productions during the season that runs from late September through January. Nevertheless, if you stop by the corner of Madison Street and Wacker early on the evening of a performance, you may find ticket holders with the extra ticket to sell, perhaps at a premium, should Pavarotti be singing that night.

⑭ We'll turn right onto Madison and continue west to Clinton Street and the eastern end of the smashing new **Northwestern Atrium Center** (500 W. Madison), which replaced the old Northwestern Station. The building combines a boxlike office tower with glass half-cylinders piled one atop the other at the lower levels. Broad contrasting horizontal bands of mirrored and smoked glass alternate up the building for a ribbon effect that is reminiscent of a similar theme—by the same architects—at the State of Illinois Center. Inside, the marble floors and exposed girders, painted a soft grayish blue, remind you of the appearance of the grand old railroad stations in this country and in Europe, yet at the same time they are completely contemporary. The girders seen against the rippling exterior glass make beautiful geometric patterns. The area over the entrance simulates a rose window in steel and clear glass. The gates to the tracks, elevated above street level to allow street traffic to proceed east and west via underpasses, are reached by going up one level and heading to the north end of the building. Go up another flight for a grand view northward looking out over the tracks; this level is the entrance to the office spaces of the building.

⑮ One block west is the **Social Security Building** (600 W. Madison), once a distant outpost in a dangerous neighborhood that was selected by the federal government because it was a low-rent district. Today the structure is one of several good-looking contemporary and renovated buildings in the area. Of interest here is the Claes Oldenburg sculpture *Batcolumn*, a gigantic baseball bat that failed to get critical acclaim when it was unveiled in 1977. Yet a 100-foot-high baseball bat is an amusing sight, and the current development west of the river will allow even more people the opportunity for a twice-daily smile at this whimsical construction.

⑯ Directly across from the *Batcolumn* are the buildings that make up the **Presidential Towers** residences. The easternmost and main building of the four is at 555 West Madison. Best seen from a distance, these attractive, if not architecturally distinguished, structures have lured some suburbanites back to the city and persuaded other young adults not to move away. The amenities are good: an attractive bistro restaurant (Zincs), an upscale supermarket, several fast food restaurants, a drug store, and other shops catering to the daily needs of the residents. The complex extends two blocks east to Desplaines Street and a block south to Monroe Street, with the buildings aligned on a southwesterly diagonal.

⑰ To the east of Presidential Towers, just opposite the Northwestern Atrium Center, is the ugly, windowless, poured-concrete **AT&T Building**. All that can be said in its defense is that when it was built, it must have seemed unlikely that visitors would stray so far from the heart of downtown.

⑱ As you recross the river on Madison, regard the pale grape colored buildings to your right; they are the twin towers of the **Chicago Mercantile Exchange** (10 and 30 S. Wacker). The visitor's gallery of the Merc, open weekdays from 7:30 AM to 3:15 PM, looks down on the frenetic activity on the trading floor. Here is where hog belly futures (they have to do with the supermarket price of bacon), soybeans, and dollars are traded on national and international markets.

Stop at the northwest corner of Madison and Wells streets for a look at a Louise Nevelson sculpture of 1983—a vigorous, forceful (19) construction of darkened steel incongruously titled *Dawn Shadows.*

Farther along Madison, the **First National Bank of Chicago,** designed by Perkins and Will in 1973, was a sensation when it was built because this structure slopes upward from its base in a shape that looks like an ornate letter A. Today it's just another good-looking downtown office building. On your left is the very different recent addition to the First National complex, **3 First National Plaza.**

Now turn right onto Dearborn. Halfway down the block is the (20) famous **First National Bank Plaza,** which runs the length of the block from Dearborn to Clark. In the summer the plaza is the site of outdoor performances by musicians and dancers and a hangout for picnickers and tanners. In any season you can visit the Chagall mosaic known as *The Four Seasons* (1974) at the northeast end of the plaza, between Madison and Monroe on Dearborn. It is said that when Chagall arrived in Chicago to install the mosaic, he found it a more vigorous city than he had remembered, and he began immediately to modify the work to reflect the stronger and more vital elements he found around him. Not one of Chagall's greatest works, it is nevertheless a pretty, pleasing, sometimes lyrical piece.

If you continue east on Madison and turn left on State, you'll (21) come to the **Reliance Building** (32 N. State). Designed by Daniel Burnham in 1890, it was innovative for its time in its use of glass as well as terra-cotta for its exterior, and once it was quite beautiful. Today, the building is not much to look at; the street level houses the kind of sleazy shop that is typical of State Street, and the whole building needs a good cleaning.

(22) Return to Madison to find **Carson Pirie Scott** (1 S. State), known to architecture students as one of Louis Sullivan's outstanding works. The building illustrates the Chicago Window, a large fixed central window with smaller movable windows on each side. Notice also the fine exterior ornamentation at street level, particularly the exquisite work over the entrance on the southeast corner of Madison and State. Dedicated shoppers may be less interested in the architecture of the building than in its contents; Chicago's "second" department store (always mentioned after Marshall Field & Co.) would be a standout anywhere else. Its Corporate Level offers tasteful clothing for male and female executives, while its main-floor InPulse store lures the teenage set.

From the south end of Carson's, head east on Monroe and south on Michigan to Adams Street and the imposing entrance to the (23) marvelous **Art Institute of Chicago.** You'll recognize the Art Institute by its guardian lions on each side of the entrance. (The lions have a special place in the hearts of Chicagoans, who outfitted them with Chicago Bears helmets when the Bears won the Superbowl.) A map of the museum, available at the Information Desk, will help you find your way to the works or periods you want to visit. The Art Institute has outstanding collections of Medieval and Renaissance paintings as well as Impressionist and Post-Impressionist works. Less well-known are its fine holdings in Asian art and its photography collection. Be sure to visit the Rubloff paperweight collection; a Chicago real estate magnate donated these shimmering, multicolored functional objects. The Thorne Miniature Rooms show interior decoration in every historical style; they'll entrance anyone who's ever furnished a dollhouse or built a model. And don't miss the Stock Exchange room, a splendid reconstruction of a part of the old Chicago Stock Exchange, which was demolished in 1972. The newest attraction at the Institute is the Daniel F. and Ada L. Rice Building, opened in September 1988, with three floors of exhibition galleries, a large space for temporary exhibitions, and a skylit central court dotted with sculpture and plantings.

If you have a youngster with you, make an early stop at the Children's Museum downstairs. Your child will be given a set of Gallery Games, including "I Spy" (which challenges small folk to locate particular works in the museum's collections), "Scrutinize" (which includes a set of postcards to be taken home), and "Bits and Pieces." The delightful and informative games will keep your youngster from becoming hopelessly bored as you tramp through the galleries. The museum store has an outstanding collection of art books, calendars, merchandise related to current exhibits, and an attractive selection of gift items. When you're ready for refreshments, the Institute provides a cafeteria, a dining room serving Continental cuisine, and a terrace café (in warm weather). *S. Michigan at Adams, tel. 312/443–3600. Admission: $5 adults, $2.50 children and senior citizens, free Tues. Open weekdays 10:30–4:30 (Tues. until 8), Sat. 10–5, Sun. noon–5. Closed Christmas Day.*

㉔ **Orchestra Hall** (220 S. Michigan, tel. 312/435–6666), opposite the Art Institute, is the home of the internationally acclaimed Chicago Symphony Orchestra. Don't expect to find symphony tickets at the box office; subscription sales exhaust virtually all the available tickets. (You'll have better luck at hearing the symphony during the summer if you make the trek to Ravinia Park in the suburb of Highland Park.) Sometimes it pays to stop by Orchestra Hall about an hour before a concert; there may be last-minute ticket returns at the box office, or there may be street-corner vendors. If you'd like to see the inside of Orchestra Hall, regardless of who's performing, buy a ticket to one of the recitals that are scheduled frequently, particularly on Sunday afternoons. For an incredible view, get a balcony ticket. The balconies are layered one atop the other in dramatic fashion, and because the seats are steeply banked, the view is splendid and the acoustics are excellent. Also at the top of Orchestra Hall is the private, handsomely understated Cliff Dweller's Club, whose membership consists principally of performers and supporters of the arts.

㉕ The **Palmer House** (17 E. Monroe, tel. 312/726–7500), one of Chicago's grand old hotels, is reached by returning to Adams and proceeding west one block. Cross Wabash, turn right, and enter about halfway down the block. The ground-floor level is an arcade with patterned marble floors and antique lighting fixtures where you'll find upscale shops, restaurants, and service establishments. But it's the lobby—up one flight of stairs—that you must see: Richly carpeted, outfitted with fine furniture, and lavishly decorated (look at the ceiling murals), this room is one of the few remaining examples of the opulent elegance that was once de rigueur in Chicago's fine hotels.

26 Exit the Palmer House on the State Street side, walk north to Monroe, and turn left. The **Xerox Building** (55 W. Monroe) was designed in 1982 by the same firm (Murphy/Jahn) that would be responsible three years later for the State of Illinois Center. The building's wraparound aluminum and glass wall ex ends from the Monroe Street entrance around the corner onto Dearborn, communicating both vitality and beauty. On the corner is **The Sharper Image**, with every kind of gadget and exercise machine for the upscale young professional. While it's great fun to browse here, the store reminds one of the aphorism that "the difference between the men and the boys is the price of their toys."

27 Now head south half a block on Dearborn. The **Marquette Building** (140 S. Dearborn) of 1894, by Holabird and Roche, features an exterior terra-cotta bas relief and interior reliefs and mosaics depicting scenes from early Chicago history.

28 Continue south to Adams and then jog a bit eastward to have a look at the westernmost building of the **Berghoff Restaurant** (17 W. Adams). Although at first glance it appears as though the front is masonry, it is in fact ornamental cast iron. The practice of using iron panels cast to imitate stone was common in the latter part of the 19th century (this building was constructed in 1872), but this building and the **Page Brothers Building** on State Street, built in the same year, are the only examples known to have survived. The iron front on the Berghoff building was discovered only a few years ago, and other such buildings may yet be extant, waiting to be found.

29 Return now to Dearborn and the **Federal Center and Plaza.** The twin Federal Buildings, the Kluczyinski (219 S. Dearborn) and the Dirksen (230 S. Dearborn), built in 1964, are classic examples of the trademark Mies van der Rohe glass and steel box. In the plaza, on the southwest side of Dearborn and Adams, is the wonderful Calder stabile *Flamingo*, dedicated on the same day in 1974 as Calder's *Universe* at the Sears Tower. It is said that Calder had a grand day, riding through Chicago in a brightly colored circus bandwagon accompanied by calliopes, heading from one dedication to the other.

30 Continue west on Adams. At La Salle is **The Rookery** (209 S. La Salle). An imposing redstone building designed in 1886 by Burnham and Root. The Rookery was built partly of masonry and partly of the more modern steel frame construction. The magnificent lobby was remodeled in 1905 by Frank Lloyd Wright. The building was closed for several years, but at press time it was receiving a $2.5 million restoration, which may be completed by 1991.

As you leave The Rookery, look to your left at the **Chicago Board of Trade**, at the foot of the La Salle Street canyon, framed by the buildings on each side.

31 Cross La Salle and head west on the little two-block lane called Quincy Street. At its terminus on Franklin you will be directly opposite the entrance to the **Sears Tower** (233 S. Wacker Dr.). A Skidmore, Owings & Merrill design of 1974, Sears Tower has 110 stories and is almost 1,500 feet tall. Although this is the world's tallest building, it certainly isn't the world's most livable one. Despite costly improvements to the Wacker Drive entrance (most of the street traffic is on the Franklin Street side) and the main floor arcade area, the building doesn't really attract the passerby.

Once inside, you'll probably be baffled by the escalators and elevators that stop on alternate floors (the elevators have double cars, one atop the other, so that when one car has stopped, say, at 22, the other is at 21). If you need to go to the upper reaches of the building (other than to go via direct express elevator to the 103rd-floor Skydeck), you'll find that you have to leave one elevator bank, walk down the hall and around a corner, and find another to complete your trip. Stories have been told about new employees on the upper stories spending their entire lunch hour trying to find a way out. In high winds the building sways noticeably at the upper levels and, most alarming, in 1988 there were two occasions on which windows were blown out. According to the architects and engineers, the odds against this happening even once were astronomical; imagine how red their faces must have been the second time it happened. When it did happen, the streets surrounding the building were littered with shards of glass and papers were sucked out of offices that had lost their windows. On a clear day, however, the view from the Skydeck is unbeatable. (Check the visibility ratings at the security desk before you decide to ride up and take it in.) And don't miss the Calder mobile sculpture *Universe* in the lobby on the Wacker Drive side.

From the south end of the Sears Tower we'll head west on Jackson Boulevard and across the river to Canal Street. The **32** wonderful old (1917) **Union Station** (210 S. Canal) is everything a train station should be, with a 10-story dome over the main waiting room, a skylight, columns, and gilded statues.

33 We return east on Jackson to the **Chicago Board of Trade** (141 W. Jackson), one of the few important Art Deco buildings in Chicago (the Civic Opera House and the Carbide and Carbon building are the others). It was designed in 1930 by the firm of Holabird and Roche; at the top is a gilded statue of Ceres, the Greek goddess of grain, an apt overseer of the frenetic commodities trading that goes on within. The observation deck that overlooks the trading floor is open to the public weekdays, 9 AM–2 PM. The lobby is well worth your attention.

Farther east, taking up a good portion of the block from Jackson to Van Buren Street, is the massive, darkly handsome **34** **Monadnock Building** (53 W. Jackson). The north half was built by Burnham and Root in 1891, the south half by Holabird and Roche in 1893. This is the tallest building ever constructed entirely of masonry. The problem with all-masonry buildings is that the higher they go, the thicker the walls at the base must be to support the upper stories, and the Monadnock's walls at the base are six feet thick. Thus you can see why the introduction of the steel frame began a new era in construction. The building was recently and tastefully renovated inside (the original wrought-iron banisters, for example, have been retained) and cleaned outside, restoring it to its former magnificence from the rather dilapidated and slightly creepy hulk it had become. This is a popular office building for lawyers because of its proximity to the federal courts in the Kluczynski Building. The **ArchiCenter,** where Chicago Architecture Foundation tours originate, is located here.

㉟ Across the street is the **Fisher Building** (343 S. Dearborn), designed by D. H. Burnham & Co. in 1896. This Gothic-style building, exquisitely ornamented in terra-cotta, is for some reason (perhaps because of favorable rents) the headquarters of dozens of arts and other not-for-profit organizations. Turn left onto Van Buren for a view of the beautifully carved cherubs frolicking over what was once a side entrance to the building, now glassed in.

㊱ Proceed east again on Jackson to Wabash for a look at the rust-colored **CNA Building.** On no one's list of landmarks, the structure is interesting principally because it leaves such a noticeable mark on the skyline. Chicagoans who thought the color was an undercoat of rustproofing paint that would be covered over by something more conventional were wrong.

㊲ Farther along Jackson, at Michigan, is the **Railway Exchange Building** (80 E. Jackson; enter on Michigan), better known as the Santa Fe building, because of the large "Santa Fe" sign atop it that is part of the nighttime skyline. Designed in 1904 by Daniel Burnham, who later had his office there, it underwent extensive and very successful renovation a few years ago. The interior atrium is spectacular.

㊳ One block south is the **Fine Arts Building** (410 S. Michigan). Notice first the handsome detailing on the exterior of the building; then step inside to see the marble and the woodwork in the lobby. The motto engraved in the marble as you enter says, "All passes—art alone endures." The building once housed artists and sculptors in its studios; today its principal tenants are professional musicians and those who cater to musicians' needs. A fine little music shop is hidden away on the ninth floor, and violin makers and other instrument repair shops are sprinkled about. The building has an interior courtyard, across which strains of piano music and soprano voices compete with tenors as they run through exercises and arias. The ground floor of the building, originally the Studebaker Theatre (the building was constructed to house the showrooms of the Studebaker Co., then makers of carriages), was converted into four cinemas in 1982, and the individual theaters have preserved much of the beautiful ornamentation of the original. The Fine Arts Theatres are an asset to the city for their exceptional selection of foreign films, art films, and movies by independent directors.

㊴ Continue on Michigan to the Congress Parkway and **Roosevelt University,** a massive building that houses the remarkable **Auditorium Theatre** (430 S. Michigan). Built in 1889 by Dankmar Adler and Louis Sullivan, the hall seats 4,000 people and has unobstructed sightlines and near-perfect acoustics. The interior ornamentation, including arched rows of lights along the ceiling, is breathtaking. Though it's normally closed to the public unless there's a show or concert, ask for a tour of this elegant hall that was allowed to fall into disrepair and even faced demolition in the 1950s and early 1960s. (Determined supporters raised $3 million to provide for the restoration, which was undertaken by Harry Weese in 1967.) Another beautiful, though less well-known, space is the library on the 10th floor of the building.

㊵ Head east on Congress to Columbus Drive and, set in its own plaza, **Buckingham Fountain.** Between Memorial Day and Labor Day you can see it in all its glory, when it's elaborately illuminated at night.

Return west on Congress to Dearborn and look ahead and to your right. The odd, triangular, poured-concrete building **41** looming up on the right-hand side of Clark is the **Metropolitan Detention Center** (71 W. Van Buren). A jail (rather than a penitentiary, where convicted criminals are sent), it holds people awaiting trial as well as those convicted and awaiting transfer. When erected in 1975, it brought an outcry from citizens who feared large-scale escapes by dangerous criminals. (Their fears have not been realized.) The building was designed by the same Harry Weese who saved the Auditorium Theatre; with its long, slit windows (five inches wide, so no bars are required), it looks like a modern reconstruction of a medieval fort, where slits in the walls permitted archers to shoot at approaching invaders.

Continue west on Congress to the striking building of 1985 by **42** Skidmore, Owings & Merrill known as **One Financial Place** (440 S. La Salle), which has an exterior and interior of Italian red granite and marble. Among its striking features is the arched section that straddles the rushing traffic on the Congress Parkway/Eisenhower Expressway below. The building's tenants include the Midwest Stock Exchange, whose visitor's gallery is open weekdays, 8:30–4, and the La Salle St. Club, which offers limited but elegant hotel accommodations and is the home of the superb Everest Room restaurant.

Another walk west across the river will take you to Chicago's **43** **Main Post Office** (433 W. Van Buren), the world's largest. Tours of this mammoth, highly automated facility are given weekdays at 10:30 AM.

Tour 2: Downtown South

Numbers in the margin correspond with points of interest on the Tour 2: Downtown South map.

The Downtown South area, bounded by Congress Parkway/Eisenhower Expressway on the north, Michigan Avenue on the east, Roosevelt Road on the south, and the Chicago River on the west, presents a striking and often fascinating contrast to the downtown area we have just visited. Once a thriving commercial area and the center of the printing trades in Chicago, it fell into disrepair as the printing industry moved south in search of lower costs. Sleazy bars, pawnbrokers, and pornographic shops filled the area behind what was then the Conrad Hilton Hotel, crowding each other on Wabash Avenue and State Street and on the side streets between. Homeless winos found a place to sleep at the Pacific Garden Mission (646 S. State). Declining business at the mammoth Hilton meant decreasing revenues; floors were closed off, too expensive to maintain, and the owners considered demolishing the building.

Then, about a decade ago, investors became interested in renovating the run-down yet sturdy loft and office buildings in the old printing district. With the first neighborhood rehab efforts just beginning, Michael Foley, a young Chicago restaurateur from an old Chicago restaurant family, opened a restaurant on the edge of the redevelopment area. Making the most of very limited funds, he decorated his restaurant warmly but sparely, relying on illusion as much as accessories to create a cozy, contemporary ambience. His innovative cuisine attracted favorable notice, and the restaurant became and has remained a success in spite of its once unlikely location. Another restaurant opened across the street from Foley's Printer's Row, and an attractive upscale bar took renovated quarters on Harrison Street. Today the Printer's Row district is a thriving urban neighborhood enclave; at press time the area bounded by Congress Parkway, Polk Street, Plymouth Court, and Federal Street was being considered for city landmark status.

At about the time that the first renovations were being undertaken in Printer's Row, a consortium of investors, aided by preferential interest rates from downtown banks, obtained a large parcel of land in the old railroad yards to the south and put up an expansive new development. This was Dearborn Park, affordable housing targeted at young middle-class families. Although its beginnings were rocky—the housing was attractive but there was no supermarket, no dry cleaner, and no public school nearby—Dearborn Park, too, became successful.

To the west, the architect and developer Bertrand Goldberg (of Marina City fame) acquired a sizable tract of land between Wells Street and the Chicago River. Driven by a vision of an innovative, self-contained city within a city, Goldberg erected the futuristic River City, the massed, almost cloudlike complex that seems to rise from the river at Polk Street. This development has been less commercially successful than Dearborn Park, yet the willingness of a developer to make an investment of this size in the area was an indication that the neighborhood south of downtown was here to stay.

Spurred by signs of revitalization all around, the owners of the Conrad Hilton scrapped their plans to abandon the hotel and instead mounted a renovation of tremendous proportion. Now one of the most beautifully appointed hotels in the city, the Chicago Hilton and Towers once again attracts the business it needs to fill its thousands of rooms.

We'll begin our tour of Downtown South at the corner of Balbo and Michigan. You can drive here—traffic and parking conditions are far less congested in the Downtown South area than they are in Downtown—or you can take the Jeffery Express (No. 6) bus from the north (catch it at State and Lake streets) or from Hyde Park.

❶ East of the intersection of Balbo and Michigan is the heart of beautiful **Grant Park**. On a hot summer night during the last week of August 1968, the park was filled with young people protesting the Vietnam War and events at the Democratic presidential nominating convention that was taking place at the Conrad Hilton Hotel down the street. Rioting broke out; heads were cracked, protesters were dragged away screaming, and Mayor Daley gave police the order to "shoot to kill." Later investigations into the events of that evening determined that a "police riot"—not the misbehavior of the protesters, who had been noisy but not physically abusive—was responsible for the violence that erupted. Those who remember those rage-filled days cannot visit this idyllic spot without recalling that time.

❷ The **Blackstone Hotel** (636 S. Michigan), on the northwest corner of the intersection, is rich with history. Presidential candidates have been selected here, and presidents have stayed here. Note the ornate little roofs that cap the first-floor windows. Inside, the elegant lobby has impressive chandeliers, sculptures, and handsome woodwork. Next door is the **Blackstone Theatre,** another vintage building, where Broadway-bound shows were once booked; the theater was recently acquired by De Paul University for its own use and that of local theater companies.

❸ Head north on Michigan to the **Spertus Museum of Judaica,** a small museum housed in Spertus College. The permanent collections include Medieval Jewish art, which is surprisingly like the better-known Christian art of the same period, without the central Christian themes and imagery. The museum regularly mounts exhibitions on topics broadly relevant to Judaism; a recent one displayed drafts, sketches, and correspondence between the wine making House of Rothschild and the artists who were commissioned (a new artist is chosen each year) to design the annual label for the bottles of Rothschild wines. *618 S. Michigan, tel. 312/922–9012. Admission: $3 adults, $2 children. Open Sun.–Thurs. 10–5, Fri. 10–3.*

❹ Continue to the corner of Harrison Street, turn left, and walk three blocks to Dearborn Street. The pioneering **Printer's Row Restaurant** (550 S. Dearborn, tel. 312/461–0780) is a wonderful place to stop for an elegant (but not inexpensive) lunch during the week. Nearby on Dearborn is one of Chicago's newest hotels, the **Hotel Morton** (538 S. Dearborn, tel. 312/663–3200).
❺ Beautifully appointed, the hotel is located in a group of renovated old buildings that have been interconnected. On the corner is the equally new **Prairie Restaurant** (500 S. Dearborn, tel. 312/663–1143).

Turn left and walk west to Federal Street and turn left again. On your right as you head south is a massive beige-gray brick
❻ renovated apartment complex, **Printer's Square** (640 to 780 S. Federal).

Continue south, turn west on Polk, and walk to Wells. Turn left
❼ at Wells and continue to the entrance to **River City** (800 S. Wells). Apartments, all with curving exterior walls (making it a bit difficult to place square or rectangular furniture), ring the circumference of the building. Interior spaces are used for shops, walkways, and tenant storage closets. The building boasts a state-of-the-art health club. The west side of River City fronts on the river, providing a splendid view for apartment dwellers on that side, and 70 spaces for mooring boats are available. If you'd like to take a tour, speak to the guard.

Taylor Street, south of the River City entrance, will take you east to Sherman Street; turn left on Sherman, right on Polk, and left on Dearborn. If you're driving, this is a good place to park. We'll walk up the west side of Dearborn to the end of the block and return on the east side.

❽ The first building on your left is the grand old **Franklin Building** (720 S. Dearborn), originally "The Franklin Co.: Designing, Engraving, Electrotyping" and now condominium apartments. The decorative tilework on the facade leads up to the scene over the front door, *The First Impression;* representing a medieval event, it illustrates the first application of the printer's craft. Above the entryway is the motto "The Excellence of Every Art Must Consist in the Complete Accomplishment of Its Purpose."

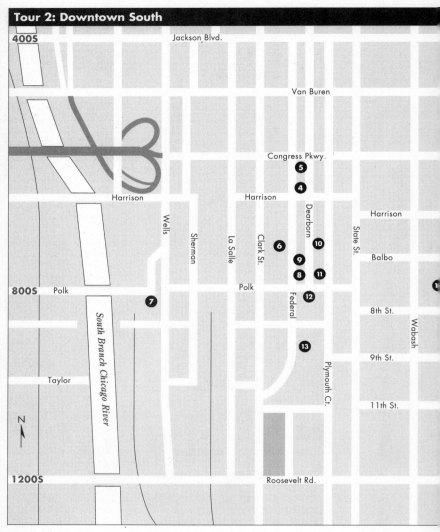

Tour 2: Downtown South

400S

Jackson Blvd.

Van Buren

Congress Pkwy.

5

4

Harrison

Harrison

Harrison

Wells

Sherman

La Salle

Clark St.

Dearborn

Balbo

State St.

6

10

9

8

11

800S   Polk

Polk

Polk

7

Federal

12

1

8th St.

9th St.

Wabash

South Branch Chicago River

13

Taylor

N

Plymouth Ct.

11th St.

1200S

Roosevelt Rd.

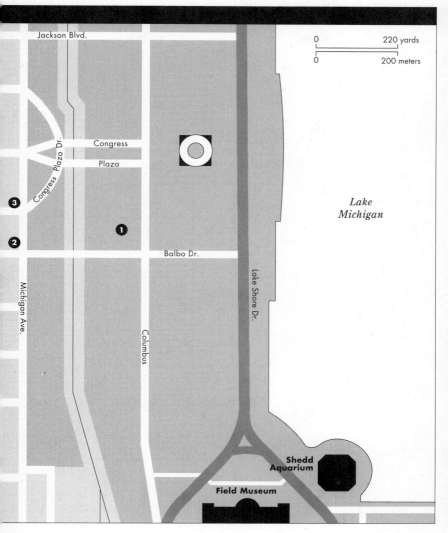

Jackson Blvd.

Congress Plaza Dr.

Congress

Plaza

❸

❷

Michigan Ave.

❶

Balbo Dr.

Columbus

Lake Shore Dr.

Lake Michigan

0   220 yards

0   200 meters

Shedd Aquarium

Field Museum

❾ Next door, **Sandmeyer's Bookstore** (714 S. Dearborn, tel. 312/922–2104) has an iron stairway set with glass bricks and a fine selection of books about Chicago.

In June this street is the locale of the Printer's Row Book Fair, a weekend event where dealers offer a wide variety of books and prints, demonstrations of the papermaking and bookbinding crafts are given, and street performers and food vendors add to the festivity.

Across the street a rehabbed brick building is hung with ban-
❿ ners announcing **Grace Place** (637 S. Dearborn). This is not the newest condo on the block but a consortium of two churches: Grace Episcopal Church and Christ the King Lutheran Church. Each of the congregations is too small to support its own church building, so the two have joined together to share facilities.

Another renovated building houses **Paper Row** (705 S. Dear-born), a card and gift shop. The distinguished **Prairie Ave. Bookshop** (707 S. Dearborn, tel. 312/922–8311) concentrates on new and out-of-print books about architecture, planning, and
⓫ design. These shops are part of the grand **Donohue Building**, whose main entrance is at 711 S. Dearborn. The entrance is flanked by marble columns topped by ornately carved capitals, with tile work over the entrance set into a splendid granite arch. Note also the beautiful ironwork and woodwork in the doors and frames of the shops as you proceed south.

Time Out For a quick pick-me-up, stop at the **Deli on Dearborn** (723 S. Dearborn) or at the **Moonraker Restaurant and Tavern** (733 S. Dearborn). In summer, you can sit outside at either establish-ment, although the cool interior of the Moonraker may be more welcome after a tramp through the city streets.

⓬ The recently restored **Dearborn Station** (47 W. Polk) at the foot of Dearborn, designed in Romanesque-Revival style in 1885 by the New York architect Cyrus L. W. Eidlitz, has a red sand-stone and red brick facade ornamented with terra-cotta. While the main building has been preserved, a train shed at the back was demolished and replaced by a glassed-in, very contempo-rary addition that has not shared the critical enthusiasm that the restoration of the station proper has earned. The striking features inside the station are the brass fixtures set against the cream and white walls and woodwork and the white, rust, and jade marble floor. Since its opening in 1985, Dearborn Station has been successful in attracting office tenants, less so in at-tracting retail tenants. A small, pretty market competes with only limited success with a White Hen Pantry in Dearborn Park and a larger market on 8th Street.

Walk east, turn right on Plymouth Court, and look south,
⓭ where you can see **Dearborn Park.** A planned mix of high-rise, low-rise, and single-family units, some in red brick and some in white, the development has a tidy look. The residents are en-thusiastic about Dearborn Park, and they have developed a warm and supportive community life.

Walk down Plymouth Court to 9th Street and turn left. Walk one block to State Street and turn left again. Look at the at-tractive high rise on the northeast corner. Built recently on a site that would have been unthinkable only a few years earlier, this building has reinforced the resurgent residential community of the area. If you look to the south from here, you can see that redevelopment is under way now in many of the nearby buildings. The Cineplex Odeon (826 S. Wabash) opened in 1988 and shows first-run movies on five screens.

⑭ Walk east on 8th Street, across Wabash, to the **Chicago Hilton and Towers** (720 S. Michigan, tel. 312/922–4400). Enter by the revolving doors, head a bit to your right and then straight, and stroll through the opulent lobby, tastefully done in shades of mauve and soft sea green. Notice the gilded horses that flank the main entrance on the inner wall and the sweeping stairway to your right off the main entrance that leads to the Grand Ballroom. Sneak a peek at the Grand Ballroom if possible; there isn't a more spectacular room in the city. On opening night at the Opera, when a midnight supper and dance is held here, a brass quintet stationed at the top of this stairway plays fanfares as the guests arrive. Be sure not to miss the exquisite Thai hanging on the north wall of the lobby (directly behind and above the concierge's desk).

Time Out | The **Lobby Cafe** at the Hilton has an attractive light lunch and dinner menu. The food is good, and the setting is wonderful for those who enjoy people-watching. Should you prefer a cocktail in the lobby lounge, choose a table by the windows looking out on Michigan Avenue, sit back, relax, and listen to the music of the string ensemble that plays here afternoons until 5 PM.

When you're ready to leave, the Jeffery Express (No. 6) bus to Hyde Park stops on Balbo, directly across Michigan Avenue from the Hilton. Or you can catch any bus that stops on the northeast corner and then transfer to a Michigan Avenue bus at Randolph Street.

Tour 3: Hyde Park and Kenwood

Numbers in the margin correspond with points of interest on the Tour 3: Hyde Park and Kenwood map.

Site of the World's Columbian Exposition of 1893, residence at the turn of the century of the meat-packing barons Swift and Armour, home of the University of Chicago, locale of five houses designed by Frank Lloyd Wright, and the nation's oldest stable racially integrated neighborhood (in the nation's most segregated city), Hyde Park and the adjoining Kenwood may be Chicago's most interesting community: important historically, intellectually, and culturally.

Although farmers and other settlers lived in Hyde Park in the early 1800s and Chicago's oldest Jewish congregation was founded here in 1847, the growth and development of the area really got under way as a result of two events: the World's Columbian Exposition of 1893 and the opening of the University of Chicago in 1892. The Columbian Exposition was responsible for the creation of the Midway Plaisance and the construction of numerous buildings, of which the Museum of Science and Industry is the most famous survivor. To accommodate visitors to the exposition, and to afford a resortlike experience to vacationers, several grand hotels were constructed along what was then the lakefront; the Windermere Apartments (then the Windermere Hotel) survives.

In the same period, the University of Chicago embarked on a program to build housing for its faculty members, and the mansions that line Woodlawn Avenue were the result. Then the neighborhood began to attract well-to-do private individuals who commissioned noted architects to construct homes suitable to persons of great wealth. Many of their houses still stand in Kenwood.

With the coming of the Depression, followed by World War II, the neighborhood entered a period of decline. Grand homes fell into disrepair as the numbers of those with the resources to maintain them dwindled. Wartime housing shortages led to the conversion of stately houses into multifamily dwellings.

Alarmed by the decline of the neighborhood, concerned citizens formed the Hyde Park-Kenwood Community Conference. Aided by $29 million from the University of Chicago, which was anxious that it might not be able to retain—never mind recruit—faculty members, this group set about restoring the neighborhood. Prizes were offered to those who would buy and "deconvert" rooming houses, and the city was pressured to enforce the zoning laws.

The effort that was to have the most lasting effect on the neighborhood was urban renewal, one of the first such undertakings in the nation. Again with the backing and support of the University of Chicago, 55th Street from Lake Park Avenue to Cottage Grove Avenue was razed. Most of the buildings on Lake Park Avenue and on many streets abutting 55th Street and Lake Park were torn down as well. With them went the workshops of painters and artisans, the quarters of "little magazines" (some 20 chapters of James Joyce's *Ulysses* were first published at one of them), the Compass Theatre—where Mike Nichols and Elaine May got their start—and Second City (since relocated to Lincoln Park), and more than 40 bars where jazz and blues could be heard nightly. In their place came town houses designed by I. M. Pei and Harry Weese and a shopping mall designed by Keck and Keck. Cynics have described the process as one of "blacks and whites together, shoulder to shoulder—against the poor."

In the end, these efforts were successful beyond the wildest imaginings of their sponsors, but more than 20 years elapsed before the neighborhood regained its luster. The 18-room houses on Woodlawn Avenue that sell today for $600,000 could still be had for $35,000 in the early 1960s.

To reach the start of our Hyde Park tour, take the Jeffery Express southbound from the Loop (board it anywhere on State Street between Lake and Congress streets) and get off at 56th Street and Hyde Park Boulevard. Or you can take the Illinois Central Gulf (ICG) RR train from Randolph Street and Michigan Avenue; get off at the 55th Street stop and walk east through the underpass one block and south one block. By auto, take Lake Shore Drive south to the 57th Street exit, turn right at the first traffic light (Hyde Park Boulevard), and continue half a block west.

Our exploration of Hyde Park and Kenwood begins at 56th Street and Cornell Avenue. Walk half a block east on 56th ❶ Street to the **Windermere House** (1642 E. 56th St.), designed in 1920 by Rapp and Rapp, known generally for their movie palaces. Notice the grand gatehouse in front of the sweeping semicircular carriage path at the entrance; notice as well the heroic scale of the building, with its ornate carvings.

2 Turn south for a fine view of the Greek Revivalist **Museum of Science and Industry,** built for the Columbian Exposition as a Palace of Fine Arts. Like much of the Exposition construction, the building was intended to be splendid but temporary, and an enormous investment was required to make the structure a permanent one.

3 Continue east to South Shore Drive to the **Promontory Apartments** (5530 S. South Shore Dr.), designed by Mies van der Rohe in 1949. The building was named for **Promontory Point,** which juts out into the lake just east of here; it's a favorite spot for picnics and frisbee, and it can be reached by an underpass just north of 55th Street at Lake Shore Drive. From the Promontory, continue north to 55th Street, turn left, and continue west on 55th Street until you cross under the ICG tracks.

4 At Lake Park Avenue stands the **"Chevrolet" building** (5508 S. Lake Park Ave.), named for the car dealership that formerly occupied it. The beautiful terra-cotta border decorates an otherwise functional building, one of only two buildings in the
5 area left standing after urban renewal. The other is the **Hyde Park Historical Society** (5529 S. Lake Park Ave., tel. 312/493–893), a research library halfway down the block.

Proceeding west on 55th Street, we find one of the fruits of ur-
6 ban renewal, **1400–1451 East 55th Street,** an apartment building designed by I. M. Pei, as were the town houses that border it on the north, between Blackstone and Dorchester avenues. Turn right and head up Blackstone, passing a variety of housing stock between 55th and 51st streets. Although these houses command prices in the hundreds of thousands of dollars today, they were originally cottages for workingmen, attractively located near the cable car line that ran west on 55th Street.

Continue north on Blackstone, across 53rd Street, and half a
7 block east to the entrance to **Harper Court.** Another product of urban renewal, Harper Court was built to house the craftspeople who were displaced from their workshops on Lake Park Avenue. Despite subsidized rents, it never caught on with the craftspeople, who moved elsewhere, while Harper Court evolved into a successful shopping center and community gathering place. People meet here in summer to play chess, eat ice cream, and chat. Among the occupants are **Artisans 21,** a gallery run by artists, and **Art Directions,** an artists' supply store that survived the departure of the artists it was intended to serve.

Time Out   A relative newcomer to Harper Court, **Cafe Coffee** (5211 S. Harper) serves an invigorating selection of coffees, pastries, and snacks. Those who are very hungry might prefer the **Valois Cafeteria** (1518 E. 53rd St.) half a block away, where you can have an inexpensive meal at any time of day or evening.

Leave Harper Court at 52nd Street and Harper, continue north to 51st Street, called Hyde Park Boulevard here, and cross it. You have now entered Kenwood. Turn left and walk a short
8 block to Blackstone and **Kenwood Academy** (5015 S. Blackstone), the local public high school and a "magnet" school for students from elsewhere in Chicago (its students must pass an

Tour 3: Hyde Park and Kenwood

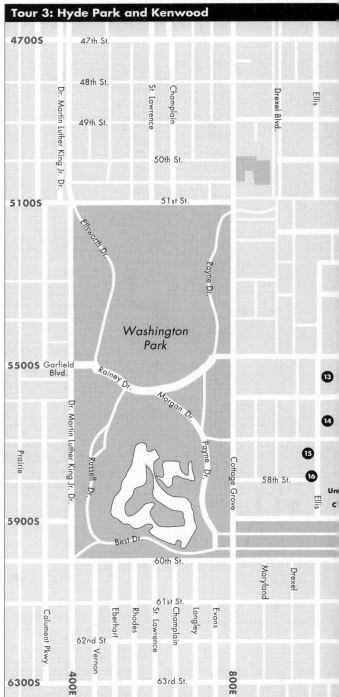

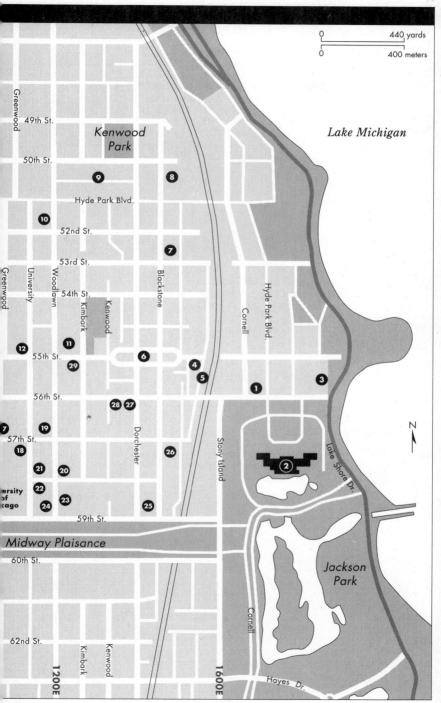

Lake Michigan

0 ——————— 440 yards
0 ——————— 400 meters

Greenwood

49th St.

Kenwood Park

50th St.

9

8

Hyde Park Blvd.

10

52nd St.

53rd St.

7

Blackstone

54th St.

Cornell

Hyde Park Blvd.

Greenwood

University

Woodlawn

Kimbark

Kenwood

12

11

55th St.

6

4

29

5

3

1

56th St.

28 **27**

Dorchester

7

19

57th St.

26

18

21

20

N

22

Stony Island

Lake Shore Dr.

University of cago

24

23

2

25

59th St.

Midway Plaisance

60th St.

Jackson Park

Kimbark

Kenwood

Cornell

62nd St.

Hayes Dr.

1200E

1600E

entrance exam). This was once a street of single-room occupancy hotels—and a supermarket that urban renewal has not adequately replaced.

⑨ Walk north to 50th Street, west to Woodlawn, and south to reach **Madison Park**, a private street that runs two blocks east to Dorchester. Originally a country estate, this tract was subdivided by the owner's heirs. A great range of housing exists here, from the grand old building at the northwest corner (5029 S. Woodlawn), now condominiums, to elegant single-family houses and perfectly ordinary dormitorylike construction (1313–1325 E. Madison Park) that is in fact University of Chicago married-student housing. The architect Y. C. Wong was responsible for the buildings at 1239–1243 and 1366–1380. Both are characterized by blank exterior walls—a device used during the urban renewal period to protect the occupants from the potentially hostile outside world. The houses at 1366–1380 are quite lovely inside: The rooms are constructed around a central atrium, giving them plenty of sunlight and a feeling of spaciousness.

⑩ Return to Woodlawn and turn south. The **Heller House** (5132 S. Woodlawn) was built by Frank Lloyd Wright in 1897; note the plaster naiads cavorting at the top.

⑪ Continue south on Woodlawn. On the east side of the street is **St. Thomas the Apostle School** (5467 S. Woodlawn), built in 1922 and now a national landmark. Note its terra-cotta ornamentation.

Time Out **The Woodlawn Tap** (1172 E. 55th St.), or Jimmy's, is a neighborhood institution, the sole bar on 55th Street to survive urban renewal. Students hang out here, professors sometimes hold classes here, and poetry-reading groups meet here. Despite the sloping floors and the rather grimy demeanor, the beer is cold and the food—standard tavern fare—is good.

---

⑫ Continue west to University Avenue and the **Lutheran School of Theology** (1100 E. 55th St.). Built in 1968 by the firm of Perkins and Will, the massive structure seems almost to float from its foundation, lightened by the transparency of its smoked-glass exteriors. Across the street is **Pierce Hall** (5514 S. University), a student dormitory designed by Harry Weese.

⑬ Walk west on 55th Street to Ellis and the **Court Theatre** (5535 S. Ellis, tel. 312/753–4472), a professional repertory company that specializes in revivals of the classics. An intimate theater, the Court has unobstructed sight lines from every seat in the house. A flag flies atop the theater when a show is on.

⑭ Continue south on Ellis about half a block beyond 56th Street; on your left is the Henry Moore sculpture *Nuclear Energy,* commemorating the first controlled nuclear chain reaction, which took place below ground roughly where the sculpture stands, in the locker room under the bleachers of what was then Stagg Field. Across 57th Street, set into the small quadrangle

⑮ on your right, is the **John Crerar Science Library.** Inside the library is John David Mooney's splendid sculpture *Crystara,* composed of enormous Waterford crystal pieces made to order for this work, which was commissioned for the site. *Tel. 312/ 702–7715.*

⓰ Farther down the block, the **University of Chicago Bookstore** has, in addition to scholarly books, a large selection of general-interest books, an outstanding collection of cookbooks, and clothing, mugs, and other souvenir goods. *5750 S. Ellis, tel. 312/702–8729. Open weekdays 9–5.*

Across Ellis Avenue stands the **University of Chicago Administration Building.** Just to the south of this edifice is a small passageway to the **Quadrangle** of the university. Here is a typical college campus, green and grassy, with imposing neo-Gothic buildings all around. Cross the Quadrangle, heading east, to the circular drive. Bear left, then turn left at the intersecting road. Follow this path north and you will pass a reflecting pool (Botany Pond) before you exit through the wrought-iron gate.

⓱ Directly ahead, the **Joseph Regenstein Library** is framed in the gate. The "Reg," the main library of the university, was designed by Skidmore, Owings, and Merrill and built in 1970.

Turn right on 57th Street and continue east. The massive building on the corner, **Mandel Hall** (5706 S. University, tel. 312/**⓲** 702–8511; enter on 57th St.), which also houses the student union, is a gem of a concert hall that has been tastefully restored. Peek in, if you can, for a glimpse of gold leaf and soft greens against the dark wood of the theater. Professional musical organizations, including ensembles from the Chicago Symphony and groups such as Les Arts Florissants from France, perform in the 900-seat hall throughout the year.

Continue east on 57th Street one block to Woodlawn. On **⓳** the northwest corner is the **First Unitarian Church** (5750 S. Woodlawn, tel. 312/324–4100), whose graceful spire is visible throughout the area. Turn right on Woodlawn and head south, noting the stately brick mansions that line both sides of the street. To the north, the building at 5605 is on the National Register of Historic Places. Many of the buildings were built by the University of Chicago in the 1890s to provide housing for professors. Professors continue to live in several of them; others have been repurchased by the university for institutional use.

⓴ Continue south on Woodlawn to Frank Lloyd Wright's **Robie House.** Built in 1909, Robie House exemplifies the Prairie style. Its cantilevered roof offers privacy while allowing in the light. The house sits on a pedestal; Wright abhorred basements, thinking them unhealthful. You can enter Robie House and examine the interiors, including the built-in cupboards, the leaded-glass windows, and the spacious kitchen. Rescued by the university from the threat of demolition, the building now houses the University Alumni Office, and it is used for small official dinners and receptions. *5757 S. Woodlawn, tel. 312/702–8374. Free tours daily at noon.*

㉑ Cross Woodlawn and continue west one block to the **Chicago Theological Seminary** (5757 S. University). Its basement accommodates the **Seminary Cooperative Bookstore,** which has an extensive selection of books in the humanities among its wide offerings. Defying all the rules of marketing, this store—which does not advertise, is not visible from the street, and has no parking—has more sales per square foot than any other bookstore in Chicago. Upstairs in the chapel is the Reneker Organ, donated by the widow of a university trustee.

Free concerts are given Tuesday at noon on this exquisitely handcrafted replica of an 18th-century organ.

㉒ On your left, on 58th Street, the **Oriental Institute** focuses on the history, art, and archaeology of the ancient Near East, including Assyria, Mesopotamia, Persia, Egypt, and Syro-Palestine. Permanent displays include statuary, small-scale amulets, mummies, limestone reliefs, gold jewelry, ivories, pottery, and bronzes from the 2nd millennium BC through the 13th century AD. *1155 E. 58th St., tel. 312/702–1062 (312/702–9521 for recorded information). Admission free. Open Tues.–Sat. 10–4, Sun. noon–4.*

㉓ Turn around and return to Woodlawn, cross 58th Street, and head south. Halfway down the block is **Woodward Court** (5825 S. Woodlawn), a student dormitory. It is hard to believe that this pedestrian structure, with its interior cell-like hive of student rooms, was designed in 1958 by Eero Saarinen, an architect known for soaring forms.

㉔ A bit farther along on the right, set back on a grassy expanse, is the neo-Gothic **Rockefeller Memorial Chapel** (5850 S. Woodlawn, tel. 312/702–7000), designed by Bertram Goodhue and named in honor of the founder of the university. The interior, which recently underwent extensive structural and cosmetic renovation, has a stunning vaulted ceiling; hand-sewn banners decorate the walls. A university carilloneur gives regular performances on the carillon atop the chapel.

Continue south again, crossing 59th Street and entering the **Midway Plaisance.** Created for the World's Columbian Exposition, this green, hollowed-out strip of land was intended to replicate a Venetian canal. When the "canal" was filled with water, houses throughout the area were flooded as well, and the idea had to be abandoned.

A two-block detour west to the **School of Social Service Administration** (969 E. 60th St.) presents an undistinguished example of the work of Mies van der Rohe. Just beyond University is the **Laird Bell Law Quadrangle** (1111 E. 60th St.); this attractive building, with fountains playing in front, is a much more successful example than Woodward Court of the work of Eero Saarinen. Farther east, a building that was once a Center for Continuing Education, housing conferences and visitors to the University, has been converted into the **New Graduate Residence Hall** (1307 E. 60th St.). This poured-concrete structure, elaborately ornamented, is reminiscent of the American Embassy in New Delhi, India—unsurprisingly, since the architect is the same: Edward Durrell Stone.

㉕ Cross the Midway again and continue east. The neo-Gothic structure just past Dorchester is **International House** (1414 E. 59th St., tel. 312/753–2270), where many foreign students live during their tenure at the university. It was designed in 1932 by the firm of Holabird and Roche. Continue east to Blackstone and turn left. **5806 S. Blackstone,** a house designed in 1951 by Bertrand Goldberg of Marina City and River City fame, is an early example of the use of solar heating and natural cooling.

㉖ Continue north on Blackstone to 57th Street and turn right. **Powell's Bookstore** (1501 E. 57th St., tel. 312/955–7780) generally has a box of free books out front, and inside you'll find a tremendous selection, on two floors, of used and remaindered books, especially art books, cookbooks, and mysteries. Walk west on 57th Street to Dorchester; on your left, at 5704 South Dorchester, is an Italian-style villa constructed before the Chicago Fire. Two additional houses that predate the fire are at 5642 and 5607 South Dorchester.

On 57th Street, spanning the block between Kenwood and Kimbark, is the **Ray School** complex. One of the best public elementary schools in the city, Ray hosts the annual Hyde Park Art Fair, one of the oldest (1947) annual outdoor art fairs in the country.

27 Farther west, **O'Gara & Wilson Ltd.** (1311 E. 57th St., tel. 312/363–0993) has another outstanding selection of used books.

28 Nearby, **57th St. Books** (1301 E. 57th St., tel. 312/684–1300), a cooperatively owned bookstore that is sister to the Seminary Cooperative Bookstore on University Avenue, specializes in current books of general interest. Copies of the *New York Times Book Review* and the *New York Review of Books* are always on a table toward the rear, next to the coffeepot. An extensive children's section has its own room, where reading aloud to youngsters is encouraged.

Turn right at Kimbark and take notice of **5630 South Kimbark Avenue,** an Italian-style house built in the 1860s. Continue north to 55th Street and turn right to confront several blocks of **29** **I. M. Pei town houses** that line the street from Kimbark to Lake Park. With their unwelcoming overhangs in front of the doorways, they are a part of the "new" Hyde Park that was a legacy of urban renewal. As you continue east along this broad, peaceful boulevard toward the ICG station or the Jeffery Express, you might reflect on what this strip was like when it teemed with the indigenous life of artists, craftsmen, and musicians—and what it might have become if urban renewal had never taken place.

Tour 4: South Lake Shore Drive

The South Lake Shore Drive tour offers spectacular views of the downtown skyline; it serves as a bonus for those who have visited Hyde Park and Kenwood and are returning north via car or the Jeffery Express (No. 6) bus or (during the afternoon rush hour) the Hyde Park Express (No. 2).

Enter Lake Shore Drive at 47th Street northbound, with the lake to your right. At 35th Street you will pass, on your left, the **Stephen Douglas Memorial.** Douglas was the U.S. Senator who debated the merits of slavery with Abraham Lincoln; you can see the monument, Douglas at the top, from the drive, but you'd have to go inland to Lake Park Avenue to visit the lovely park and gardens there.

Directly ahead, the **Sears Tower** (233 S. Wacker Dr.) is the world's tallest building. In case the perspective makes it appear unfamiliar, you can recognize it by the angular setbacks that narrow the building as it rises higher. Ahead and to your right is the low-rise, dark **McCormick Place Convention Hall** (2300 S. Lake Shore Dr.); opposite it, to your left, is the **McCormick Hotel.** Immediately north of the hotel, the low-rise **McCormick Place North** is the latest addition to the complex, its completion having been delayed by almost a year because of political machinations and scandals, in true Chicago style.

The rust-color building to the east is the **CNA Building** (55 E. Jackson Blvd.). When it was newly constructed, Chicagoans believed that the color was that of a first coat of rustproofing paint. They were wrong. The **Associates Center** (150 N. Michigan), the building with the more or less diamond-shaped, angled face at the top, was the first building in Chicago to be constructed fully wired for computer and telecommunications use. Its exterior rim of light bulbs is colored to reflect the seasons and the holidays (red, white, and blue for the Fourth of July, red and green for Christmas). Unfortunately, each of the more than 300 bulbs must be changed by hand.

The tall white building to the right of the Associates Center is the **Amoco Building** (200 E. Randolph), the world's largest marble-clad building. Because the marble cladding has shown a propensity in recent years to fall off, corrective techniques are under review.

The building with the twin antennae, to the right of the Amoco Building, is the **John Hancock Center** (875 N. Michigan), the world's third-tallest building, at 98 stories. Off to the right, seemingly out in the lake, are the sinuous curves of **Lake Point Towers** condominium apartments (505 N. Lake Shore Dr.).

Coming up on the left, the building with the massive columns on an ancient Grecian model is **Soldier Field** (425 E. McFetridge Dr.), the home of the Chicago Bears. A new stadium on the near west side is in the planning stages, and many Chicagoans look forward to having Lake Shore Drive to themselves again on fall and winter Sunday afternoons. To the right is **Meigs Field,** Chicago's third airport, used principally by commuter airlines and private planes. Farther to the right, the dome of the **Adler Planetarium** (1300 S. Lake Shore Dr.) is visible, while straight ahead is the **John G. Shedd Aquarium** (1200 S. Lake Shore Dr.). A modern Oceanarium has been added in back, housing several whales and other forms of marine life. Opposite the Shedd Aquarium, just north of Soldier Field on the left, is the **Field Museum of Natural History** (Lake Shore Dr. and E. Roosevelt Rd.).

As you round the curve past the Shedd Aquarium, look to your right for a view of the harbor. Off to the left looms the handsome, massive complex of the **Chicago Hilton and Towers** (720 S. Michigan), and soon thereafter the **Buckingham Fountain** will appear immediately to your left. To the far right, at the north and east, you can just see the ornate towers of **Navy Pier.**

Having reached the Loop, we've come to the end of the South Lake Shore Drive tour.

Tour 5: River North

Numbers in the margin correspond with points of interest on the Tour 5: River North map.

Bounded on the south and west by branches of the Chicago River, River North has eastern and northern boundaries that are harder to define. As in many neighborhoods, the limits have expanded as the area has grown more attractive; today they extend roughly to Oak Street on the north and Clark Street on the east. This neighborhood, richly served by waterways and by railroad tracks that cut along its western edge, was settled by Irish immigrants in the mid-19th century. Toward the end of the century, as cable lines came to Clark, La Salle, and Wells streets, it developed into a vigorous commerical, industrial, and warehouse district.

The typical River North building, made of the famed Chicago red brick, is a large, rectangular, solidly built structure with high ceilings and hardwood floors. Even those buildings of the period that were intended to be strictly functional were planned with an often loving attention to detail in the fine woodwork in doors and door frames, in the decorative patterns set in the brickwork, in the stone carvings and bas reliefs, and in the wrought-iron and handsome brass ornamentation.

In the early 1970s economic conditions changed. As factories moved away, their owners seeking lower costs and cheaper labor, the buildings fell into disuse and disrepair. Despite its location less than a mile from Michigan Avenue and the bustling downtown, the neighborhood became just another deteriorated urban area, the deterioration underscored by the depressed quality of life in the massive Cabrini-Green public housing project at the neighborhood's northern and western fringe.

As commerce moved away, artists and craftspeople moved into River North, attracted by the spacious abandoned storage areas and shop floors and the low rents. Toward the end of the 1970s, foresighted developers began buying up the properties with an eye toward renovation. Today, although some buildings remain unrestored and patches of the neighborhood retain their earlier character, the area has come through a renaissance. Scores of art galleries, dozens of restaurants (the owner of Gordon was mocked for locating here in 1980), and trendy, upscale shops have opened in River North, bringing life and excitement to a newly beautiful yet hardly new neighborhood. Walking through River North, one is aware of the almost complete absence of contemporary construction; the handsome buildings are virtually all renovations of properties nearly a century old.

To reach the start of our River North tour, take the Lake Street (No. 16) bus westbound (board it on Wacker Drive east of Wabash Avenue) and get off at Canal Street just after the bus crosses the Chicago River. Walk one long block north, crossing the railroad tracks.

① At **355 North Canal Street,** the riverfront commercial building renovated by Harry Weese is now a condominium complex. On the river side (turn east at the corner and cross the bridge) are docks for the owners' boats. Note the odd little new building just north of here, with its sharply angled east face open to the morning sun and river life. Immediately to your left when you **②** have crossed the bridge is the **East Bank Club** (500 N. Kingsbury, tel. 312/527–5800), a fitness and social center open on a membership basis to those who pay the rather stiff fees.

As you continue east on Kinzie Street toward the intersection with Orleans Street, note the attractive ornamental woodwork **③** on the windows of **Orleans Plaza** (414 N. Orleans), the renovated brick building at Hubbard Street one block to the north. The **Apparel Center** (350 N. Orleans) is a Midwest clothing display center. East of the Apparel Center is the rear of the **Merchandise Mart** (on the river between Orleans and Wells).

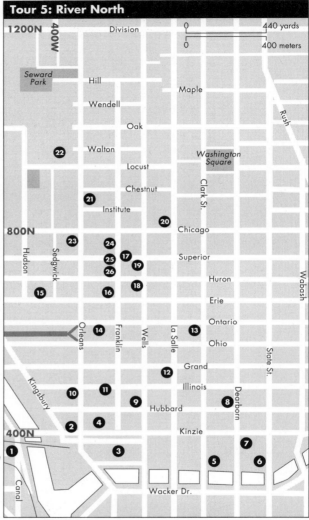

Tour 5: River North

❹ Continuing east, you'll pass **George's** (230 W. Kinzie, tel. 312/644–2290), a restaurant that once served outstanding northern Italian food; after a fire and renovation, the quality of the food declined while George's became one of the best spots in the city for late-night jazz. All the buildings on Kinzie between Franklin and Wells streets, once nondescript and run-down, have been attractively restored. Look up and straight ahead for a spectacular view, framed between the buildings on each side of Kinzie, of the **Wrigley Building** half a mile away on Michigan Avenue.

Proceed east on Kinzie, cross Clark Street, and look to your right to see two recent additions to Chicago's architecture scene. At the river's edge, and a veritable extension of the

downtown business district, is the massive, glass-skinned box
❺ designed by Skidmore, Owings & Merrill that **Quaker Oats**
built to house its world headquarters after decades in the nearby Merchandise Mart. This handsome office building dwarfs
the nouveau-Japanese **Hotel Nikko** (320 N. Dearborn, tel.
312/744–1900) to its east. Hotel Nikko was built by a consortium headed by Japan Air Lines to provide both top-quality
Japanese-style accommodations to Japanese businessmen and
luxury Western-style facilities to traveling Americans. Farther east, you can see the circular towers of Bertrand Gold-
❻ berg's **Marina City** and Mies van der Rohe's classic boxlike **IBM
Building.**

Before you turn left on Dearborn Street, notice the splendid
❼ ornamental brickwork of **33 West Kinzie Street,** a Dutch Renaissance style building. Once a commercial building, it was renovated and for years housed the Kinzie Steak House. Recently it
was again renovated, and is now the home of the sportscaster
Harry Caray's restaurant.

❽ Proceed north to Hubbard, turn left, and pause at **Courthouse
Place** (54 W. Hubbard), a splendid granite building that has
been beautifully renovated; notice the bas reliefs over the
arched, pillared doorway. Continuing west, you come to
Rowbottoms & Willoughby (72 W. Hubbard, tel. 312/329–
0999), an upscale casual clothing store. Peer around the corner
to your left to see a remnant of the neighborhood's former condition, a sleazy porno peep-show shop, two doors down from
Quadrant (406 N. Clark), a trendy little snack shop featuring a
large selection of homemade muffins.

Continue two blocks west on Hubbard, cross Wells, and you'll
❾ find yourself in a new shopping strip. **Kinko's Copy Center** (444
N. Wells), open 24 hours, shows how attractive the setting for a
rather unglamorous business can be: The high ceilings and ex-
posed-brick walls combine with carpeting and neon lighting to
provide a warm, airy environment for the chuk-chuk-chuk of
the machines. Don't fail to notice, across the street, the unusual building of peach-colored brick and granite, **445 North Wells
Street. Table of Contents** (448 N. Wells) is an unusually pretty
store devoted to crystal, china, silver, and other traditional and
modern tableware.

❿ Turn left onto Illinois Street and continue to **Assumption
Church** (323 W. Illinois). Built in 1881, the simple church is constructed of brick, as is so much of the rest of the area. But with
its slender arched windows running the height of the building
and its grassy courtyard dotted with religious statuary, the
church seems incongruous in an industrial setting.

Backtrack on Illinois to the first of dozens of galleries we will
⓫ see on this tour: **Caledonian Antiques** (209 W. Illinois, tel. 312/
923–0098), housed in a gemlike renovated brick building, has
one of the most extensive collections of English antique furniture in this country.

Walk east to the corner of Illinois and Wells and turn left into a
small shopping district. **Improvisations** (504 N. Wells, tel.
312/782–6387) is a comedy club. Inside **Galleria Renata** (507 N.
Wells, tel. 312/644–1607), you'll find a tasteful collection of contemporary paintings and sculpture. **Superior Lighting** (503 N.
Wells, tel. 312/644–4188) offers an attractive collection of
contemporary lamps. **Posey Fisher** (501 N. Wells, tel. 312/

Park, northward along the lakefront, and into the northern 644
–1749) has fine leather footwear in European styles for men and
women.

Turn left and continue one block east to La Salle Street, then
turn left and proceed to Grand Street. The funny, charming
⑫ building on the southwest corner is the home of the **Anti-
Cruelty Society** (153 W. Grand, tel. 312/644–8338), designed by
the whimsical Chicago architect Stanley Tigerman.

The largely unrenovated strip north on La Salle is a reminder
of earlier times in River North. On the southeast corner of Ohio
and La Salle is the **River North Hotel** (tel. 312/467–0800), recently refurbished in shades of mauve and gray; on the northwest corner is the **Ohio House Motel** (tel. 312/943–6000).

⑬ Walk north to Ontario Street and turn right. The **Rock and Roll
McDonald's** at Clark and Ontario has a standard McD's menu
(with slightly higher prices), 24-hour service, and a profusion
of rock and roll artifacts, '50s and '60s kitsch, and just plain bizarre items to entertain you while you savor your $2.30 Big
Mac. Jukeboxes blast at all hours, and vintage '50s cars often
crowd the parking lot on Saturday nights. It's one of the
highest-grossing McDonald's franchises in the world, and so
the company lets the operator decorate as he pleases. Even if
you don't like the food, it's worth sticking your head in the door
just to admire the Howdy Doody puppets, the '59 Corvette, and
the rest of the collection.

Now double back and head west on Ontario Street. Beyond
Wells, the new art deco–style building on your left houses
⑭ Ditka's (*see* Chapter 6) and **City Lights** (223 W. Ontario, tel.
312/280–1790), a trendy sports-oriented restaurant and a
nightclub owned in part by Mike Ditka, the coach of the some-
time Superbowl champion Chicago Bears. Next door is the **Chicago Sports Hall of Fame**, housing a modest collection of
memorabilia. *227 W. Ontario, tel. 312/915–4500. Open Mon.–
Sat. 10–4. Admission: $3 adults, $2 senior citizens and children.*

Time Out In warm weather, the tables outside will tell you that you've arrived at **Sieben's River North Brewery** (436 W. Ontario); in cold
weather, you'll have to look for the number. Sieben's is one of
several new "brew pubs" in Chicago, neighborhood pubs that
make their own specialty beers. A lager, a golden ale, an amber
beer, and a dark stout are always available, and there are several specials. This is beer for savoring as well as for quenching
thirst; brewed from a denser combination of ingredients, it is
more flavorful than the standard American products because a
lower level of carbonation permits more of the flavor to come
through. With your beer, you might enjoy some Wisconsin
bratwurst or a Hildesheimer sausage sandwich. The gleaming
copper vats behind glass walls in the center of the pub are
where the beer is made. And don't hesitate to come here with
your youngsters; the atmosphere at Sieben's is more like that of
a family restaurant than that of a neighborhood saloon. Closed
Monday.

Proceed to Kingsbury, turn and walk a block north, and turn
right on Erie Street. **The Factory** (445 W. Erie) is a particularly handsome loft building renovation. On the other side of the
⑮ street, the **Peace Museum** presents often unconventional exhi-

bitions on themes of war and peace, using art, photography, and multimedia shows. *430 W. Erie, tel. 312/440–1860. Admission: $3.50 adults, $1 children and senior citizens. Open Tues.–Sun. noon–5, Thurs. noon–8.*

Farther along Erie, an ironwork archway tells you that you've reached **Flair Lane** (214–216 W. Erie). Walk into this narrow, unprepossessing alley and look to your left, where a carefully tended strip of flowers and ornamental plantings front the stained oak door, with carriage lamp, of a single residence in the side of the building. Built in 1883 and restored in 1966, this elegant Victorian harbors an award-winning collection of antiques. The Erie Street face of the building houses the charming **Petites Choses** (tel. 312/642–0149), a store partly obscured by graceful trees.

At Wells turn left and walk to Huron Street. Huron, Superior (one block north), and Hudson streets form an area known as **SuHu**—a double play on New York's SoHo, for this, too, is an arts district, the home of more than 50 art galleries, showing every kind of work imaginable. Don't be shy about walking in and browsing; a gallery's business is to sell the works it displays, so most galleries welcome interested visitors and, time permitting, the staff will discuss the art they are showing. On Friday evening many galleries schedule openings of new shows and serve refreshments; you can sip jug wine as you stroll through the newly hung exhibit. Consider a gallery tour an informal, admission-free alternative to a museum visit. While each gallery sets its own hours, most of them are open weekdays and Saturday 10–5 or 11–5 and are closed Sunday. For announcements of openings and other news of the art scene, write for the *Chicago Gallery News*, 107 West Delaware Place, Chicago, IL 60610.

Turn left at Huron Street. A beautifully rehabbed brick building houses the **Leather Center** (233 W. Huron, tel. 312/943–9415); have at least a look in the window at the handsome leather furniture within. The building at 325 W. Huron contains several galleries and **Hat Dance** (tel. 312/649–0066), a popular Mexican-style restaurant that will be enjoyed by those who like a noisy ambience and long waits.

The parking lot at Huron and Orleans used to be the site of several gallery buildings, razed in a catastrophic fire in 1989. Accusations of code violations and neglect died down as a dozen galleries scrambled to relocate.

Virtually every building on Superior between Orleans and Franklin houses at least one gallery. Two of the more interesting occupants of 301 West Superior are **Eva Cohon** (tel. 312/664–3669), with contemporary American and Canadian painting, sculpture, and works on paper, and **Prairie Lee** (tel. 312/266–7113), with Southwest regional and American Indian art.

Superior east of Franklin harbors another large collection of galleries. At the corner of Wells, **Janis** (200 W. Superior, tel. 312/280–5357) looks like an avant-garde women's clothing store, which it is; the creations spring from experimental efforts in clothing as art. Turn the corner onto Wells and look across the street at the unrenovated building opposite, the ornamental work in the brick, the oak doors, and the decorative ironwork.

Wells Street boasts an attractive shopping strip. **Littman Bros.** (734 N. Wells, tel. 312/943–2660) advertises Casablanca Fans, and the store has a beautiful selection of contemporary lamps. **Elements** (738 N. Wells, tel. 312/642–6574) offers one-of-a-kind plates, pens, and other decorative accessories.

㉘ Ahead on your right when you reach Chicago Avenue is the **Moody Bible Institute** (820 N. La Salle, tel. 312/329–4000), a handsome, if massive, contemporary brick structure. Here students of various conservative Christian denominations study and prepare for religious careers. For a view of the front of the institute, go a block east and cross the street to the north.

Fans of contemporary furniture and design may want to go west on Chicago two blocks, turn left on Orleans Street, and **㉑** follow it three blocks to Chestnut Street to visit **Luminaire** (361 W. Chestnut, tel. 312/664–9582) and **World of Leather** (820 N. Orleans, tel. 312/943–5700). One block farther to the north and west, on Sedgwick and Locust streets, is the southeastern edge **㉒** of the infamous **Cabrini Green** public housing project.

The city is embroiled in controversy surrounding the ultimate fate of Cabrini Green. Although it is widely agreed to be among the most dangerous and unhealthful areas of the city, the government has resisted pressures to tear the structures down and relocate the inhabitants in scattered-site, low-rise housing elsewhere in the city. While many who support this move are disinterested observers who have the welfare of project residents in mind, others are those developers who would stand to profit handsomely from the availability of vast tracts of land in a location whose desirability is newly appreciated. On the other hand, city council members elected by voters in Cabrini Green and other public housing may be reluctant to scatter their constituencies to other parts of the city, because such a move might jeopardize their city council careers.

㉓ **The River North Concourse** (750 N. Orleans at Chicago Ave.) houses numerous galleries along with a collection of stores and businesses. The striking lobby is done in exposed brick and glass block, and a bank of television monitors decorates the Orleans Street entrance. On the ground floor is Gallery Vienna, specializing in furniture and decorative arts from turn-of-the-century Vienna. Others include the Brandywine Fantasy Gallery, which features American painting and "fantasy art," and Chiaroscuro, a gallery/shop with jewelry, clothing, furniture, and paper goods that could all be classified as objets d'art.

Time Out If you're weary from gallery hopping, **Cafe Tête-à-Tête,** on the second floor of 750 North Orleans, is a good spot for a croissant and espresso, a sandwich, or a more substantial entrée. Roomy and airy, it's billed as a "cafe in the European tradition" and has gelati and Viennese-style pastries for that sweet but cosmopolitan flavor. The art on the walls (from the building's various galleries) is for sale.

㉔ Return now to Franklin Street, just south of Chicago Avenue, for the last leg of the River North exploration. A long building at 750 North Franklin houses several attractive shops. **Village Loom** (tel. 312/943–4777) has unusual carpets of all sizes, cushion covers, and "Oriental rugs at village prices." **Techline Chicago** (tel. 312/664–0190) offers contemporary furniture and kitchenware; **Cose** ("Things"; tel. 312/787–0304) has a pretty selection of household accessories, including wrapping paper, tea kettles, fireplace tools, and decorative bottles.

25 On the next block south, don't miss **Aquariums by Design** (730 N. Franklin, tel. 312/944–5566). While custom-made aquariums may not sound exciting, the works here are as aesthetically pleasing as they are functional; the beautiful shapes, objects, and lighting make them a visual pleasure with or without fish. Notice, too (as in many other River North shops), the extensive and creative use of neon lights and signage. Like the area itself, neon has made a comeback in new and often quite lovely forms.

26 An equally beautiful store, **J. T. Monckton Ltd.** (730 N. Franklin, tel. 312/266–1171), has rare books, antique maps, and fine prints. Across the street, 301 West Superior houses more galleries and small shops.

To return by public transportation to Michigan Avenue in the near north, walk north to Chicago Avenue, turn right, and walk east to La Salle. Here you can catch the eastbound Lincoln (No. 11) bus, which takes Chicago Avenue to Michigan Avenue and turns south on Michigan. Or you can take the Chicago (No. 66) bus from the same stop, eastbound to Michigan Avenue and transfer to the Water Tower Express (No. 125) for points north between Chicago Avenue and Walton Street.

Tour 6: Lincoln Park

Numbers in the margin correspond with points of interest on the Tour 6: Lincoln Park map.

In the early years of the 19th century, Lincoln Park, an area that extends from North Avenue (1600 N.) on the south to Diversey Parkway (2800 N.) on the north, the lake on the east and the Chicago River on the west, was a sparsely settled community of truck farms and orchards that grew produce for the city of Chicago three miles to the south.

By the mid-1860s the area had become more populated. Germans predominated, and there were Irish and Scotch immigrants. The construction in 1860 of the Presbyterian Theological Seminary (later the McCormick Seminary, which moved to Hyde Park in 1977) brought modest residential construction. By the end of the century, immigrants from Eastern Europe— Poles, Slovaks, Serbians, Hungarians, Romanians, and some Italians as well—had swelled the population, and extensive construction to house the new residents was taking place.

The recent history of Lincoln Park has interesting parallels to that of Hyde Park and Kenwood. Between the world wars, expensive new construction, particularly along the lakefront and the park, was undertaken in Lincoln Park. At the same time, the once elegant houses to the west that had begun to deteriorate were being subdivided into rooming houses—a process that was occurring at roughly the same period in Hyde Park, 10 miles to the south. By 1930 a group of blacks had moved to the southwestern corner of Lincoln Park. Italians were feared because the "black hand" was active here. The St. Valentine's Day Massacre and the FBI shooting of John Dillinger at the Biograph Theatre were neighborhood events.

Following World War II, the ethnic groups that had been first to arrive in Lincoln Park, having achieved some affluence, began to leave for the suburbs and the northern parts of the city. Poor Appalachians, Hispanics, and blacks, who did not have the resources to maintain their homes, moved in. By 1960 nearly a quarter of the housing stock in Lincoln Park had been classified as substandard.

As housing prices fell, artists and others who appreciated the aesthetic value of the decaying buildings and were willing to work to restore them moved to the southeastern part of the area. The newcomers joined established residents in forming the Old Town Triangle Association; residents to the north, who had successfully resisted subdivision, formed the Mid-North Association. Neighborhood institutions, including De Paul University, the McCormick Seminary, four hospitals, a bank, and others dismayed by the decline of the area, formed the Lincoln Park Conservation Association in 1954. As the University of Chicago had done in Hyde Park, this association began exploring the possibilities of urban renewal as a means of rejuvenating the area.

As renewal plans progressed, blacks and Hispanics became incensed by what appeared to be minority removal, but the sit-ins and demonstrations that followed were ultimately unsuccessful. As you head west on North Avenue to begin this tour, notice that virtually all the construction on the north side of the street is new; the original buildings were bulldozed. Behind the houses to the north, moreover, many streets have been closed off, precluding access from the North Avenue side. Just as Hyde Park and Kenwood did with the Athletic Club that stretches for blocks along 47th Street, Lincoln Park created its own Maginot Line along North Avenue.

Since the 1960s the gentrification of Lincoln Park has moved steadily westward. We will see areas that were run-down and poor a few years ago, and have since been renovated or bulldozed and replaced. One can still see poor blacks in the neighborhood, particularly in its southwest corner, but they now live alongside the newly arrived upper middle class, and their numbers seem to decrease daily.

To give you the flavor of several areas within Lincoln Park, our exploration is divided into three parts. In Sheffield/De Paul, in the western section of the neighborhood, we go from undeveloped and redeveloping areas, through some of Lincoln Park's most beautiful housing, to the handsome campus of De Paul University and the gemlike grounds of the old McCormick Seminary. Then we head north on Lincoln Avenue to visit the shops and the Biograph Theatre where John Dillinger met his end. Finally, we explore the Old Town Triangle, including the Midwest Buddhist Center, St. Michael's Church, one of the oldest streets in Chicago, and one of the most expensive.

Sheffield/De Paul To reach the start of the tour, drive north on Clark Street or La Salle Street to North Avenue, turn left, continue west to Sheffield Avenue, and turn right. Or take the La Salle Street (No. 156) bus north to North Avenue, transfer to the westbound North Avenue (No. 72) bus, and get off at Sheffield.

Proceed north on Sheffield to Willow Street. As you approach and cross Clybourn Avenue, notice the severely deteriorated housing in the area and, interspersed with it, the buildings that have been or are being renovated. The upscale shopping/entertainment complex at 1800 North Clybourn is one of several along the Clybourn corridor. This is gentrification in action.

● **958 West Willow Street,** on the corner, the building with the Italianate corner bay supported by a single square column, ropelike detailing in stonework around the windows and entryway, and a contrast of stone with brick, was once the Delicious Cookie Factory; it is now condominium apartments.

Turn east on Willow, go one block, and take Bissell Street southeast two blocks. Notice in the extensive new construction under way here that an effort has been made to match the style of the new construction to that of the older buildings in the neighborhood; stonework detailing inset in the brick structure, for example, updates an earlier theme. This area, just a few years ago, was poor and run-down. At the corner of Bissell and Dayton streets look to the south. Beyond the railroad overpass the street has been turned into a dead end; beyond a grassy strip south of the dead end is busy North Avenue.

Turn north on Dayton and continue to Willow, where new construction is interspersed with the old. Turn left on Willow, go one block, turn right on Fremont Street, and proceed to Wisconsin Street. The beautifully restored houses on Fremont make quite a contrast to the streets we've just seen.

On Wisconsin walk one block west to Bissell. At the corner, ● **1875 North Bissell Street** is a brick building with contrasting stone and classical columns done in iron. Once a saloon, it has been turned into two condominium apartments. The building across the street, at 1901 North Bissell, is almost a duplicate of the saloon; it, too, is of brick with contrasting stone and ironwork pillars with capitals.

As you proceed through Lincoln Park, watch for the numbers designed in the half-moon leaded-glass windows that often cap the doorways of the neighborhood. Many of the numbers have no relation to the address of the building in which they are set. Renovators pay high prices for leaded-glass windows that fit the openings in their houses; the "misnumbered" windows once graced other homes. (The theft of leaded-glass windows was a serious crime problem in Lincoln Park a few years ago.)

Before returning to Fremont, have a look inside the pretty vest-pocket park across from the intersection on the west side of Bissell. Sheffield has many beautiful private gardens as well, and the neighborhood hosts an annual garden walk with some 150 stops. The profusion of flowers and the old, leafy trees contribute to the attractiveness of the neighborhood.

Retrace your steps on Wisconsin and turn left on Fremont. As you proceed north toward Armitage Avenue, notice again the beautifully restored houses. At the intersection, **859 West Armitage Avenue** has an angled corner bay with wood framing ● and decorations in brick. Notice at **2130–2136 North Fremont Street** the painted woodwork framing the windows of the Federal-style brick houses. Note especially the detail work in the wood; some homeowners have painted the detail in contrasting colors to highlight it.

Continuing north on Fremont, you come to an unusual ● group of houses on your left. At **2216 North Fremont Street** notice the leaded glass window and the arch over it in the front room of the house. There is more beautiful leaded glass at **2218 North Fremont Street,** where the number in the glass is not the

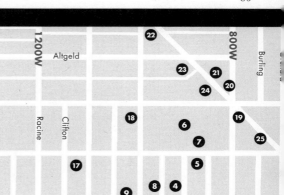

Tour 6: Lincoln Park

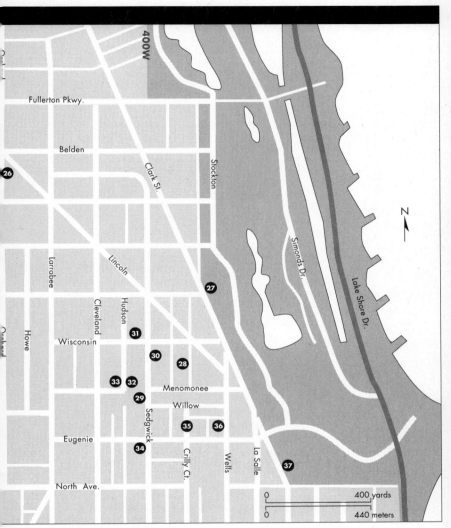

same as the number of the house. **2222 North Fremont Street** is one of only a few Romanesque-style houses in Sheffield; stone below and brick above, it boasts a corner bay, arched entrance, and leaded glass. At **2244 North Fremont Street** note the contrast of the stone inlays with the brick structure and the detail work around the windows. The lacy wrought-iron work surrounding the miniature widow's walk over the doorway is a frequently used element in houses in the area; it appears again in the house across the street, **2241 North Fremont Street.**

Take Fremont north to Belden Avenue and turn right. The De Paul University campus is to your left, on the north side of Belden. On your right, at **845–839 West Belden Avenue,** is a particularly handsome row of four stone houses. The brown stone house at 845, Romanesque in style, has a three-level tower and exquisite cutouts in the stone porch balustrade. All four houses are characterized by great arches, bay windows, and turrets. On the other side of the street, **832 West Belden Avenue** is a Queen Anne with a tower the full height of the building.

Continue east to the entrance to the **De Paul University** campus. This portion of the campus is the former **McCormick Seminary** grounds, where antislavery groups met during the Civil War and Chicagoans sought refuge from the Great Fire in 1871. Note the elegant New England-style church on your right as you enter. The small street inside the U on your left is Chalmers Place. The massive Queen Anne building on the north side has decorative shingles aligned in rows of different shapes; at the west end of the building is a great turret. Now enter the cul-de-sac, where the brick houses, more than 100 years old and once faculty residences at McCormick Seminary, are now privately owned. Note the semicircular brickwork around the windows. At the west end of the street is the Gothic seminary building. Continue south past the seminary, east on Chalmers Place, and south again to exit the university grounds where you entered on Belden.

Turn right on Belden, proceed two blocks to Bissell, and turn left. Notice the arched windows framed with wood and the flowers in the leaded glass of the front window of the brick building at **2244 North Bissell Street.** At the northeast corner of Bissell and Webster note the unrenovated building, **924 West Webster Avenue;** with its black turrets and bays overhanging Bissell contrasting with the white of the building, it will not remain unrenovated for long. Turn west onto Webster. **St. Vincent's Church** (1010 W. Webster) is characterized as Late Gothic, yet it has an enormous Queen Anne-style bay on its north face (turn right on Sheffield and walk up the block a bit to see it on your left). Notice, too, the ornamental stonework around the stained-glass windows of the church.

Return to the intersection of Webster and Bissell and continue south on Bissell to the 2100 block. This street is noteworthy for the detailed stone and terra-cotta insets in many of the houses, especially the row at **2135–2127 North Bissell Street,** and for the elaborately carved cornices, window overhangs, and turrets on the buildings, typical of the Queen Anne style that you see throughout Sheffield/De Paul.

Continue another block south to Armitage and turn right. **1024 West Armitage Avenue** is a variant of a building we've seen, with a rounded corner bay supported by a single ornate column. This one has ornate scrollwork in stone, and the building is red brick, with a handsome dome.

Continue west on Armitage to the intersection with Clifton Street, where two corner buildings have corner bays supported by single columns. The building on the east side of the street has been badly remodeled and has lost the fine detailing and the grace of the style. The building opposite, **2000 North Clifton Street,** has curlicues and ornamental work in beautiful condition. Another vintage brick building at **1143 West Armitage Avenue** has been painted to highlight the detailing around the windows and under the eaves.

(12) Turn right and stop at the handsome red brick building with an oak door at **2022 North Clifton Street;** note the ornamental stones placed in a radiating semicircular pattern around the door and the windows. Turn right again, walk to Seminary Avenue, and turn left. **2018 North Seminary Avenue** is a brick
(13) building whose top half is shingled. An arched window is in the front room. Note the raised entryway; this is a one-and-a-half-story building, typical of an early style of construction known as Chicago cottage. Many buildings in the area have a steep flight of steps leading to the entry and a small story below, at ground level.

(14) The farmhouse at **2023 North Seminary Avenue,** built in 1863, is one of the few buildings to survive the Fire in 1871. **2029 North Seminary Avenue** is an old frame building that looks as if it may fall down at any time—as well it might, for it, too, predates the fire. **2031 North Seminary Avenue** is a vintage brick building with the raised first floor of the Chicago cottage style. Across the street, **2034 North Seminary Avenue** is a brick house with cut-out stonework, limestone around the front window and doorway, gingerbread over the doorway, and lots of leaded-glass windows; this is a typical Queen Anne–style house. **2037 North Seminary Avenue** is a handsome Romanesque redstone building, with pretty windows, a big bay in front, and columns.

(15) Continue to Dickens Street and turn right. **1051 West Dickens Street** is a large ivy-covered building, its number hidden behind an evergreen bush. This 135-year-old structure was originally a schoolhouse and is now condominium apartments. Note the overhanging roof, the arched doorway and windows, and the period carriage lamps at the front door. **2058 North Seminary Avenue,** at the corner, is a brick building whose woodwork has been painted in contrasting colors to reveal the detailing.

(16) Now turn around and walk west on Dickens to Clifton and turn north. **2101 North Clifton Street,** the corner house, is similar in style to the old saloon and its companion building that we saw on Bissell, and it is undoubtedly of the same era. The handsome stone building at **2106 North Clifton Street** has beautiful leaded glass. Note the curlicues in the facade of the building next door, **2108 North Clifton Street,** as well as the Italianate cornices and window decorations.

(17) Proceed north to Belden, and just before you reach the intersection, regard the building on your right, **1125 West Belden Avenue,** with its stately bays extending out over Clifton. As you turn east, you'll see that this building has what is now a familiar design feature: the ornate corner bay, supported by a single column. As you continue east on Belden, you'll find that the very contemporary poured-concrete buildings of the De Paul University campus to your left are an interesting juxtaposition.

The painted brick building at **1055 West Belden Avenue** has ornate cutouts and doweling in the roof over the entryway, columns, and tall arched windows on the first floor; all are typical elements of the Queen Anne style. At **1035 West Belden Avenue** is a building whose style parallels that of number 1125, with ornate bays but without the rounded corner bay.

Turn left at Kenmore Avenue and continue north, the De Paul University campus on your left. Turn right at Fullerton Avenue and right again at Sheffield. The massive brick building complex extending halfway down the block on your right and now known as the **Sanctuary** (2358 N. Sheffield) was built in 1895 as the St. Augustine Home for the Aged.

North Lincoln Avenue The second portion of our Lincoln Park exploration begins at Fullerton and Lincoln. You can take the eastbound Fullerton (No. 74) bus or, if you're driving, you can take Fullerton to Lincoln—and look for a place to park, since this stretch should be done on foot.

Lincoln Avenue is a diagonal that creates a three-way intersection with Fullerton and Halsted Street. At the northwest corner of the intersection, directly across from the northeast end of the De Paul University campus, the **Seminary Restaurant** (2402 N. Lincoln, tel. 312/549–5193) is a neighborhood hangout frequented by De Paul students and area residents. It had lots of "atmosphere" until its renovation a few years ago; now it looks like any other coffee shop, yet the food remains pleasant and inexpensive. To the southeast, where Halsted and Lincoln come together at a point, the huge **Children's Memorial Resale Shop** (2374 N. Lincoln, tel. 312/281–3747) carries every kind of used merchandise imaginable: furniture, clothing, kitchenware, china, books, and more.

We'll head up the east side of Lincoln and return on the west side. Like most urban strips (as opposed to suburban malls), this shopping strip tells a good deal about the neighborhood. Upscale and trendy without being avant-garde, the strip caters to well-educated, young and middle-aged professionals, emphasizing recreation and leisure time needs over more mundane requirements. You'd be hard pressed to find a drugstore or a shoemaker's shop on this strip. That might be inconvenient if you lived here, but it makes it all the more fun for browsing.

The **Biograph Theater** (2433 N. Lincoln, tel. 312/348–1350), where the gangster John Dillinger met his end at the hands of the FBI, is now on the National Register of Historic Places. The Biograph shows first-run movies with an emphasis, as you might expect from the neighborhood, on foreign and art films.

Time Out Next door to the Biograph is a **Vie de France** bakery and café (2441 N. Lincoln). Although Vie de France is part of a chain, the breads, muffins, and pastries here are unusually tasty, and the coffee is generally fresh and good. If you've just walked through Sheffield/De Paul, you'll find this a welcome spot to sit and have some refreshment.

Next to Vie de France is **Bookseller's Row** (2445 N. Lincoln, tel. 312/348–1170), one of several bookstores on the strip, where you'll find used, out of print, and fine books and a few new ones as well. **Wax Trax Records** (2449 N. Lincoln, tel. 312/929–0221), the place for everything in popular music, including oldies and imports, is a "must" stop if you have teenagers with you. **Fiber Works** (2457 N. Lincoln, tel. 312/327–0444) has an attractive selection of clothing and yarns in natural fibers. The **Children's Bookstore** (2465 N. Lincoln, tel. 312/248–2665) is probably the best of its kind in the city. **Finders Keepers** (2469 N. Lincoln, tel. 312/525–1510), a resale shop for the Latin School of Chicago, has more of the kind of used merchandise we found at the Children's Memorial Resale Shop.

㉒ Across Lincoln, the **Apollo Theatre Center** (2540 N. Lincoln, tel. 312/935–6100) offers local productions of Broadway and off-Broadway hit shows.

Time Out If you passed up the opportunity for a snack at Vie de France, you can reconsider your decision at **Periwinkle** (2511 N. Lincoln), an attractive small café that expands to its adjacent garden outdoors in summer. The coffee is outstanding, but the food is uneven and sometimes disappointing.

㉓ **Omiyage** (2482 N. Lincoln, tel. 312/477–1428) is a Japanese shop that has a little of lots of different things: jewelry, plates, cookware, miscellany. The items are attractive and tasteful, the prices reasonable.

Lincoln Park is known for its clubs and its music. **The Earl's Pub** (2470 N. Lincoln, tel. 312/929–0660) has live music.

On the corner of Montana Street is **Guild Books** (2456 N. Lincoln, tel. 312/525–3667). Unlike the two bookstores we visited earlier, this one has new and remaindered titles; like the other two stores, it's a good spot for bargain hunters. Next to the Guild Bookstore is **Blake** (2448 N. Lincoln, tel. 312/477–3364), a trendy clothing store. If your tastes run to more practical items, you might prefer **Uncle Dan's Army Navy Store** (2440 N. Lincoln, tel. 312/477–1918), a treasure trove of camouflage outfits, hats, camp cookware, tents, sleeping bags, duffel bags, footlockers, and badges.

㉔ The **Threepenny Theatre** (2424 N. Lincoln, tel. 312/935–5744) used to be a revival house where golden oldies lived again, but that business died when VCRs became ascendant. The Threepenny now shows new films in competition with the Biograph across the street.

㉕ The buildings at **2312–2310 North Lincoln Avenue** were designed by Adler & Sullivan in the 1880s. Another folk music club is the **Wise Fools Pub** (2270 N. Lincoln, tel. 312/929–1510). Across the street, **Artwear Originals** (2273 N. Lincoln, tel. 312/248–2554), has an unusual selection of hand-painted and embroidered clothing.

The **John Barleycorn Memorial Pub** (636 W. Belden, tel. 312/348–8899) is one of Chicago's better-known pubs, and hun-㉖ gry or not, you'll want to step inside the **Potbelly Sandwich Works** (2264 N. Lincoln, tel. 312/528–1405). The walls are decorated with old-fashioned signs, the tables are covered in tile. Vintage malted-milk machines whir behind the counter. A massive old Toledo scale sits against the wall. In the oaken loft is a player piano and a small potbellied stove. And the centerpiece of the restaurant is a huge potbellied stove that you'll have to walk around to get to the service counter.

Notice the red 1950s vintage Chevrolet that hangs out of the building at **Jukebox Saturday Night** (2251 N. Lincoln, tel. 312/525–5000), one of Chicago's better-known nightspots. Next door are **The Body Politic** and the **Victory Gardens Theatre** (2261 N. Lincoln, tel. 312/871–3000), two long-established and respected small theater groups; like many others, they share space and facilities to reduce expenses.

This stretch of Lincoln now has two hospitals, **Children's Hospital** and **Grant Hospital**. A third, **Lutheran General**, closed in 1990 because the market was too crowded. At press time, neighbors were fighting its proposed conversion into condominiums. You may want to take the Lincoln Avenue (No. 11) bus for a few blocks and give your feet a rest.

Before you leave the neighborhood, be sure to have a look at the elegant row of gracious old painted brick buildings at **1850–1858 North Lincoln Avenue.**

Take Lincoln southeast to Armitage, turn left and continue to Clark to reach the imposing classical-style building that houses ㉗ the **Chicago Academy of Sciences.** Despite its scholarly name, this is not an institution of higher learning but a museum specializing in the natural history of the Midwest. The permanent exhibits include dioramas showing the ecology of Chicago millions of years ago, before it was settled by man, and back-lit ceiling images of the nighttime sky as seen from Chicago. Special exhibits are mounted regularly; DinoRama, which featured 12 life-size animated dinosaur models that roared and lunged, was a hit in the summer of 1988. *2001 N. Clark, tel. 312/549–0343. Admission: $4 adults, $2.50 children and senior citizens, free Mon. Open daily 10–5.*

Old Town Triangle Old Town Triangle is filled with courts and lanes that run for only a block or so; to complicate matters, many of the streets have been made one-way in a pattern that can make it difficult to get from one place to another. (Urban planners commonly use this device in redeveloped areas to discourage the inflow of unwanted traffic; Hyde Park and Kenwood have been designed in similar fashion.) Therefore, if you're driving, you may find it easier to park your car near the start of the tour and explore on foot. If you came by public transportation, you are now rewarded by not having to find a place to park.

To reach Old Town Triangle, take Clark or Lincoln south to Wisconsin, turn west, and proceed to Lincoln Park West.

A left turn onto Lincoln Park West will lead you to two marvel- ㉘ ous frame houses at **1838 and 1836 North Lincoln Park West.** By now you know that frame houses are relatively uncommon in Lincoln Park, in part because of the restrictions on wood construction that went into effect following the Chicago Fire in 1871. (Some poorer areas in the southwest of Lincoln Park do have extensive frame construction; the regulations were not always strictly enforced.)

The smaller of the two buildings, 1836, was built just after the Fire; it has narrow clapboards, bays, leaded glass, and decorative iron grillwork around the miniature widow's walk above the front entrance. Note also the decorative cutouts in the wood over the front door. The exterior painting has been done in contrasting colors of brown, beige, and white to reveal the detail work in the wood.

The larger house, 1838, is a grand structure built of wider clapboards and painted—in true Victorian style—in vividly contrasting gray, green, and salmon. Ornaments and traceries are outlined. (The painter, James F. Jereb, has signed his work at the south end of the house, a foot or so above the ground.) Notice, too, the overhanging veranda, the twin attic windows, and the ornately carved supports under the veranda and eaves. The wrought-iron fence is of the appropriate period in style.

Continue south, turn west on Menomonee and go one block to Sedgwick. On the southwest corner of the intersection is **Marge's Pub** (1750 N. Sedgwick, tel. 312/944–9775), the oldest commercial property in Lincoln Park. The beer, however, is fresh and good. The building, with its red brick construction, decorated in stone around the windows, is a familiar style in older Lincoln Park buildings and is reminiscent of the converted saloon we saw at 1875 North Bissell.

Turn right onto the **1800 North Sedgwick Street** block and proceed about halfway up the block. On the right, you will notice a change from the traditional brick architecture with which you have become familiar. These houses begin with a handsome contemporary red brick and move on to a poured concrete, an oddly colored brick, and a gray wood, among others. This strip may be the most expensive in all of Chicago. Each of the houses was custom-designed for its owner, at an astronomical price, by a world-renowned architect. Such were the egos involved that the architects could agree on nothing, not style, not materials, not lot size, not even the heights of the buildings. While some of the structures might look good on another site, particularly if surrounded by some land, here they look like transplanted misfits, jammed in together and for the most part out of character with the neighborhood and with each other. Despite their monetary value, little about them is aesthetically pleasing.

Continue on Sedgwick to the intersection with Wisconsin. On the north side of **Wisconsin Street,** extending west to Hudson Avenue, is another example of new construction, a massive condominium complex that fails aesthetically for just the opposite reason that the Sedgwick Street custom-designed buildings fail. Here the architect has augmented basic red brick construction with virtually every design element one might see in turn-of-the-century buildings of the neighborhood, including bays and huge arched windows. The mammoth scale of the building is an anachronism; worse, the overuse of traditional stylistic elements makes the building look like a parody of, rather than a complement to, the buildings it seeks to imitate. Now look at the period brick building on the northeast corner of Sedgwick and Wisconsin for a reminder of how satisfying elegant simplicity can be.

Walk west on Wisconsin, turn south on Hudson, and proceed one block to Menomonee. The Oriental-looking building where the street curves is the **Midwest Buddhist Temple** (435 W. Menomonee, tel. 312/943–7801). In mid-June, Old Town Triangle hosts the Old Town Art Fair, which claims to be the oldest juried art fair in the country, and the Midwest Buddhist Temple is one of the most popular food vendors at the fair.

33 Before you turn on Menomonee, regard the half-timbered house at the corner, **1800 North Hudson Avenue,** a particularly handsome example of a style that, as you know by now, is an unusual one for Lincoln Park.

34 Go west one block on Menomonee, then south on Cleveland Avenue to Eugenie Street and **St. Michael's Church** (458 W. Eugenie, tel. 312/664–1511). This massive, ornate Romanesque building was constructed on land donated in the 1850s by Michael Diversey (the early beer baron after whom Diversey Parkway was named) to provide a church where the area's German community could worship. The structure partially withstood the Fire of 1871, and the interior of the church was restored after the Fire by the German residents of the neighborhood. Their work is a legacy of exquisite craftsmanship. Outside, notice the classical columns of different heights, the elaborate capitals, the many roofs with stonework at the top, and the elegant spire.

35 Walk east on Eugenie about five blocks and turn left onto **Crilly Court,** one of the oldest streets in Chicago. For nearly half a century this little enclave was also one of Chicago's stablest neighborhoods, with residents who had lived here for more than 40 years. Then, a few years ago, the buildings were acquired by developers who converted them into condominiums. Even though the existing tenants were given the option to buy, most of them—some quite elderly—could not afford it and had to move away. This is a classic urban story: Some fine buildings have been maintained, some developers have made money, and a close-knit community has been destroyed.

36 When you come to St. Paul, turn east, proceed to Wells Street, and turn right. **Green, Inc.** (1716 N. Wells, tel. 312/266–2806), is a plant-lover's delight, with shrubs and trees set out on the sidewalk in good weather and a marvelous selection of cactus, many of which are displayed in the window. The building that houses the stores on this block has designs stamped in tin between the upper and lower bay windows.

Continuing south on Wells, you'll find an attractive shopping strip. **Collector's Nook** (1714 N. Wells, tel. 312/642–4734) specializes in authentic Early American furniture; **Design Source/Light Source** (1710 N. Wells, tel. 312/751–2113) has contemporary furniture and lighting, unusual accessories, and splendid (and near life-size) pottery animals; **Handle With Care** (1706 N. Wells, tel. 312/751–2929) carries women's clothing and accessories; **A Joint Venture** (1704 N. Wells, tel. 312/440–0505) has toys, salt and pepper shakers, picture frames, and jewelry.

Time Out For a pick-me-up, stop at **Savories** (1700 N. Wells), a coffee, tea, and spice shop that also sells pots, mugs, and other accessories. The coffee is fresh and delicious (try the daily special), and so are the iced coffees and teas. Sample one of the rich scones or the sour-cherry cobbler; the muffins, buns, and pastries, too, are delectable.

With Old Town Triangle behind us, we have just one more stop to make in Lincoln Park. Continue south on Wells, turn left on North Avenue, and walk east to Clark.

37 Across Clark, the **Chicago Historical Society** has been outfitted with a sparkling, all-glass addition to the front of the structure

that gives this face of the building a dramatically different appearance from that of the stately brick building you see from the westbound La Salle Street exit from Lake Shore Drive. The new section contains a café at the south end of the building (the curved portion); in the café's north wall is a terra-cotta arch designed by Daniel Burnham more than 100 years ago. The Historical Society's permanent exhibits include the much-loved diorama room that portrays scenes from Chicago's history—and has been a part of the lives of generations of Chicago children; collections of costumes; and the famous statue of Abraham Lincoln, whose nose gleams from having been rubbed by countless numbers of those children. In addition, the Society mounts current exhibitions: two recent photographic exhibits were "The Chicago Street: 1865–2000" and a six-month study of O'Hare Airport. *1601 N. Clark, tel. 312/642–4600. Admission: $1.50 adults, 50¢ students 6–17 and senior citizens, free Mon. Open Mon.–Sat. 9:30–4:30, Sun. noon–5.*

The southbound Clark Street (No. 22) bus will return you to the near north or downtown.

Tour 7: North Clark Street

A car or bus ride up North Clark Street north of Lincoln Park provides an interesting view of how cities and their ethnic populations grow and change. Before the late 1960s the Clark Street area was solidly white middle class. Andersonville, the Swedish community centered at Foster (5200 N.) and Clark, extended north half a mile and included residential buildings to the east and west as well as a vital shopping strip on Clark. Then, in the early 1970s, immigration from the Far East began. Chicago's first Thai restaurant opened at 5000 North Clark. (Chicago's Thai population has since dispersed itself throughout the city without establishing a significant concentration here.) The Japanese community, which had shops and restaurants at the northern end of the North 3000s on Clark, became more firmly entrenched, joined by substantial Korean immigration. Korean settlement has since grown to the north and west, along north Lincoln Avenue. As the 1970s ended, the Asian immigrants were being joined by newcomers from the Middle East. Together these groups have moved into the neighborhood, in classic fashion, as the old established group (the Swedish community) moved out to the suburbs. Today the shops on north Clark bear witness to the process of ethnic transition.

You can board the northbound Clark Street (No. 22) bus on Dearborn Street in the Loop or on Clark north of Walton Street. Or you can drive to Clark and North Avenue, where we'll begin our ride. North Avenue (1600 N.) is the southern boundary of the Lincoln Park neighborhood, which extends north to Diversey Avenue (2800 N.). The drive through Lincoln Park affords views of handsome renovated housing, housing in the process of being restored, upscale shops, and youthful joggers.

As you cross Belmont (3200 N.), you'll notice that the character of the neighborhood has changed. In the 3300 North block of Clark the **Happi-Sushi** restaurant and the **Suehiro** restaurant provide for Japanese tastes in food and are long-time denizens of this strip. You can get all the ingredients for authentic Japanese dishes at **Star Market** (3349 N. Clark, tel. 312/472–0599), including exquisitely fresh (and astronomically expensive) fish to be used raw, sliced thinly, for sashimi.

Continuing north to the intersection with Addison Street, you'll find **Wrigley Field,** the home of the Chicago Cubs. The surrounding neighborhood of Wrigleyville is the last solidly white middle-class neighborhood remaining on this strip. Until the summer of 1988, area residents were successful in fighting the installation of lights for night games at Wrigley Field, and the Cubs played all their home games in the afternoon.

At Clark and Irving Park Road (4000 N.), you'll find **Graceland Cemetery**, the final resting place of many 19th-century millionaires and other local luminaries. In the 4500 N. block are **K-World Trading** and **Bee Tradin' Co.**, and a bit farther north is **Nice Trading Co.** All are East Asian import and export firms who aren't much to look at—they don't do business with the public—but whose names speak volumes.

North of Wilson Avenue, pictures of fish swim across the window of the **Clark St. Fishmarket,** where very little English is spoken; the customers and the shop owners are Korean immigrants. **Charming Woks** (4628 N. Clark, tel. 312/989–8768) prepares Hunan and Szechuan food. The **Korean Restaurant** (4631 N. Clark, tel. 312/878–2095) advertises carryouts. **Oriental Food Mart Wholesalers and Importers** is just south of Leland. **Tokyo Marina** restaurant (5058 N. Clark, tel. 312/878–2900) comes up on your left *(see* Chapter 6).

Foster Avenue is the old southern boundary of Andersonville. Around the corner on Foster, west of Clark, is the **Middle Eastern Bakery and Grocery** (1512 W. Foster, tel. 312/561–2224). Here are felafel, meat pies, spinach pies, baba ghannouj (eggplant puree dip), oil-cured olives, grains, pita bread, and a seductive selection of Middle Eastern sweets—flaky, honey-dipped, nut-filled delights. In the 5200 North block just north of Foster the **Beirut Restaurant** serves *kifta* kebabs (grilled meatballs), *baba ghannouj, kibbee* (ground lamb with bulghur wheat), felafel (deep-fried chick-pea balls), meat and spinach pies, and more. Across the street the original **Ann Sather's** restaurant, with its white wood on red brick storefront, specializes in Swedish cuisine and generally does a good business. South of Ann Sather the **Mediterranean Snack Shop and Grill** advertises steak sandwiches, Italian beef, burritos, and tacos; the specials of the day are potato stew with rice, *kheema* (ground beef) stew with rice, okra stew with rice, and other traditional dishes of the Mideast and Indian subcontinent.

Across the street on the same block the **Byblos I Bakery and Deli** offers Lebanese Middle Eastern bread and groceries. If you arrive at the right time, you'll see the window filled with pita breads still puffed. Opposite the bakery, the **Swedish-American Museum Center** has beautifully decorated papier-mâché roosters and horses, place mats, craft items, tablecloths, and candelabras. North of the Byblos Bakery is the **Scandinavian Furniture Center.** The wares of **Nelson's Scandinavian Bakery** are classical European pastries: elephant ears and petit fours with chocolate, for example. The **Svea Restaurant** has pretty blue and white tablecloths and a counter; business seems slow. **Erickson's Delicatessen** has glögg in bottles, crispbreads, Ramlösa, hollandaise sauce mix, and homemade herring and imported cheese.

Just north of Erickson's the **Andersonville Artists Original Arts and Crafts Display** features the work of local artisans, which includes hand-painted china, small sculptures, and paintings. On the other side of the street, the shelves of **Wikstrom's Gourmet Foods** contain Wasa bread, Swedish pancake mix, coffee roll mix, lingonberries, dilled potatoes, and raspberry dessert. Just north of Wikstrom's is **G. M. Nordling Jeweler.** At **Reza's Restaurant** (5255 N. Clark) you can dine on kebabs, *must* and *khiyar* (yogurt and cucumber), pomegranate juice, charbroiled ground beef with Persian rice, and other Middle Eastern entrées in an attractive setting.

On the 5400 North block are **Seoul House,** which carries food, groceries, and general merchandise, and the **Kotobuki Japanese Restaurant.** On the 5600 North block are **Gabriel Philippine Food** and the **Korean Chap Chae House.**

Phil House (5845 N. Clark) is a Philippine market stocking fresh fish, taro root, fresh shrimp of all sizes, crayfish, langostinos, *longaniza* (Philippine sausage), and a huge selection of spring roll skins. Chicago is home to a very large group of Philippine immigrants, but like the Thais (and unlike the Indians and the Koreans) they have not concentrated in a single area.

Here ends our ride up Clark Street, an urban tour through time and the waves of ethnic migration and replacement. In that respect, Clark—like north Milwaukee Avenue, which has gone from being Polish to Hispanic to Polish again as new immigrants have arrived in the 1980s—is a microcosm of the city of Chicago and the continuing ebb and flow of its populations.

Tour 8: Argyle Street and Uptown

In many cities, *uptown* suggests an elite residential area, as opposed to *downtown*, the central business district. Something like that must have been in the mind of the Californian who bought Chicago's Uptown National Bank sight unseen a few years ago; ever since he got a look at his property and its neighborhood, he's been trying to sell it. In Chicago, Uptown—an area bounded by Irving Park Road (4000 N.) on the south, Foster Avenue (5200 N.) on the north, the lake on the east, and Clark Street and Ravenswood Avenue (1800 W.) on the west—is the home of the down-and-out: Appalachians who came to Chicago in search of jobs following World War II, blacks, American Indians, families on welfare, drug addicts, winos, and others of Chicago's most disadvantaged residents live here. The neighborhood is rough, the rents are low.

Given the characteristics of the neighborhood, numerous social service agencies are located here. Because of that, and the low rents, Uptown is where Vietnamese immigrants were placed when they began arriving in Chicago in substantial numbers following the end of the Vietnam War. Hmong refugees—tribal mountain folk from Vietnam—likewise joined a polyglot community whose common bond, if any, was a shared destitution.

Yet the arrival of the Vietnamese groups brought interesting developments in Uptown. The first years were difficult: Although some of the families were educated and well-to-do in Vietnam, they came here with no money and no knowledge of English. The Hmong were further disadvantaged by having had no urban experience; they were transplanted directly from remote, rather primitive villages into the heart of a modern urban slum. Nonetheless, like earlier immigrants who came to America, these people arrived with the determination to make new lives for themselves. They took any job that was offered, no matter how menial or how low the pay, and they worked two jobs when they could find them. From their meager earnings, they saved money. And they did two other important things: They sent their children to school and zealously oversaw their studies, and they formed self-help associations. Through the associations, they used pooled savings as rotating funds to set one, then another, up in business: grocery stores and bakeries to sell the foods that tasted like home, clothing shops and hairdressing salons to fill the needs of the community, and finally restaurants that attracted not only people from the old country who were beginning to have discretionary funds but also Americans from all over the city.

As their businesses prospered, they bought property. And the property they bought was the cheapest they could find, on the most depressed street in this crumbling neighborhood, Argyle Street (5000 N.). Today Argyle Street, a two-block strip between Broadway on the west and Sheridan Road on the east, is thriving. Its commercial buildings have been upgraded, thereby attracting the shops and restaurants of other Asian communities in Chicago, principally the Chinese and Thai. As "New Chinatown" or "Chinatown North," the area became so attractive that the old Chinatown merchant's association, representing the stores along Wentworth Street on the south side, considered relocating there en masse. While that plan fell through, some stores moved on their own. The Argyle Street group has been so successful that there is now a rivalry between the two Chinatowns for the custom of the Asian (and American) communities in Chicago.

If you've never been to Southeast Asia, a walk down Argyle Street is the next best thing. The neighborhood bustles with street traffic, and the stores are crowded with people buying fresh produce, baked goods, kitchen equipment, and 50-pound sacks of rice. Few signs are in English, though merchants know enough English to serve customers who don't speak their native language. Often older children and teenagers who learned English in school are pressed into service to help visitors. If you've been to Southeast Asia and long again for those tastes, smells, and sights, you must visit Argyle Street. Only here will you find, for example, the wonderful, vile-smelling durian fruit—an addiction for many, anathema to some—and other staples of Southeast Asian cuisine. Here, too, you will find two of the best Vietnamese restaurants in the city, **Mekong** (4953 N. Broadway) and **Hue** (1138 W. Argyle; *see* Chapter 6), as well as Chinese restaurants serving noodles and barbecued duck and pork (which you might enjoy munching as you walk).

Today, fueled in part by the success of the Vietnamese and, more generally, the prosperity that that success has brought, Uptown is changing. Renovators are buying once fine old properties and restoring them, and young middle-class folk, driven here by the high prices in such neighborhoods as Lincoln Park to the south, are beginning to move in. The area has become a political battleground between those who claim to represent the poor and downtrodden, who are likely to be displaced (as they always are) when gentrification comes, and those who believe that the undeniable social costs of rehabbing are less than the social costs of allowing the neighborhood to fall further and further into decay.

A walk on Argyle Street is one of the most complex experiences you can have in Chicago. You'll become totally immersed in the tastes and sounds of another culture; you'll see the classic immigrant pattern, the process of successful Americanization; and you'll appreciate the pushes and pulls at work as cities decay, are restored, and grow again.

Tour 9: Devon Avenue

As immigration laws were made more lenient in the 1970s and 1980s, the number of immigrants arriving in Chicago increased substantially. In the 1970s, newcomers from the Indian subcontinent began to arrive, and in the 1980s they were followed by Asians from Thailand, Korea, the Phillipines, and Vietnam; as well as large numbers from the Middle East, including Palestinians, Syrians, Lebanese, and Turks. The Soviet relaxation of restrictions on Jewish emigration has turned many Jewish refuseniks into American residents.

Several of these diverse cultures mingle along a mile-long strip of Devon Avenue between Sacramento and Oakley streets, near the northern edge of the city. A stroll down the strip on any sunny Sunday afternoon or hot summer evening will allow you to appreciate the avenue's variety of cultures. At the eastern end is the hub of the Indian community, with stores catering to both Muslims and Hindus. As you walk west, you will see saree stores give way to Korean restaurants and Russian grocery stores. At the western end is an orthodox Jewish neighborhood, dotted with kosher bakeries and butchers, and religious bookstores.

To get to Devon Avenue (6400 N.), take Lake Shore Drive north to Hollywood Avenue. Stay in one of the left lanes and go west on Hollywood to Ridge Avenue. Turn right on Ridge and head north for about a mile to Devon. Turn left on Devon, drive about two miles west to Oakley Street (2200 W.), and park your car. Your tour will take you down Devon as far as Sacramento Avenue (3000 W.).

Starting on the south side of Devon at Oakley, you'll see **Suleiman Brother Farm City Meats** (2255 W. Devon), purveyors of *Halal* meat, from animals slaughtered according to the provisions of Islamic law. The store sells baby goat meat, as well as a large selection of fish. As you walk west, you'll see many stores, such as **Video Palace** (2315 W. Devon), that sell or rent Indian and Pakistani movies and videotapes.

There are also at least a dozen stores that sell the colorful sarees worn by Indian women, including the **Taj Saree Palace** (2553 W. Devon), **Sarees Sapne** (2623 W. Devon), **Sharada Saree Center** (2629 W. Devon), and **ISP Indian Saree Palace** (2524 W. Devon).

Numerous grocery stores along your route sell Indian foods, condiments, and kitchenwares; the exotic smells are enticing. Take a look at the **Middle East Trading Co.** (2505 W. Devon),

Patel Brothers (with three locations at 2542, 2600, and 2610 W. Devon), and **Foods of India** (2331 and 2614 W. Devon).

For a quick snack, try the Indian food at the **Pakistani Indian Chat House** (6357 N. Claremont, at the corner of Devon), or **Annapurna Fast Food Vegetarian Snacks and Sweets** (2608 W. Devon).

Several Indian restaurants along Devon Avenue are good choices for a meal, including **Viceroy of India** (2518 W. Devon), **Moti Mahal** (2525 W. Devon), and the vegetarian **Natraj** (2240 W. Devon). Try the tandoori chicken or fish, which is marinated and grilled, the *sagh paneer* (a creamy mixture of spinach and cheese), or the *dal* (a lentil puree).

Several stores specialize in Russian cuisine and are easily recognized by the signs in Cyrillic writing hanging outside. Among them are **Globus International Foods and Delicatessen** (2837 W. Devon), **Three Sisters Delicatessen** (2854 W. Devon), and **Kashtan Deli** (2740 W. Devon). Three Sisters has a large selection of *matrioshkas* (the popular Russian dolls that are stacked one inside another). At 2845 West Devon, you'll see the **Croatian Cultural Center.**

When you reach the western end of Devon Avenue, notice the many stores and restaurants catering to the orthodox Jewish community. The restaurants and bakeries are good bets for either a sit-down meal or a snack to eat while you walk. Watch for **Miller's Market** (2527 W. Devon), **Tel Aviv Kosher Bakery** (2944 W. Devon), **The Bagel Restaurant** (3000 W. Devon), **Kosher Karry** (2828 W. Devon), and **Levinson's Bakery** (2856 W. Devon). The **Midwest Fish Market** (2942 W. Devon) has lox and other smoked fish for sale.

Several stores along the way sell Hebrew books and sacramental items, including **Rosenblum's Hebrew Bookstore** (2910 W. Devon) and the **Chicago Hebrew Bookstore** (2942 W. Devon). Rosenblum's has a large selection of unusual cookbooks, including several on Yemeni and Sephardic cuisine.

Tour 10: Oak Park

Ernest Hemingway once called Oak Park—his birthplace and childhood home from 1899 to 1917—a town of "broad lawns and narrow minds." The ethnic and political leanings of this neighborhood have diversified since Hemingway played on its streets, however, due in part to the past decade's influx of young professionals fleeing the city with their children in search of safer streets, better public schools, and easy access to the Loop. Restoration activity and property values have increased accordingly.

Founded in the 1850s, just west of the Chicago border, Oak Park is not only one of Chicago's oldest suburbs, but also a living museum of American architectural thought. Oak Park has the world's largest collection of Prairie School buildings, an architectural style created by Frank Lloyd Wright, to reflect the expanses of the Great Plains. Constructed from materials indigenous to the region, Prairie School houses hug the earth with their emphatic horizontal lines; inside, open spaces flow into each other, rather than being divided into individual rooms.

To get to the heart of Oak Park, take the Eisenhower Expressway (I–290) west to Harlem Avenue and exit to the left. Turn right at the top of the ramp, head north on Harlem Avenue to Chicago Avenue, turn right, and proceed to Forest Avenue.

On the southeast corner of Forest and Chicago avenues you'll see the **Frank Lloyd Wright Home and Studio.** In 1889, the 22-year-old Wright began building his own Shingle Style home—financed by a $5,000 loan from his then-employer and mentor, Louis Sullivan (of the noted firm Adler & Sullivan)—at the same time as he began to develop the Prairie School of architecture. Over the next 20 years, Wright expanded his business as well as his original modest cottage, establishing his own firm in 1894 and adding a studio in 1898.

In 1909 Wright left his wife and six children for the wife of a client; the focus of his career changed, too, as he spread his innovative designs across the United States and abroad. Sold by Wright in 1925, his home and studio were turned into apartments that eventually fell into disrepair. In 1974, a group of local citizens calling itself the Frank Lloyd Wright Home and Studio Foundation, together with the National Trust for Historic Preservation, embarked on a 13-year, $2.2 million restoration that returned the building to its 1909 appearance.

Wright's home, made of brick and dark shingles, is filled with natural wood furnishings and earth-tone spaces; Wright's determination to create an integrated environment prompted him to design the furniture as well. The leaded windows have colored art glass designs, and several rooms feature skylights or other indirect lighting. A spacious playroom on the second floor is built to a child's scale. The studio is made up of four spaces—an office, a large reception room, an octagonal library, and an octagonal drafting room that uses a chain harness system rather than traditional beams to support its balcony, roof, and walls. A testimony to Wright's somewhat eccentric regard for nature, the house was built around a tree that grew through the wall of a hallway and up through the ceiling; though the original tree died years ago, the restoration includes a replacement branch. *951 Chicago Ave., tel. 708/848–1500. Admission: Mar.–Oct., $5 adults, $3 senior citizens and children 10–18; Nov.–Feb., $4 adults, $2 senior citizens and children 10–18. Tours weekdays at 11 AM, 1 PM, and 3 PM, and continuously on weekends 11–4. Reservations required for groups of 10 or more. Closed Thanksgiving, Christmas, and New Year's Day.*

Several other examples of Wright's work are within easy walking or driving distance from his home and studio. Except for the Unity Temple, though, these are all private homes, so you'll have to be content with what you can view from the outside. One block east on Chicago Avenue takes you past **1019, 1027,** and **1031 Chicago Avenue.** Turn left on Marion Street and then left again on Superior Street to reach **1030 Superior Street.** Continue down Superior Street, turn right onto Forest Avenue, and take a look at **333, 318, 238,** and **210 Forest Avenue.** Head left for a detour to **6 Elizabeth Court.** Follow Forest Avenue a few blocks south to Lake Street and turn left. On the corner of Lake Street and Kenilworth Avenue is **Unity Temple** (875 Lake St., tel. 708/848–6225), built for a Unitarian congregation in 1905.

If you still have some energy, head back up Forest Avenue to Chicago Avenue. One block east and two blocks north brings you to **Ernest Hemingway's boyhood home** (600 N. Kenilworth). This gray stucco house is privately owned and not open to the public.

Maps, tour information, and recorded tours of other historic buildings in the River Forest/Oak Park area (including those by Prairie School architects E. E. Roberts and George Maher) are available through the **Oak Park Visitors Center** (158 N. Forest Ave., tel. 708/848-1500).

Chicago for Free

Like all great cities, Chicago offers a wealth of things to see and do that cost no more than the price of transportation to them.

Concerts **Chicago Public Library Cultural Center** (78 E. Washington St., tel. 312/346-3278) presents the Dame Myra Hess Memorial Concert Series Wednesday at 12:15, a program of recitals by rising professional classical musicians.
Petrillo Bandshell in Grant Park is the site of summertime concerts sponsored by the Chicago Park District. In mid-June the Jazz Fest and the Gospel Fest are three-day events in which numerous performances take place on several stages. The Grant Park Symphony Orchestra and Chorus perform three to four times a week, late June through August. The Blues Festival comes to town in late August and early September. *The Reader* (free at stores and other locations in The Loop, Near North Side, Lincoln Park, and Hyde Park on Thursday and Friday) gives program details and performance times.
Daley Plaza (Washington between Clark and Dearborn Sts.) and **First National Bank of Chicago Plaza** (Dearborn to Clark between Monroe and Madison Sts.) have performances of light music, including folk and pop, during the noon hour in the summertime.
Chicago Chamber Orchestra (tel. 312/922-5570), under the direction of Dieter Koeber, gives free chamber concerts throughout the year at various locations. The performances are funded by corporate and foundation grants and individual memberships; the organization's goal is to bring live performances of fine music to those who cannot afford to pay for them.

Many Chicago churches offer free concerts, frequently organ recitals, choral programs, and gospel music. *The Reader* lists programs and locations.

Museums Several Chicago museums do not charge admission fees, among them: **Chicago Public Library Cultural Center, Czechoslovakian Society of America Heritage Museum and Archives, Mexican Fine Arts Center Museum, Museum of Science and Industry, Oriental Institute, Polish Museum of America, Telephony Museum.** Of the museums that have admission fees, many of them schedule one day a week when admission is free to all: **Art Institute of Chicago** (Tuesday), **Chicago Academy of Sciences** (Monday), **Chicago Historical Society** (Monday), **Field Museum of Natural History** (Thursday), **Museum of Contemporary Art** (Tuesday), **John G. Shedd Aquarium** (Thursday). Though there is a fee for the Sky Show, the exhibits are free at the **Adler Planetarium.**

Music School Chicago has several fine music schools and university departPrograms ments of music, where faculty and students frequently give recitals (public performances are often a part of degree requirements).

University of Chicago Concert Office (tel. 312/702–8068) schedules concerts by a number of performing ensembles: the Motet Choir, the University of Chicago Chorus, the University of Chicago Orchestra, and the Collegium Musicum (an instrumental and vocal ensemble that performs music of the Renaissance and Baroque periods).

American Conservatory of Music (17 N. State St., tel. 312/263–4161) offers student and faculty recitals, at noon and in the evening, when school is in session. A program is scheduled almost every day except Sunday, and most performances are free.

De Paul University School of Music (804 W. Belden Ave., tel. 312/341–8373) has concerts by a chorus, an orchestra, a jazz band, and other performing ensembles as well as recitals. There are daily events throughout the school year.

Chicago Musical College of Roosevelt University (Rudolf Ganz Memorial Hall, 430 S. Michigan Ave., tel. 312/341–3787) schedules recitals and orchestral, chamber, woodwind, and jazz concerts. Early in the semester there are two to three events a week; later there's something every day.

Sherwood Conservatory of Music (1014 S. Michigan Ave., tel. 312/427–6267) has faculty and student recitals most Sunday afternoons and some Saturdays.

Picnics Between April and October, picnicking can be delightful almost anywhere along the lakefront. Favorite spots include Grant Park and Navy Pier.

Tours Many institutions offer free guided tours of their operations; most require reservations.

Chicago City Hall (121 N. La Salle St., tel. 312/744–6671) has one tour daily at 10 AM that takes in the City Council chambers and an exhibit of gifts presented to the late Mayor Harold Washington. City council meetings are open to the public and are famous for their often heated debates. Call 312/744–6800 for meeting times.

Chicago Police Department (1121 S. State St., tel. 312/744–5571) gives weekday 45-minute tours of its communication facility and the crime lab.

The main **U.S. Post Office** in Chicago (433 W. Van Buren St., tel. 312/765–3009), the largest postal facility in the world, offers tours of its mail processing division weekdays at 10:30 and 12:30. Call one week in advance; no children under nine.

James Jardine Water Purification Plant (Navy Pier, tel. 312/744–3692), the largest facility of its kind in the world, shows you the entire purification process in tours Tuesday and Thursday at 9:30 and 1:30.

Federal Reserve Bank (230 W. LaSalle St., tel. 312/322–2386) explains how checks are processed and how money travels; tours are given daily 9–1. Call for reservations.

What to See and Do with Children

Among the outstanding activities Chicago has in store for family groups are several museums that provide hours of fascination for youngsters, where dozens of exhibits not only do not forbid you to touch them but actually require that you interact with them.

Adler Planetarium (*see* Museums and Galleries in Sightseeing Checklists, below). The Sky Shows enthrall young and old alike.

Brookfield Zoo (*see* Zoos in Sightseeing Checklists, below). Here are elephants, dolphins, a rain forest, and animals enough to keep you busy all day.

Chicago Academy of Sciences (*see* Tour 6: Lincoln Park, above) has many exhibits that will fascinate children.

Chicago Public Library Cultural Center (78 E. Washington St., tel. 312/269–2900). Programs for youngsters take place throughout the year.

Children's Bookstore (2465 N. Lincoln Ave., tel. 312/248–2665). Browsing is encouraged among a superb collection of carefully selected books for children; story hours for children under six are scheduled several times a week.

Express-Ways Children's Museum (*see* Museums and Galleries in Sightseeing Checklists, below). Designed specifically for very young children, Express-Ways has many things to see and touch.

Facets Multimedia (1517 W. Fullerton Ave., tel. 312/281–4114). Movies for youngsters are programmed Saturday and Sunday afternoons, October to May. The children's international film festival in October includes shorts, features, and TV videos from other countries.

Field Museum of Natural History (*see* Museums and Galleries in Sightseeing Checklists, below). Three rooms are filled with the touchy-feely stuff that small folk love, and many of the regular exhibits have considerable appeal for children.

57th St. Books (1301 E. 57th St., tel. 312/363–0993). In addition to the excellent selection of children's books, the store has a play and reading area where youngsters can browse or grown-ups can read to them.

Lincoln Park Zoo (*see* Zoos in Sightseeing Checklists, below). The Children's Zoo, the Farm-in-the-Zoo, and the Kids' Corner Discovery Place are the special attractions prepared just for youngsters.

Museum of Science and Industry (*see* Museums and Galleries in Sightseeing Checklists, below). Children and parents may find themselves competing here to see who gets to use the instruments or take part in the activities first.

John G. Shedd Aquarium (*see* Museums and Galleries in Sightseeing Checklists, below). The display of sea creatures is guaranteed to captivate every visitor, regardless of age.

Off the Beaten Track

If you're at McCormick Place, take a walk on the promenade that runs between the convention center and the lake. You can watch small planes take off from and land at tiny Meigs Field and, in the summer, observe the sailboats as they bob in Burnham Harbor.

The **Trompe l'oeil Building** (1207 W. Division) is on the northeast corner of La Salle and Division streets, but you should study its appearance from a block east, at Clark and Division, or approach it from the south for the full effect of its rose window, ornate arched doorway, stone steps, columns, and sculptures. As you move closer to the building, you'll discover that an ordinary high rise has been elaborately painted to make it look like an entirely different work of architecture.

Olive Park juts out into Lake Michigan a block north of Lake Point Towers (505 N. Lake Shore Dr.); to find it, walk east on Grand Avenue, pass under Lake Shore Drive, and bear left. It has no roads, just paved walkways and lots of benches, trees, shrubs, and grass. The marvelous and unusual views of the city skyline from here, in addition to the absence of vehicular traffic, make it seem as though you're miles from the city, not just blocks from the busy Near North side.

Slightly northwest of Hyde Park, at the corner of Drexel Boulevard and 50th Street, is the headquarters of **Operation PUSH** (930 E. 50th St., tel. 312/373–3366), Jesse Jackson's black self-help organization. A former synagogue, you'll recognize the building by its splendid columns before you see its colorful cloth banner. Three blocks east and one block north you'll find **4995 South Woodlawn Avenue**, the home of the controversial black leader Louis Farrakhan, who has made it a headquarters of the Nation of Islam. The great house was built by Elijah Mohammed, the Nation's founder; its $3 million funding was rumored to have come from the Libyan despot Muammar Khadafi.

Nearby, at 49th Street and Kenwood Avenue, stand two early works by Frank Lloyd Wright, **Blossom House** (4858 S. Kenwood) and **MacArthur House** (4852 S. Kenwood), both built in 1892. Across from Blossom House is **Farmers' Field**, a park where animals grazed as recently as the 1920s. A few blocks away, at 49th Street and Ellis Avenue, (4901 S. Ellis), is the 22-room Prairie Style **Julius Rosenwald mansion** built by the Sears Roebuck executive in the early 1900s. After a stint as a home for boys, followed by years of disuse, the mansion was purchased by a family and extensively restored.

A treeless hill near Lincoln Park's **Montrose Harbor** draws kite-flying enthusiasts of all ages on sunny weekends. Take Lake Shore Drive north from the Loop about five miles, exit at Montrose, turn right into the park, and look for colorful stunt kites on your left. Windsurfers often practice at nearby **Montrose Beach.**

Sightseeing Checklists

Historical Buildings and Sites

This list of Chicago's principal buildings and sites includes both attractions that were covered in the preceding tours and additional attractions that are described here for the first time.

Amoco Building (Tour 1. Downtown)

Art Institute of Chicago (Tour 1. Downtown)

Associates Center (Tour 1. Downtown)

Auditorium Theatre (Tour 1. Downtown)

Biograph Theatre (Tour 6. Lincoln Park)

Blackstone Hotel (Tour 2. Downtown South)

Blackstone Theatre (Tour 1. Downtown)

Buckingham Fountain (Tour 1. Downtown)

Carbide and Carbon Building (Tour 1. Downtown)

Carson Pirie Scott (Tour 1. Downtown)

"Chevrolet" Building (Tour 3. Hyde Park and Kenwood)

Chicago Board of Trade (Tour 1. Downtown)

Chicago City Hall–Cook County Building (Tour 1. Downtown)

Chicago Academy of Sciences (Tour 6. Lincoln Park)

Chicago Hilton and Towers (Tour 1. Downtown)

Chicago Historical Society (Tour 6. Lincoln Park)

Chicago Mercantile Exchange (Tour 1. Downtown)

Chicago Public Library Cultural Center (Tour 1. Downtown)

Chicago Temple (Tour 1. Downtown)

Chicago Theatre (Tour 1. Downtown)

Chicago Theological Seminary (Tour 3. Hyde Park and Kenwood)

Civic Opera House (Tour 1. Downtown)

Clarke House (1800 S. Prairie Ave., tel. 312/326–1393). Chicago's oldest building, Clarke House was constructed in 1836 in Greek Revival style. Period furniture enlivens the interior. Part of the Prairie Avenue Historical District.

Crilly Court (Tour 6. Lincoln Park)

Daley Center (Tour 1. Downtown)

Dearborn Park (Tour 2. Downtown South)

Dearborn Station (Tour 2. Downtown South)

Donohue Building (Tour 2. Downtown South)

Drake Hotel (*see* Lodging)

Federal Center and Plaza (Tour 1. Downtown)

Fine Arts Building (Tour 1. Downtown)

First National Bank of Chicago (Tour 1. Downtown)

Fisher Building (Tour 1. Downtown)

Franklin Building (Tour 2. Downtown South)

Glessner House (1801 S. Prairie Ave., tel. 312/326–1393). The only surviving building in Chicago by the architect H. H. Richardson. Glessner House was designed in 1886. Part of the Prairie Avenue Historic District.

Heller House (Tour 3. Hyde Park and Kenwood)

Hull House (800 S. Halsted St., tel. 312/413–5353). The columned, red brick, turn-of-the-century Hull House seems out of place on its site, surrounded by the massive and modern buildings of the University of Illinois campus. Here Jane Addams wrought social work miracles in a neighborhood that was then a slum. Here, too, Benny Goodman learned to play the clarinet. Open to the public weekdays 10 AM–4 PM, Sunday noon–5. Closed most holidays.

IBM Building (Tour 5. River North)

Illinois Institute of Technology (31st–35th Sts. on S. State St., tel. 312/567–3000). The campus was designed principally by

Mies van der Rohe, with participation by Friedman, Alschuler and Sincere; Holabird and Roche; and Pace Associates. Built between 1942 and 1958, the structures have the characteristic box shape that is Mies's trademark. Unlike most of his work, they are low-rise buildings. Crown Hall (3360 S. State St.) is the jewel of the collection; the other buildings have a certain sameness and sterility.

International House (Tour 3. Hyde Park and Kenwood)

Laird Bell Law Quadrangle (Tour 3. Hyde Park and Kenwood)

Lutheran School of Theology (Tour 3. Hyde Park and Kenwood)

Marquette Building (Tour 1. Downtown)

McCormick Seminary (Tour 6. Lincoln Park)

Metropolitan Detention Center (Tour 1. Downtown)

Midway Plaisance (Tour 3. Hyde Park and Kenwood)

Moody Bible Institute (Tour 6. Lincoln Park)

Monadnock Building (Tour 1. Downtown)

Museum of Science and Industry (Tour 3. Hyde Park and Kenwood)

Northwestern Atrium Center (Tour 1. Downtown)

One Financial Place (Tour 1. Downtown)

Oriental Institute (Tour 3. Hyde Park and Kenwood)

Orchestra Hall (Tour 1. Downtown)

Page Brothers Building (Tour 1. Downtown)

Palmer House (Tour 1. Downtown)

Promontory Apartments (Tour 3. Hyde Park and Kenwood)

Quaker Oats Building (Tour 5. River North)

Railway Exchange Building (Tour 1. Downtown)

Joseph Regenstein Library (Tour 3. Hyde Park and Kenwood)

Reliance Building (Tour 1. Downtown)

River City (Tour 2. Downtown South)

Robie House (Tour 3. Hyde Park and Kenwood)

Rockefeller Memorial Chapel (Tour 3. Hyde Park and Kenwood)

The Rookery (Tour 1. Downtown)

Julius Rosenwald Mansion (Tour 3. Hyde Park and Kenwood)

The Sanctuary (Tour 6. Lincoln Park)

Sears Tower (Tour 1. Downtown)

State of Illinois Center (Tour 1. Downtown)

Tribune Tower (435 N. Michigan Ave., tel. 312/222–3232). Col. Robert McCormick held an international design competition for a new building to house the *Chicago Tribune*. Faced with a slew of functional modern designs, he chose instead this ultra-traditional, crenellated Gothic building. Look for chunks of other famous buildings (such as Westminster Abbey) embedded in the outside of the tower.

Union Station (Tour 1. Downtown)

U.S. Post Office (Tour 1. Downtown)

University of Illinois at Chicago (705 S. Halsted St., tel. 312/996–7000). Designed by Walter Netsch, of Skidmore, Owings, and Merrill, the university buildings seem to surge and weave toward each other.

333 North Wacker Drive (Tour 1. Downtown)

Water Tower (Michigan and Chicago Aves.). A survivor of the Great Fire of 1871, the distinctive yellow stone Water Tower of 1869 is now a tourist information center.

Windermere House (Tour 3. Hyde Park and Kenwood)

Wrigley Building (400 N. Michigan Ave., tel. 312/923–8080). The graceful Wrigley Building, which is illuminated at night, is the corporate home of the Wrigley chewing gum empire.

Xerox Building (Tour 1. Downtown)

Museums and Galleries

Museums **Adler Planetarium.** The planetarium is a museum with exhibits about the stars and the planets and a popular program of Sky Shows. Past Sky Shows have included "The Space Telescope Story" and "Planetary Puzzles." *1300 S. Lake Shore Dr., tel. 312/322–0304 (general information), 312/322–0300 (Sky Show information), 312/322–0334 (information on the skies for the month). Admission free. Sky Show admission: $3 adults, $1.50 children 6–17, free under 6 for the Sat. 10 AM show only. Open Mon.–Thurs. 9:30–4:30, Fri. 9:30–9, weekends 9:30–4:30.*

American Police Center Museum. The museum's exhibits are concerned with police work and relationships between the police and the public. Safety, crime and punishment, and drugs and alcohol are among the subjects. One exhibit shows how the police communication system works; another details the history of the Haymarket Riot. A memorial gallery is dedicated to policemen who have lost their lives in the line of duty. *1717 S. State St., tel. 312/431–0005. Admission: $2 adults, $1.50 senior citizens, $1 children 6–11. Open weekdays 9–4.*

Art Institute of Chicago (Tour 1. Downtown)

Balzekas Museum of Lithuanian Culture. The little-known Balzekas Museum offers a taste of 1,000 years of Lithuanian history and culture on its three floors. You'll find exhibits on rural Lithuania; concentration camps; rare maps, stamps, and coins; textiles; and amber. The library can be used for research. *6500 S. Pulaski Rd., tel. 312/582–6500. Admission: $2 adults, $1.50 students and senior citizens, $1 children under 12. Open daily 10–4.*

Chicago Academy of Sciences (Tour 6. Lincoln Park)

Chicago Historical Society (Tour 6. Lincoln Park)

Chicago Public Library Cultural Center (Tour 1. Downtown)

Czechoslovakian Society of America Heritage Museum and Archives. The collections of the Czechoslovakian Society include crystal, marble, dolls, musical instruments, china, ornamented eggs, vases, paintings, and statues. A library is part of the museum. *2701 S. Harlem Ave., Berwyn, tel. 708/242–2224. Admission free. Open weekdays 10–noon and 1–4.*

DuSable Museum of African American History. A 10-foot mural in the auditorium of the museum, hand-carved by Robert Witt Ames, depicts black history from Africa to the 1960s. Another gallery features great history makers: Martin Luther King, Jr., Rosa Parks, Paul Robeson, Sojourner Truth, and others. Special exhibits change frequently; a recent one on the cultural history of Haiti included paintings, papier-mâché crafts, flags, and other cultural artifacts. *740 E. 56th Pl., tel. 312/947–0600. Admission: $2 adults, $1 senior citizens and students, 50¢ under 13. Open weekdays 9–5, weekends noon–5.*

Express-Ways Children's Museum. Here are major exhibits of African art, architecture, and a recycling center, but the big draws are the three "hands-on" exhibits for children 2–12 and a "touch and feel" exhibit for preschoolers. *435 E. Illinois St. (North Pier building), tel. 312/527–1000. Admission: $3 adults, $2 children. Open Tues.–Fri. 12:30–4:30 and Thurs. eve. 5–8, weekends 10–4:30; closed Mon.*

Field Museum of Natural History. The Field is one of the country's great natural history museums, and the breadth of its collections is enormous. You can hear songs and stories about Pawnee life while sitting in a reconstructed Pawnee earth lodge (built in conjunction with the Pawnee of Oklahoma) and touch tools and artifacts. You can return to ancient Egypt by visiting the museum's newest permanent exhibit, a reconstructed Mastaba tomb complex that houses Unis-ankh, the son of a fifth-dynasty pharaoh. Two of the original chambers, excavated in 1908, are reached by a 35-foot descent. The exhibit includes a working canal and a living marsh where papyrus is grown; a shrine to the cat goddess Bastet; burial ceremonies; and 23 mummies and 1,400 rare artifacts, many of which have never before been seen by the public. A gem room contains more than 500 gemstones and jewels. Place for Wonder, a three-room exhibit for children, lets youngsters handle everything on display, including a half-ton polar bear (named Earthquake Charlie), shells, animal skins, stuffed animals, clothing and toys from China, aromatic scent jars, and gourds. Music, dance, theater, and film performances are also scheduled. *Lake Shore Drive at E. Roosevelt Rd., tel. 312/922–9410. Admission: $10 families, $3 adults, $2 students and senior citizens; free Thurs. Open daily 9–5.*

International Museum of Surgical Sciences. The surgical sciences museum has medical artifacts from around the world. *1524 N. Lake Shore Dr., tel. 312/642–3555. Open Tues.–Sat. 10–4, Sun. 11–5.*

Mexican Fine Arts Center Museum. The exhibits of the work of contemporary Mexican artists change every two to three months. *1852 W. 19th St., tel. 312/738–1503. Admission free. Open Tues.–Sun. 10–5.*

Museum of Broadcast Communications. Thousands of tapes of old TV and radio programs are collected here, and 10 study bays allow visitors to view or listen to them. Among the exhibits are the original Charlie McCarthy and Mortimer Snerd puppets. A reconstructed WGN radio studio broadcasts Saturday 1–5, and visitors to the museum can attend the broadcasts. Recent special exhibits were "40 Years of WGN-TV" and "A Salute to the TV Western." *800 S. Wells St., tel. 312/987– 1500. Admission: $3 adults, $2 students, $1 senior citizens and children under 13. Open Wed.–Fri. and Sun. noon–5, Sat. 10–5.*

Museum of Contemporary Art. The Museum of Contemporary Art, started by a group of art patrons who found the great Art Institute unresponsive to modern work, concentrates on 20th-century art, principally that after 1940. Limited display space means that the collection of more than 4,000 works can be shown only in rotation; about six major exhibitions and 12 smaller ones are mounted each year. Because the museum must close to prepare a major exhibition, you should call before planning a visit. The museum expects to move to a new building on the site of the old armory on Chicago Avenue in 1993. *237 E. Ontario St., tel. 312/280–5161. Admission: $4 adults, $2 children under 16, students, and senior citizens; free Tues. Open Tues.–Sat. 10–5, Sun. noon–5; closed Mon.*

Museum of Holography. Holograms are three-dimensional images produced by lasers. If you have never seen a hologram, consider this museum a must stop; the images seem to leap out at you from their frames. The exhibits of holographic art from around the world include computer-generated holograms, moving holograms, pulsed portraits of people, and color holograms. Two to three special exhibits are mounted annually. *1134 W. Washington Blvd., tel. 312/226–1007. Admission: $2.50. Open Wed.–Sun. 12:30–5.*

Museum of Science and Industry. Visit a U-505 submarine, descend into a coal mine, experience an auditory miracle in the whispering gallery, learn how telephones work, trace the history of computing and the development of computer hardware, explore spacecraft and man's history in space, visit Main Street of Yesterday, learn how the body works, and much more. Many of the exhibits are hands-on, and you could spend days here and still not see everything. The museum's restaurants and cafeterias are ready when you get hungry. When you must sit down, take in the show at the Omnimax Theatre. *5700 S. Lake Shore Dr., tel. 312/684–1414. Admission free. Open Memorial Day to Labor Day, daily 9:30–5:30; Labor Day to Memorial Day, weekdays 9:30–4, weekends and holidays 9:30–5:30.*

Newberry Library. This venerable research institution houses superb book and document collections in many areas and mounts exhibits in a small gallery space. *60 W. Walton, tel. 312/ 943–9090. Admission free. Open Fri.–Sat. 9–5; Tues.–Thurs. 9–7:30; closed Mon.*

Oriental Institute (Tour 3. Hyde Park and Kenwood)

Peace Museum (Tour 5. River North)

Polish Museum of America. Dedicated to collecting materials on the history of the Polish people in America, the Polish Museum has an eclectic collection that includes an art gallery, an exhibit on the Shakespearean actress Modjeska, one on the American Revolutionary War hero Tadeusz Kosciusko, and another on the pianist and composer Ignaczi Paderewski that includes the last piano on which he performed and the chair he carried everywhere and without which he could not perform. The Stations of the Cross from the first Polish church in America (which was located in Texas) are on display. A library is available. *984 N. Milwaukee Ave., tel. 312/384–3352. Admission free. Open daily noon–5.*

John G. Shedd Aquarium. The Coral Reef is the big draw at the aquarium. Sharks, tarpon, turtles, and myriads of smaller fish and other aquatic forms live here, just as they do on reefs in nature. The fish are fed daily at 11, 2, and 3; the feeders narrate the process. Hundreds of other watery "cages" display fish from around the world, some bizarre and many fantastically beautiful. A new oceanarium was expected to open in early 1991, housing several killer whales and other marine life. *1200 S. Lake Shore Dr., tel. 312/939–2426. Admission: $3 adults, $2 children and senior citizens. Open daily 10–5.*

Maurice Spertus Museum of Judaica (Tour 2. Downtown South)

Swedish-American Museum Association of Chicago. Permanent exhibits here include a history of Swedish immigrant travel to the United States and a survey of the textile arts and industry in Sweden. Special exhibits, often on loan from other museums, come every six weeks. *5211 N. Clark St., tel. 312/728–8111. Admission: $1 adults, 50¢ children and senior citizens. Open Tues.–Fri. 11–4, Sat. 11–3.*

Terra Museum of Art. The museum began with Ambassador Daniel Terra's superb private collection of American art, which he made available to the city of Chicago. *666 N. Michigan Ave., tel. 312/664–3939. Admission: $4 adults, $2.50 senior citizens and children 12–18. Open Wed.–Sun. 10–5, Tues. 10–8.*

Ukrainian Institute of Modern Art. Located in the heart of Ukrainian Village on the west side, this museum focuses on contemporary paintings and sculpture by artists of Ukrainian descent. *2318 W. Chicago Ave., tel. 312/227–5522. Admission: $2. Open Tues.–Sun. noon–4.*

May Weber Museum of Cultural Arts. The small May Weber Museum has a new exhibit every three months; recent shows have explored the textiles and household arts of Japan and the crafts of the Yoruba tribe. *230 E. Ohio St., tel. 312/787–4477. Admission: $2. Open Tues.–Sat. noon–5.*

Galleries Chicago has more art galleries than any American city after New York. Most galleries are open weekdays and Saturday 10–5 or 11–5 and at other times by appointment. The largest concentrations of galleries are in the River North area and on Superior and Ontario streets east of Michigan Avenue. The River North tour in this chapter points out many of the buildings that house galleries. Because the galleries and their shows change frequently, the prospective visitor should consult the *Chicago Gallery News* for a full current listing.

Churches, Temples, and Mosques

For many decades the immigrants who settled in Chicago came principally from Ireland, Germany, Italy, and the Catholic countries of Eastern Europe. They struggled to build temples to their faith in the new neighborhoods, churches where the faithful could be uplifted and carried away from the often grinding struggles of their daily lives. As new waves of immigrants arrived, the churches became places where the ethnic community gathered to reinforce its cultural and artistic traditions as well as its faith. In this sense, it has been observed that the history of Chicago's churches is the history of the city.

Today many of the exquisite churches and the historical repositories they represent are threatened. City neighborhoods that once were enclaves of hardworking, increasingly affluent Catholic ethnic groups whose lives centered on the church now house new populations, largely Hispanic and black, who are too poor or too Protestant to maintain the churches. The Archdiocese of Chicago cannot take on their maintenance without adequate parish support; indeed, the churches may have fulfilled their function and outlived it, for the communities they were meant to serve are gone. Plans have been announced to demolish two churches, Holy Family on the near west side and St. Mary of the Angels in a depressed area on the north side, and replace them with smaller, simpler structures more suited to the size and resources of their parishes. Holy Family parishioners and other interested Chicagoans have mounted a massive effort to raise the funds needed to save the church; at this writing, there has been no resolution. It is rumored that as many as 25 old neighborhood ethnic churches may be demolished over the next 10 years.

Ironically, while churches in the ethnic neighborhoods languish, others—the Fourth Presbyterian Church on Michigan Avenue's Magnificent Mile, for example—whose congregations are well able to support them, are threatened because of the tremendous underlying value of the property on which they stand.

Many of Chicago's most beautiful churches may not be around much longer, and the wise visitor will take the opportunity to see these treasures while it is still possible. Always remember to call ahead before planning to visit a church; economic constraints have forced many churches to restrict the hours during which they are open to the public.

Baha'i House of Worship (100 Linden Ave., Wilmette, tel. 708/273–3838). Here is a sublimely lovely nine-sided building that incorporates a wealth of architectural styles and symbols from the world's religions—and symbolizes unity. The symmetry and harmony of the building are paralleled in the formal gardens that surround it. To reach the Baha'i House of Worship by public transportation, take the Howard St. el to the end, then cross the platform and take the Evanston train to the end of the line (Linden Avenue) and walk two blocks east. By car, take Lake Shore Drive northbound to its end at Hollywood, then turn right onto Sheridan Road and follow it about 10 miles to Linden Avenue in Wilmette.

Bond Chapel (1025 E. 58th St., tel. 312/702–8200). Bond Chapel is a jewel of a Gothic-style chapel on the quadrangle of the University of Chicago. The gargoyles outside belie its simple interior of dark wood, stained glass, and delicate ornamentation, which produces unusual intimacy and warmth.

Fourth Presbyterian Church (126 E. Chestnut). The courtyard of the church, a grassy spot adorned with simple statuary, situated between the granite church and the rectory and bounded by a covered walkway, is an oasis amid Michigan Avenue commercialism and provides a welcome respite for the weary shopper.

Holy Cross (4557 S. Wood St., tel. 312/376–3900). The Lithuanian Holy Cross Church was built in 1913 in Renaissance revival style. Its exterior has columns and twin towers; the interior has an arched ceiling, elaborate altar, and geometric-pattern marble floor.

Holy Family (1080 W. Roosevelt Rd., tel. 312/243–6125). Located on the near west side in what is now largely a poor Hispanic neighborhood, Holy Family is Chicago's second-oldest Catholic church. Icons have been added as the populations in the neighborhood changed: The original Irish saint has been joined by an Italian saint, a black saint, and recently a Hispanic saint. Built in Gothic style, Holy Family survived the Chicago Fire but may fall at last to the wrecker's ball.

Holy Name Cathedral (735 N. State St., tel. 312/787–8040). The yellow stone Victorian Gothic Holy Name of 1874–1875 is the principal church of the Archdiocese of Chicago. Although it is very grand inside, it is architecturally disappointing.

Holy Trinity Cathedral (1121 N. Leavitt Ave., tel. 312/486–6064). This Russian Orthodox church was designed by Louis Sullivan, who also did the Carson Pirie Scott building. It is said that Czar Nicholas of Russia contributed $4,000 to the construction. The interior, elaborately detailed and filled with icons, contains no pews; worshipers stand during the services.

Midwest Buddhist Temple (Tour 6. Lincoln Park)

Moody Memorial Church (1630 N. Clark St., tel. 312/943–0466). A massive Romanesque church, Moody Memorial is one of the largest Protestant churches in the nation. The fundamentalist nondenominational church is associated with the Moody Bible Institute.

Nativity of the Blessed Virgin Mary Ukrainian Catholic Church (4952 S. Paulina St., tel. 312/737–0733). Note the Byzantine domes. The interior is richly ornamented with murals, icons, chandeliers, and stained glass.

Old St. Patrick Church (718 W. Adams St., tel. 312/782–6171). Here is the oldest church in Chicago; built in 1852–1856, it withstood the Chicago Fire. Located just west of the west Loop redevelopment area and the huge Presidential Towers high-rise development, Old St. Patrick's is in the happy (and unusual) situation of finding its membership increasing. The towers, one Romanesque and one Byzantine, are symbolic of West and East.

Our Lady of Mt. Carmel Church (700 W. Belmont Ave., tel. 312/525–0453). Mother church for the north side Catholic parishes, Mt. Carmel is a serene oasis in the midst of urban cacophony.

Rockefeller Memorial Chapel (Tour 3. Hyde Park and Kenwood)

St. Alphonsus Church (2960 N. Southport Ave., tel. 312/525–0709). Having originally served a German neighborhood, the Gothic St. Alphonsus is now in the heart of the redeveloping

Lincoln Park. The beautiful interior has a vaulted ceiling and stained glass.

St. Basil Church (1850 W. Garfield Blvd., tel. 312/925–6311). Originally an Irish church, St. Basil's congregation tried unsuccessfully to stave off the white flight that hit this west side neighborhood in the 1960s.

St. Clement's Church (642 W. Deming Pl., tel. 312/281–0371). Combining both Roman and Byzantine elements in its design, St. Clement's has beautiful mosaics and lavish stained glass.

St. Gabriel Church (4501 S. Lowe, tel. 312/268–9595). Situated in the heart of the Irish Bridgeport neighborhood, St. Gabriel was designed more than 100 years ago by Daniel Burnham and John Root. Unlike many of Chicago's neighborhoods, Bridgeport has remained the Irish community it was 100 years ago, despite expansionist pressures from Hispanic Pilsen to the northwest and Chinatown to the northeast.

St. James Cathedral (65 E. Huron St., tel. 312/787–7360). Built in 1856, St. James was largely destroyed by the Chicago Fire in 1871. Rebuilt in 1875, it is Chicago's oldest Episcopal church.

St. Martin Church (5842 S. Princeton Ave., tel. 312/667–2100). This South Side church, like the North Side St. Alphonsus, was built by a German immigrant congregation. Located in the Englewood neighborhood, the church now serves an all-black congregation.

St. Michael's Church (Tour 6. Lincoln Park)

St. Michael's Italian Roman Catholic Church (2325 W. 24th Pl., tel. 312/847–2727). The beautifully ornate St. Michael's is now in a Hispanic parish in the neighborhood of Pilsen.

St. Nicholas Ukrainian Catholic Cathedral (2238 W. Rice St., tel. 312/384–7243). The Byzantine St. Nicholas is situated in the heart of Ukrainian Village, an ethnic enclave in the changing west side. The interior is decorated with mosaics, frescoes, and chandeliers; services are conducted in Ukrainian.

St. Thomas the Apostle (Tour 3. Hyde Park and Kenwood)

Second Presbyterian Church (1936 S. Michigan Ave., tel. 312/225–4951). Located in a black neighborhood just south of Downtown South, this handsome Victorian church endured years of struggles to stay afloat. In recent years, aided by new members from both Hyde Park to the south and Dearborn Park to the north, the congregation has grown and become racially integrated and ethnically diverse. The church has lovely stained glass, and oak is used lavishly throughout the interior.

Unity Temple. (Tour 10. Oak Park)

Parks and Gardens

Thanks to the Lakefront Protection Ordinance, most of Chicago's more than 20 miles of lakefront is parkland or beach reserved for public use. Visitors to the city tend to concentrate on the lakefront, even though the Chicago Park District maintains hundreds of parks in neighborhoods throughout the city. While all the lakefront land is maintained for park use, several areas have been specifically designated as parks, and these areas offer special delights.

Grant Park, just east of the Loop, boasts acres of rose gardens and other carefully tended beds; something is always in bloom here, from early spring until late fall.

Lincoln Park on the north side (1600 N. to 2800 N.) is the home of the Lincoln Park Conservatory, which has a palm house, a fernery, a cactus house, and a show house where the special annual shows are mounted: the azalea show in February, the Easter show in March–April, the chrysanthemum show in November, and the Christmas show in December. Grandmother's Garden, between Stockton Drive and Lincoln Park West and dating from 1893, is a collection of informal beds of perennials including hibiscus and chrysanthemums. A large outdoor garden has flowering plants. The No. 151 bus stops "at the door." *2400 N. Stockton Dr., tel. 312/294–4770. Admission free. Open Sat.–Thurs. 9–5, Fri. 9–9. Hours vary during shows.*

The Garfield Park Conservatory, perhaps the largest in the world, keeps more than five acres of plants and flowers indoors in near-tropical conditions throughout the year. Here are a palm house, a fern house, an aeroid house (which includes such plants as dieffenbachia and antherium), and others. Like the Lincoln Park Conservatory, Garfield Park does four major shows a year: azaleas and camellias in February, a spring show beginning in mid-March, chrysanthemums in November, and a Christmas show from mid-December. Each year the conservatory honors one nation—in 1990, the Soviet Union—with displays of the country's typical flowers and plants, from April to November. By car, take I–290 (Eisenhower Expressway) to Independence Boulevard. Turn right onto Independence and go north to Lake Street. Turn right on Lake and left at the first traffic light. *300 N. Central Park Blvd., tel. 312/533–1281. Admission free. Open daily 9–5, with extended hours during shows.*

Jackson Park, just south of the Museum of Science and Industry, features a wooded island known as Wooded Island and a Japanese Garden with authentic Japanese statuary.

The **Morton Arboretum** consists of 1,500 acres of woody plants, woodlands, and outdoor gardens; a library and a gift shop; a restaurant that serves lunch; and a coffee shop. Tours and special programs are scheduled most Sunday afternoons. Take I–290 (the Eisenhower Expressway) to the East-West Tollway, the Tollway to Route 53 north, and Route 53 about half a mile to the arboretum. *Rte. 53, Lisle, tel. 708/719–2400. Admission: $3 per car, $2 per car with senior citizen driver, walk-ins free. Open daily 9–7.*

The **Chicago Botanic Garden,** which covers 300 acres, has 15 separate gardens, among them a traditional rose garden, a three-island Japanese garden, a waterfall garden, a sensory garden for the visually impaired, an aquatic garden, a learning garden for the disabled, and a 3.8-acre fruit and vegetable garden whose yields are donated to area food kitchens. Ten greenhouses provide flowers all winter long. Special events and shows are scheduled most weekends, many of them sponsored by area plant societies. Major shows are the winter orchid show, an August bonsai show, a daffodil show, a cactus and succulent show, and Japan Fest in May. The Botanic Garden is about 25 miles from downtown Chicago, and you can get there by public transportation. Take the Evanston CTA train from the el in the Loop to Davis Street in Evanston; transfer there for the Nortran (No. 214) bus, which stops at the garden. By car, take I–94/US 41 to Lake-Cook Road, turn east and take Lake-Cook about half a mile to the garden entrance. *Lake-Cook Rd., Glencoe, tel. 708/835–5440. Admission: $3 per car. Open daily 7 AM –sunset in summer, 8 AM–sunset in winter; closed Christmas Day.*

Zoos

Lincoln Park Zoo is perfect for those who want to visit a zoo and can't spend a lot of time getting there. Youngsters will enjoy the Children's Zoo, the Farm-in-the-Zoo (farm animals plus a learning center with films and demonstrations), and the Kids' Corner Discovery Place, with hands-on activities. The 35-acre zoo is noted especially for its Great Ape House: The 23 gorillas are thought to be the finest collection in the world. Since most of them have been bred in captivity, there are always several babies around. In addition to the reptile house, the large mammal house (elephants, giraffes, black rhinos), the monkey house, the bird house, the small mammal house, and a huge polar bear pool with two bears, the zoo has several rare and endangered species. The Spectacle Bear (named for the eyeglasseslike markings around the eyes), who comes from Peru, is endangered in the wild. The Père David's deer, from China, has been extinct in the wild for centuries; it's an unusual-looking deer, with backward antlers, big feet, and a horselike face. The zoo opened in 1868, before the Chicago Fire; most of the buildings have been renovated since. A food concession is a new addition. To reach the zoo, take the northbound La Salle Street bus or the Sheridan Avenue (No. 151) bus. Metered parking is available. *2200 N. Cannon Dr., tel. 312/294–4660. Admission free. Open daily 9–5.*

Brookfield Zoo, in Brookfield, is a special place to visit when you have a day to devote to it. The animals inhabit naturalistic settings that give visitors the feeling of being in the wild rather than in a zoo environment. One exhibit, simulating a tropical rain forest in South America, Asia, or Africa, is the world's largest indoor zoo of mixed species. Monkeys, otters, birds, and other rain forest fauna cavort in a carefully constructed setting of rocks, trees, shrubs, pools, and waterfalls. Thunderstorms occur at random intervals, and it's fascinating to watch what the animals do when it begins to rain (visitors on walkways don't get wet) and after the rain has ended. In the Aquatic Bird House visitors can test their "flying strength" by "flapping their wings" on a machine that simultaneously measures wing action and speed and decides what kind of bird you are, based on how you flap. Elephant demonstrations take place outside the pachyderm house in summer, and the Animals in Action shows in the Children's Zoo in summer allow visitors to watch the behaviors of animals up close. Cow and goat milkings are done at 11 AM and 1 PM. The daily dolphin shows, a highlight of the zoo, are a favorite even of jaded adults, and the new show area accommodates 2,000 spectators. Seals and sea lions inhabit a rocky seascape exhibit that simulates a Pacific Northwest environment, and there's a splendid underwater viewing gallery. From late spring through early fall the "motorized safari" tram will carry you around the grounds; in the wintertime the heated Snowball Express does the job. To reach the zoo, take the Burlington Northern train from Union Station to Hollywood Avenue (also known as the zoo stop); it's a walk of about a half mile from the station to the zoo. By car, take I–290 (the Eisenhower Expressway) to First Avenue, or take I–55 (the Stevenson Expressway) to First Avenue, and follow the signs to the zoo. *8400 W. 31st St., Brookfield, tel. 708/485–0263. Admission: $2.75 adults, $1 children 3–11 and senior citizens; free Tues. Parking: $3 ($3.50 Tues.). Children's zoo: $1 adults, 50¢ children 3–11 and senior citizens, free under 3, free Nov.–Feb. Dolphin show: $2 adults, $1.50 children 3–11 and seniors, free under 3. Motorized safari: $1.75 adults, 75¢ children 3–11 and senior citizens. Open Memorial Day to Labor Day, daily 9:30–6; rest of year, daily 10–5. Rental strollers and wheelchairs available. Snowball Express free.*

4 Shopping

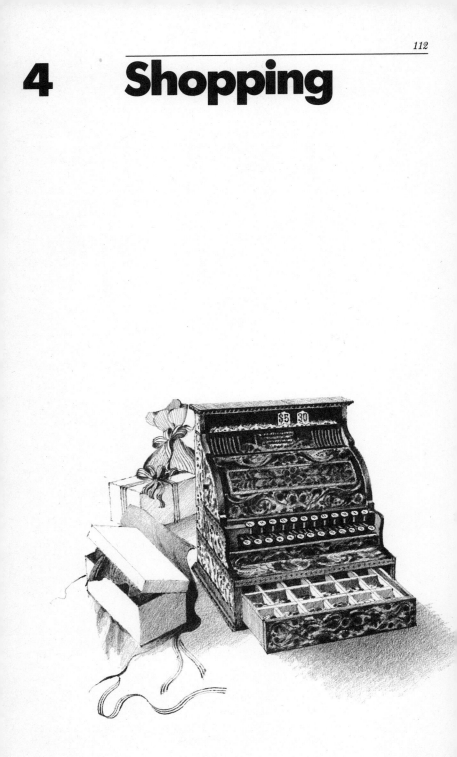

Chicago shopping is extensive and varied, ranging from elegant department stores, small boutiques, and specialty shops to malls and bargain outlets. Visa, MasterCard, American Express, and most other major credit cards are widely accepted, and traveler's checks are welcome in most establishments throughout the city. Illinois' 8% sales tax is added to all purchases except groceries and prescription medicines.

Many stores, particularly on north Michigan Avenue and the north side, are open on Sundays; call ahead for Sunday hours.

The Reader, a free weekly paper available in stores and restaurants in the downtown, Near North Side, Lincoln Park, and Hyde Park areas, carries ads for smaller shops. Sales at the large department stores are advertised in the *Chicago Tribune* and the *Chicago Sun-Times*.

There are far too many stores in Chicago to attempt a complete or fully descriptive listing here. The following pages offer a general overview of the more popular shopping areas and list some of the stores where certain items can be found. If you're looking for something in particular, check the Yellow Pages classified phone directory, but if you have no concrete shopping goals, simply choose any one of the major shopping districts and browse to your heart's content.

Major Shopping Districts

The Loop, bordered by Lake Street on the north, Michigan Avenue on the east, Congress Street on the south, and Wells Street on the west, is the heart of Chicago business and finance. The city's two largest department stores, Marshall Field & Co. and Carson Pirie Scott, anchor the Loop's State Street–Wabash Avenue area, which has declined since the years when it was known as "State Street, that great street." (Four of State Street's largest retailers—Sears, Montgomery Ward, Wieboldt's, and Goldblatt's—have closed their doors in the last decade.) Several Loop buildings, including the Stevens Building (17 N. State St.) and the Mallers Building (5 S. Wabash Ave.), contain groups of small shops on their upper floors, and there are a number of interesting specialty stores on the west end of the Loop.

The Magnificent Mile, Chicago's most glamorous shopping district, stretches along Michigan Avenue from the Chicago River (400 N.) to Oak Street (1000 N.). The street is lined on both sides with some of the most sophisticated names in retailing: Tiffany (715 N.), Gucci (900 N.), Chanel (990 N.), I. Magnin (830 N.), and Ralph Lauren (960 N.), to name just a few. Look on the Mag Mile for stores offering clothing, shoes, jewelry, and accessories, as well as for several art galleries.

Aside from dozens of designer shops, Michigan Avenue also features two "vertical malls." **Water Tower Place** (835 N. Michigan Ave.) contains branches of Lord & Taylor and Marshall Field's, as well as seven floors of specialty stores. Branches of national chains, such as The Gap, Banana Republic, The Limited, Casual Corner, Hoffritz for Cutlery, Benetton, and Rizzoli Books are all represented; the Ritz-Carlton Hotel sits atop the entire complex.

The **Avenue Atrium** (900 N. Michigan Ave.) houses the new Chicago branch of Bloomingdale's, along with dozens of smaller

Shopping North

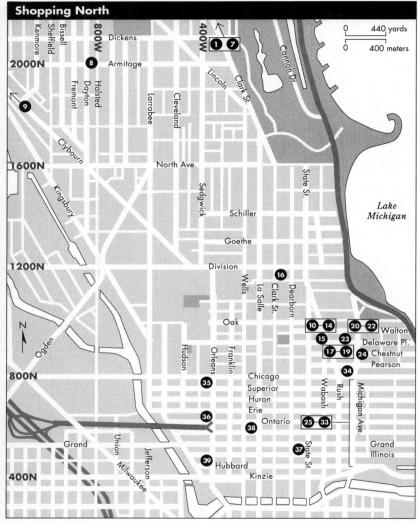

2000N
1600N
1200N
800N
400N

800W
400W

Kenmore
Sheffield
Bissell
Dickens
Armitage

Fremont
Dayton
Halsted
Larrabee
Cleveland
Sedgwick

Clybourn
Kingsbury
Ogden

North Ave.
Schiller
Goethe
Division

Lincoln
Clark St.
Cannon Dr.

State St.

Lake Michigan

Wells
La Salle
Clark St.
Dearborn

Oak
Hudson
Orleans
Franklin

Chicago
Superior
Huron
Erie
Ontario

Wabash
Rush
Michigan Ave.

Walton
Delaware Pl.
Chestnut
Pearson

Grand
Illinois

Union
Jefferson
Milwaukee

Grand
Hubbard
Kinzie

State St.

0   440 yards
0   400 meters

N

Abraham Lincoln Book Shop, **35**
Accent Chicago, **24**
Ann Taylor, **10**
Avenue Atrium, **23**
Bally, **21**
Beggar's Market, **17**
Bloomingdale's, **23**
Brittany, Ltd., **20**
Chalet, **15**
Cole-Haan, **30**

Convito Italiano, **18**
Crate & Barrel, **33**
Erehwon, **36**
Florsheim, **31**
Florsheim Thayer McNeill, **26**
Gianni Versace, **12**
Giorgio Armani, **13**
Hammacher Schlemmer, **32**
Hanig, **29**
Herman's, **34**
Jazz Record Mart, **37**

Land's End Outlet, **9**
Le Grand Tour Bookstore, **4**
Lori's, **8**
Mark Shale, **22**
MC/Mages Sports, **38**
Nieman Marcus, **25**
Nuts on Clark, **1**
Season to Taste, **3**
2nd Hand Tunes, **2**
Sonia Rykiel, **11**
SportMart, **5, 39**

Stars Our Destination, **6**
Stuart Brent, **28**
Tiffany, **27**
Treasure Island, **16**
Ultimo, **14**
Water Tower Place, **24**
Wax Trax, **7**
Williams Sonoma, **19**

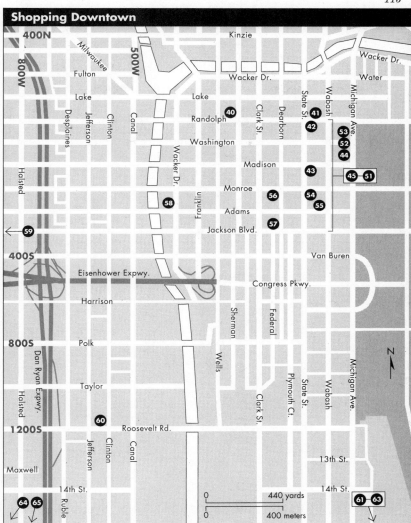

Shopping Downtown

ArchiCenter Store, **57**
Bennett Brothers, **55**
Brooks Brothers, **44**
Capper & Capper, **47**
Carl Fischer, **51**
Carson Pirie Scott, **43**
Central Camera, **50**
Chernin's, **60**
City of Chicago
Store, **40**
Crate & Barrel, **46**
C.D. Peacock, **54**
Eddie Bauer, **45**
57th Street Books, **61**
Helix, **59**

I Love a Mystery, **52**
Kroch's &
Brentano's, **48**
Marshall Field, **42**
Powell's, **62**
Rand McNally, **58**
Rose Records, **49**
Savvy Traveller, **53**
Sears, **65**
Seno Formalwear, **41**
Sharper Image, **56**
Spiegel, **64**
University of Chicago
Bookstore, **63**

boutiques and specialty stores. At this writing, a branch of the posh Henri Bendel department store is also slated to open in the Atrium. Generally, the merchandise found here is more sophisticated, and more expensive, than in Water Tower Place. The Atrium also has a hotel on top—the lavish Four Seasons. The restaurants and movie theaters found in both malls are a good option for entertainment during inclement weater.

Oak Street, between Michigan Avenue and Rush Street, is populated with stores selling designer clothing and European imports. Designers with Oak Street addresses include Giorgio Armani (113 E. Oak St.), Gianni Versace (101 E. Oak St.), Sonia Rykiel (106 E. Oak St.), and Ultimo (114 E. Oak St.).

The upscale residential neighborhoods of **Lincoln Park and Lakeview** offer several worthwhile shopping strips. **Clark Street** between Armitage (2000 N.) and Diversey (2800 N.) avenues is home to a number of clothing boutiques and specialty stores. The shopping continues north of Diversey Avenue to School Street (3300 N.), with several large antiques stores, more boutiques, and some bookstores. **Broadway** between Diversey Avenue and Addison Street (3600 N.) also offers a variety of shops. The **Century Mall,** in a former movie palace at Clark Street, Broadway, and Diversey Parkway, houses a variety of national outlets and small specialty stores. Take the Clark Street bus (No. 22) at Dearborn Street or the Broadway bus (No. 36) at State Street north to reach this neighborhood.

The North Pier development, on the Lake, at 435 E. Illinois St. is teeming with fascinating small shops, including a seashell store, a hologram showroom, and a shop that embroiders custom designs on T-shirts and jackets.

Contained by the Chicago River on the south and west, Clark Street on the east, and Oak Street on the north, **River North** boasts a profusion of art galleries, furnishing stores, and boutiques, some of which are described in the River North walking tour (*see* Chapter 3). The *Chicago Gallery News*, available from the tourist information center at the Water Tower (Michigan Ave. and Pearson St.), provides an up-to-date listing of current art gallery exhibits.

Department Stores

Marshall Field & Co. (111 N. State St., at the corner of Randolph St., tel. 312/781–1000). Though there are branches at several other locations in Chicago and its suburbs, the State Street Field's is the granddaddy of them all. Founder Marshall Field's catchphrase was "Give the lady what she wants!" and, for many years both ladies and gentlemen have been able to find everything they want, from furs to riding boots to padded hangers, on one of Field's nine floors. After a period of decline, Field's launched a $110-million-dollar renovation project and is currently restoring the building to its former glory. The bargain basement has been replaced with "Down Under," a series of small boutiques that sell clothing, luggage, picture frames, Chicago memorabilia, and Field's famous Frango mints, which many consider to be Chicago's greatest edible souvenirs. You'll find restaurants on the seventh floor and in the basement. Architecture buffs will admire the Tiffany glass dome that tops the store's southwest atrium. At press time Field's had been acquired by Dayton-Hudson Corp., Minneapolis, but observers of the retail industry don't expect the new owners to tamper with this Chicago tradition.

Carson Pirie Scott (1 S. State St., tel. 312/641–7000). Second only to Field's for many years, Carson's was operating at a loss when it was acquired recently by P.A. Bergner, a Milwaukee-based retail chain. At this writing, the fate of the State Street store is unknown, though the building itself, the work of famed Chicago architect Louis Sullivan, is protected by landmark status. Some options that have been discussed include scaling down the department store to make room for smaller retailers and office space; and replacing Carson's entirely with offices and small shops. However it is used, the building is worth visiting just to see the northwest door at the corner of State and Madison; the iron scrollwork here shows Sullivan at his most ornate.

Neiman Marcus (737 N. Michigan Ave., tel. 312/642–5900). Neiman's prices may be steep, but browsing here is fun. Be sure to take a look at the graceful four-story wood sculpture that rises between the escalators of this branch of the famous upscale Dallas department store.

Bloomingdale's (900 N. Michigan Ave., tel. 312/440–4460). Unlike both its Michigan Avenue neighbors and its New York City sibling, this branch of Bloomies, built in a clean, airy style that is part Prairie School and part postmodern, gives you plenty of elbow room to sift through its selection of designer labels. The adjacent six-floor Avenue Atrium offers a profusion of specialty stores and boutiques.

Specialty Stores

Books
General Interest

Kroch & Brentano (29 S. Wabash St., tel. 312/332–7500). The most comprehensive branch of this local chain, the Wabash Street flagship store will special-order any book they don't have in stock. The city's largest selection of technical books shares the lower level with an impressive paperback department. Upstairs, Kroch's collection of hardcover books is extensive and includes several sale tables of remaindered and slightly damaged books. There's a foreign-language department on the mezzanine and a large selection of magazines and newspapers.

Stuart Brent (670 N. Michigan Ave., tel. 312/337–6357). A Chicago literary landmark, Stuart Brent carries an extensive and tasteful, if sometimes quirky, collection of hardcover and paperback books, as well as a good selection of music and art books. The walls are covered with photographs of well-known authors posing with owner Mr. Brent, who for years has been prominent in the Chicago literary scene.

57th Street Books (1301 E. 57th St., tel. 312/684–1300). Wood floors, brick walls, and books from the popular to the esoteric distinguish this Hyde Park institution. An excellent place to while away the hours on a rainy afternoon.

University of Chicago Bookstore (970 E. 58th St., tel. 312/702–7712). Aside from the expected selection of textbooks, this bookstore also carries many works of general interest, with an emphasis on cooking and computer books.

Specialty **Rand McNally Map Stores** (150 S. Wacker Dr., tel. 312/332–2009 and 444 N. Michigan Ave., tel. 312/332–4628). Maps for everywhere from Manhattan to the moon, as well as travel books and globes, are available in abundance here.

Savvy Traveller (upstairs at 50 E. Washington St., tel. 312/263–2100). Aside from a full range of travel books, the Savvy Traveller also carries a number of odds and ends that can come in handy on the road.

I Love a Mystery (55 E. Washington St., tel. 312/236–1338). This shop specializes in—you guessed it—mysteries.

Season to Taste (911 W. School St., tel. 312/327–0210). This homey shop has all manner of cookbooks, as well as an assortment of cooking videocassettes.

The Stars Our Destination (2942 N. Clark St., tel. 312/871–2722). Science fiction fans will find a large selection of their favorites, along with the latest news on local sci-fi happenings.

Le Grand Tour Bookstore (3229 N. Clark St., tel. 312/929–1836). Foreign-language books are the specialty here, but there's a large selection of English volumes and an eclectic assortment of periodicals, as well.

Used **Powell's** (1501 E. 57th St., tel. 312/955–7780). Powell's Hyde Park store has one of the largest and most diverse selections of used books in town.

Abraham Lincoln Bookstore (357 W. Chicago Ave., tel. 312/944–3085). Civil War buffs will want to visit this shop, which specializes in Lincolniana and Civil War books. Call for hours.

Camera Equipment **Helix** (310 S. Racine St., tel. 312/421–6000). Off the beaten track in a neighborhood west of the Loop, this warehouse store sells and rents all manner of camera and darkroom paraphernalia at competitive prices. A good selection of used equipment is also available. Helix has two smaller branches in the Loop, at Three First National Plaza (tel. 312/444–9373) and 400 S. LaSalle St. (tel. 312/663–3650).

Central Camera (232 S. Wabash Ave., tel. 312/427–5580). This store, stocked to the rafters with cameras and darkroom equipment, is a Loop institution.

Catalog Stores/ Factory Outlets **Bennett Bros.** (30 E. Adams St., tel. 312/263–4800). Primarily a catalog store, Bennett's sells jewelry, silverware, kitchen appliances, cameras, and electronic equipment at discount prices. The store's second-floor showroom displays some of the merchandise available in the catalog. Closed weekends.

Spiegel (1105 W. 35th St., tel. 312/254–0091) and **Sears** (5555 S. Archer Ave., tel. 312/284–3200) both operate warehouse stores on the city's south side. The two famous mail-order establishments have ever-changing inventories of clothing, appliances, and housewares, and can offer fabulous bargains to the sharp-eyed and flexible shopper. Don't expect elegant surroundings or helpful salespeople, and do check your merchandise thoroughly before you take it home.

Land's End (men's, 2241 N. Elston Ave., tel. 312/276–2232; women's, 2317 N. Elston Ave., tel. 312/384–4710). This Wisconsin mail-order firm sells casual and business wear, luggage, housewares, and outdoor gear. The quality of the stock may be inconsistent at these outlet stores, but the discount savings can be considerable.

Clothing The major department stores are good sources of mainstream sportswear, and the smaller boutiques of the Avenue Atrium, Water Tower Place, River North, Oak Street, and Lincoln Park can provide you with more unique designer clothing.

Business Clothing **Brooks Brothers** (74 E. Madison St., tel. 312/263–0100 and 713 N. Michigan Ave., tel. 312/915–0060), **Capper & Capper** (1 N. Wabash Ave., tel. 312/236–3800), **Brittany Ltd.** (999 N. Michigan Ave., tel. 312/642–6550), and **Mark Shale** (919 N. Michigan Ave., tel. 312/440–0720). All four of these stores are good sources of high-quality business attire.

Women's **Ann Taylor** (103 E. Oak St., tel. 312/943–5411) offers a selection of classic, upscale womenswear.

Men's Evening **Seno Formalwear** (6 E. Randolph St., tel. 312/782–1115). This popular store both rents and sells tuxedos.

Food **The Chalet.** (40 E. Delaware Pl., tel. 312/787–8555). This store is one of a chain that has several branches on the near north and north sides. All stores offer a large selection of wines, beers, cheeses, coffee, and other gourmet items.

Treasure Island (75 W. Elm St., tel. 312/440–1144, and 680 N. Lake Shore Dr., tel. 312/664–0400). This Chicago institution is a combination supermarket/gourmet store. Any of its branches is ideal for buying the makings for a gourmet picnic or an elegant, edible house gift.

Nuts on Clark (3830 N. Clark St., tel. 312/549–6622). This warehouse, located just a few blocks from Wrigley Field, displays bins full of nuts, as well as an assortment of candies, spices, jams and jellies, coffee, tea, mustards, and other culinary delights.

Convito Italiano (11 E. Chestnut St., tel. 312/943–2983). Both a restaurant and an Italian food shop, Convito Italiano sells olive oil in porcelain vessels, an array of wines, Saronno biscuits, cookbooks, an enormous selection of pastas, and ready-to-eat carry-out items. Elegant party trays can be ordered.

Gifts Water Tower Place, the Avenue Atrium, Michigan Avenue, and the larger department stores are likely places to find gifts and toys. For artsy gifts with a twist, try the River North art galleries and boutiques.

C.D. Peacock (State and Monroe Sts., tel. 312/630–5700). This elegant store, which occupies the same city block as the Palmer House hotel, has been selling jewelry and silver to Chicago for more than 150 years.

Beggar's Market (15 E. Chestnut St., tel. 312/944–1835). The front of this store carries an attractive selection of cards, ribbons, and unusual wrapping papers; in the back you'll find jewelry, decorative rubber stamps, tablecloths, bedspreads, and other unique gifts.

The Sharper Image (55 W. Monroe St., tel. 312/263–4535) and **Hammacher Schlemmer** (618 N. Michigan Ave., tel. 312/664–9292). Both stores are great for browsing and can provide upscale gadgets and unusual gifts.

Kitchenware **Crate & Barrel** (101 N. Wabash Ave., tel. 312/372–0100, 646 N. Michigan Ave., tel. 312/787–5900. Warehouse store: 1510 N.

Wells Ave., tel. 312/787–4775). One of the first "lifestyle" cookware, glassware, and furniture stores, the Crate remains one of the best. There are large branches on Michigan Avenue and in the Loop and a warehouse store on Wells Street, where you may pick up a good bargain.

Williams Sonoma (17 E. Chestnut St., tel. 312/642–1593). The selection of kitchenware and cookbooks is excellent, and if you're there during an equipment demonstration you get to taste the results.

Music **Rose Records** (214 S. Wabash Ave., tel. 312/987–9044). This chain's main store on Wabash Avenue has three floors of records, tapes, and compact discs. If you're looking for movie soundtracks or Broadway musicals, Rose has an exceptionally large selection. One entire floor is devoted to "cut-outs," budget labels, and other bargains.

Wax Trax (2449 N. Lincoln Ave., tel. 312/929–0221). This crowded shop is the place to go for the latest rock and other offbeat imports.

Jazz Record Mart (11 W. Grand Ave., tel. 312/222–1467). This specialty store stocks one of Chicago's largest collections of records, in addition to compact discs and tapes. Jazz and blues fanciers will be delighted to find many rare historic recordings and obscure imports at the Record Mart.

2nd Hand Tunes (2604 N. Clark St., tel. 312/929–6325 and 1375 E. 53rd St., tel. 312/684–3375) specializes in used records.

Carl Fischer (312 S. Wabash Ave., tel. 312/427–6652). This venerable store carries the largest selection of piano, vocal, choral, and band sheet music in Chicago.

Shoes There are a great many shoe stores along Michigan Avenue, including several in Water Tower Place. Large selections can be found at: **Florsheim** (622 N. Michigan Ave., tel. 312/787–0779), **Florsheim Thayer McNeill** (727 N. Michigan Ave., tel. 312/649–9619), **Hanig** (660 N. Michigan Ave., tel. 312/642–5330), **Bally** (919 N. Michigan Ave., tel. 312/787–8110), and **Cole-Haan** (645 N. Michigan Ave., tel. 312/642–8995).

Chernin's (men's, 606 W. Roosevelt Rd., tel. 312/922–4545; women's, 610 W. Roosevelt Rd., tel. 312/939–4080). Chicago's famous bargain shoe outlet is all that remains of a once flourishing Roosevelt Road shopping district. If you're in the market for lots of shoes, it may be worth a trip down here.

Lori's Discount Designer Shoes (808 W. Armitage Ave., tel. 312/281–5655). Located in Lincoln Park, this store offers women's designer shoes below department-store prices.

Souvenirs **The Tourist Information Center** (163 E. Pearson, tel. 312/280–5740). This is an excellent source for postcards and souvenirs, as well as maps and city guides.

Accent Chicago (Water Tower Place, 835 N. Michigan Ave., 7th floor, tel. 312/944–1354) and **Down Under at Marshall Field's** (111 N. State St., basement, tel. 312/781–1000). Both stores are good spots to shop for Chicago memorabilia.

The ArchiCenter Store (330 S. Dearborn Ave., tel. 312/922–3431). A large selection of books, posters, T-shirts, toys, mugs, and other souvenirs with architectural themes can be found here.

The City of Chicago Store (174 W. Randolph St., tel. 312/332–0055). This shop carries merchandise from 35 of the city's cultural institutions and organizations, including the Art Institute and the Lincoln Park Zoo. There's also an eclectic collection of restored artifacts, such as traffic lights, ballot boxes, parking meters, and manhole covers, culled from 12 city departments. The store is closed on weekends.

Sporting Goods   **MC/Mages Sports** (620 N. LaSalle St., tel. 312/337–6151). Be sure to look at the "Wall of Fame" outside the store that shows the handprints of famous Chicago sports figures such as football's Jim McMahon, baseball's Ryne Sandberg, and hockey's Stan Mikita. Inside you will find six floors of reasonably priced sporting and camping equipment, shoes, and clothing.

Sportmart. (3134 N. Clark St., tel. 312/871–8500 and 440 N. Orleans St., tel. 312/222–0900). These large emporia, one in Lakeview and the other in River North, offer low prices and good selections as long as you're not looking for uncommon sizes.

Herman's (111 E. Chicago Ave., tel. 312/951–8282). Part of a national chain, Herman's carries a respectable selection of shoes, tennis rackets, golf clubs, skis, and workout wear.

Eddie Bauer (123 N. Wabash Ave., tel. 312/263–6005). You'll find clothing for the outdoors and some camping equipment at this chain's Wabash Avenue store. Another branch at Water Tower Place carries mostly sportswear.

Erehwon Mountain Outfitters (644 N. Orleans St., tel. 312/337–6400). For hiking, camping, rock climbing, canoeing, and other rigorous outdoor pursuits, you can probably find clothing and equipment at Erehwon, which has a rough-hewn atmosphere and friendly salespeople.

5 Sports, Fitness, Beaches

Participant Sports and Fitness

Bicycling The lakefront bicycle path extends some 20 miles along Chicago's lakefront, offering a variety of scenic views. The prospect of the harbor, created with landfill a few years ago when Lake Shore Drive's notorious S-curve between Monroe Street and Wacker Drive was straightened, is lovely. Be careful: A few blocks to the north, Grand Avenue is one of a few places along the route where the path crosses a city street (two others are parallel to Lake Shore Drive in the downtown area). Rent a bike for the day as you enter Lincoln Park at Fullerton or from Village Cycle Center (1337 N. Wells St., tel. 312/751-2488). There are many other scenic rides in the Chicago area. For information, contact the Chicagoland Bicycle Federation (Box 64396, Chicago, IL 60664, tel. 312/427-3325).

Boating Lake Michigan is right here, but those who didn't bring their sailboats or motorized craft with them to Chicago will have to content themselves with renting paddleboats in Lincoln Park or taking sightseeing boat trips (*see* Chapter 1.)

Golfing The Chicago Park District maintains six golf courses, all with nine holes, except Jackson Park (18 holes), and two driving ranges, one in Jackson Park and one at Lake Shore Drive and Diversey Avenue (where there is a miniature 18-hole course). The Jackson Park facilities are located two and three blocks east of Stony Island Avenue at 63rd Street (tel. 312/753-8670).

Ice Skating During the winter months there is ice skating at the Daley Bicentennial Plaza, Randolph Street at Lake Shore Drive. A small fee is charged, and skate rentals are available (tel. 312/294-4790).

Jogging The lakefront path accommodates both joggers and bicyclists, so you'll need to be attentive. Avoid jogging in areas where there are few other people and after dark. You can pick up the path at Oak Street Beach (across from the Drake Hotel), at Grand Avenue underneath Lake Shore Drive, or by going through Grant Park on Monroe Street or Jackson Boulevard until you reach the lakefront.

Swimming Lake Michigan provides wonderful swimming opportunities between Memorial Day and Labor Day, particularly toward the end of the period, when the lake has warmed up (*see* Beaches, below).

Tennis The Chicago Park District maintains hundreds of tennis courts, most of which can be used free of charge. The facility at the Daley Bicentennial Plaza, Randolph Street at Lake Shore Drive, is a lighted facility that can be used at night; there is a modest hourly fee, and reservations are required (tel. 312/294-4790). The Grant Park tennis courts, at 9th Street and Columbus Drive (between Michigan Avenue and Lake Shore Drive), are also lighted, and there is a modest fee; reservations are not required.

Spectator Sports

Chicago's loyal sports fans turn out regularly, year after year, to watch what are not the most winning teams in professional sports. Occasionally this virtue is rewarded: In January 1986 the Chicago Bears triumphed at the Superbowl in New Orleans. Also, the White Sox won a lone division championship during the 1980s, and the Cubs won two, though neither was able to capture a league title.

Other owners have threatened to relocate their teams, most recently the owners of the White Sox, who conducted a lengthy courtship with the city of St. Petersburg, Florida; in the end, a deal was made with the State of Illinois. At this writing, a new stadium is being constructed across the street from Comiskey Park and should be ready for the 1991 season. After the new one is completed, venerable Comiskey Park will be demolished.

Baseball The **Chicago Cubs** (National League) play at Wrigley Field (1060 W. Addison St., tel. 312/404-2827); the baseball season begins early in April and ends the first weekend in October. Wrigley Field is reached by the Howard St. el line; take the B train to Addison Street. Wrigley Field finally received lights in 1988, the last major-league ballpark in the nation to be lighted for night games. But the Cubs still play most of their home games during the day, and the bleachers are a great place to get a tan while listening to Chicagoans taunt the visiting outfielders. The grandstand offers a more sedate atmosphere. Most games start at 1:20 PM, but call for exact starting times.

The **Chicago White Sox** (American League) play at Comiskey Park (324 W. 35th St., tel. 312/924-1000 or 312/559-1212 for ticket information). Games usually start at 7:30 PM. Take an A or B Dan Ryan el train to 35th Street.

Basketball The **Chicago Bulls** play at the Chicago Stadium (1800 W. Madison St., tel. 312/943-5800); the basketball season extends from November to May, and games usually start at 7:30 PM. Avoid leaving the game early or wandering around this neighborhood at night.

Football The **Chicago Bears** play at Soldier Field (425 E. McFetridge Dr., tel. 312/663-5100) from August (preseason) through January (postseason, if they're lucky). While subscription sales generally account for all tickets, you can sometimes buy the tickets of a subscriber who can't use them at the stadium shortly before game time. (Even though you'll miss the excitement of being part of the crowd, you'll see a lot more of the game by watching it on TV.) To reach Soldier Field, take the Jeffery Express (No. 6) bus to Roosevelt Road and Lake Shore Drive and follow the crowd. The stadium is just south of the Field Museum of Natural History.

Hockey The **Chicago Blackhawks** play at the Chicago Stadium (1800 W. Madison St., tel. 312/733-5300) from October to April. Games usually start at 7:35 PM. Again, avoid leaving the game early or wandering around the neighborhood at night.

Horse Racing Hawthorne Race Course (3501 S. Laramie Ave., tel. 708/780-3700), just beyond the Chicago city limits in Cicero, features **flat racing.**

Arlington Park has **flat racing** July–October (N. Wilke Road at West Euclid Avenue, Arlington Heights, tel. 708/255–4300). Sportsman's Park (3301 S. Laramie Ave., tel. 312/242–1121) has **flat racing** Feb.–May and **harness racing** June–October. Maywood Park (North and Fifth Aves. in Maywood, tel. 708/343–4800), has **harness racing** February–May and October–December.

Beaches

Chicago has some 20 miles of lakefront, most of it sand or rock beach. Beaches are open to the public daily 9 AM-9:30 PM, Memorial Day to Labor Day, and many beaches have changing facilities. The **Chicago Park District** (tel. 312/294-2333) provides lifeguard protection during daylight hours throughout the swimming season. The water is too cold for swimming at other times of the year.

Oak Street Beach (600-1600 N.) is probably Chicago's most popular, particularly in the 1000 North Area, where the shoreline curves. You can expect it to be mobbed with trendy singles and people-watchers on any warm day in summer. There are bathrooms here, but for changing facilities you'll have to make the walk to the North Avenue Beach bathhouse. The concrete breakwater that makes up the southern part of Oak Street Beach is a popular promenade on hot summer nights. You can walk along the water all the way to Grand Avenue, where you'll find both Navy Pier and Olive Park.

North Avenue Beach (1600-2400 N.) is heavily used; the crowd tends to be more family oriented than the crowd at Oak Street Beach. There are bathrooms, changing facilities, and showers. The southern end of this beach features lively volleyball action during the summer and fall. **South Shore Country Club Beach** (7100 S.), Chicago's newest and one of the nicest beaches, is quite pretty and not overcrowded. There are bathrooms, changing facilities, and showers. Enter through the South Shore Country Club grounds at 71st Street and South Shore Drive; you may see the police training their horses in the entry area.

Other Chicago beaches are:

Leone/Loyola Beach (6700-7800 N.), changing facilities.
Foster Beach (5200 N.), changing facilities.
Montrose Beach (4400 N.), changing facilities.
12th Street Beach (1200 S. at 900 E., just south of the planetarium), changing facilities.
31st Street Beach (3100 S.), changing facilities.
Jackson Beach, Central (5700-5900 S.), changing facilities.

6 Dining

Introduction

The restaurants were selected by Paul A. Camp, former food critic of the Chicago Tribune *and author of* Paul Camp's Chicago Tribune Restaurant Guide.

For decades, fine dining in Chicago meant steak, and inexpensive dinners out meant storefront Polish or Bohemian cuisine. One of the major developments of the 1980s has been a dramatic expansion in the offerings and styles of the city's restaurants. A hungry visitor to Chicago can now find every cuisine from Afghani (the Helmand) to Yugoslavian (the Yugo Inn); Chicago has become a great city for good food.

Chicago's more than 7,000 restaurants range from those ranked among the best in the nation, and priced accordingly, to simple storefront ethnic eateries (the city has more than 80 Thai restaurants alone) and old-fashioned pubs that offer good food in unpretentious settings at modest prices. Our listing includes the restaurants we recommend as the best within each price range.

It's a good idea to make a reservation in advance, when possible, to avoid a long wait when you are ready to eat. The more expensive restaurants generally will not accommodate you without one, and the more modest establishments can serve you better when they are expecting you. Ordinarily, reservations can be made a day or two in advance, or even on the morning of the same day, but a few of the more popular restaurants require that you book a week or two—some even five or six weeks—in advance, particularly for weekend evenings. Some of the trendier restaurants do not accept reservations; standing at the bar with the crowd until your table is ready is thought to be part of the experience. Such a wait can last more than an hour, so be sure that this is the kind of evening you want before you make your plans.

As a general rule, you should expect to tip 15% in restaurants in the Inexpensive and Moderate price categories. The Chicago meal tax is 8½%, and you can double that amount for a 17% tip when you feel generous and don't want to have to do higher math. Expensive and Very Expensive restaurants have more service personnel per table who must divide the tip, so it's appropriate to leave 20%, depending on the quality of the service. In such restaurants, the maître d' who found you the table you wanted can be rewarded with $5, and an especially helpful wine steward should be acknowledged with $2 or $3.

This guide divides the restaurants of Chicago into three areas, each with its own dining map locating the restaurants: (1) Near North, River North, and Lincoln Park; (2) North Chicago; (3) Downtown and South. Within each area, the restaurants are grouped by type of cuisine. Restaurants serve lunch and dinner daily except where noted.

The restaurant price categories are based on the average cost of a dinner that includes appetizer, entrée, salad, and dessert (except as noted). Prices are for one person, food alone, not including alcoholic beverages, tax, and tip.

The following credit card abbreviations are used: AE, American Express; CB, Carte Blanche; DC, Diners Club; MC, MasterCard; V, Visa.

The most highly recommended restaurants are indicated by a star ★.

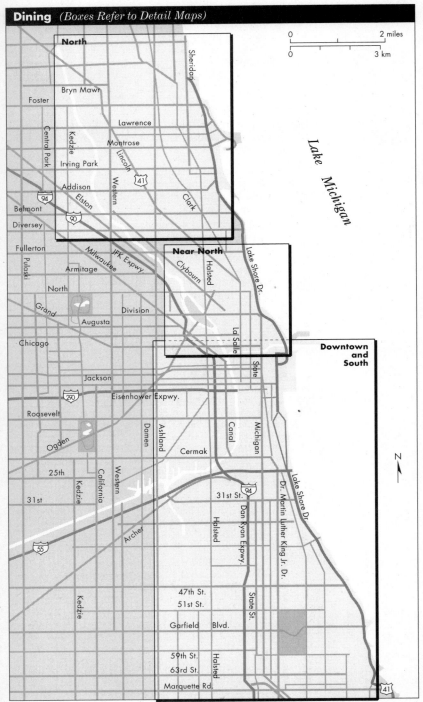

Dining *(Boxes Refer to Detail Maps)*

North

Bryn Mawr

Foster

Lawrence

Central Park

Kedzie

Montrose

Lincoln

Irving Park

Addison

Western

Elston

Belmont

Diversey

Fullerton

Pulaski

Armitage

Milwaukee

JFK Expwy

North

Grand

Augusta

Division

Chicago

Jackson

Eisenhower Expwy.

Roosevelt

Ogden

Damen

Ashland

Cermak

Canal

Michigan

25th

California

Western

Kedzie

31st

Archer

31st St.

Halsted

Dan Ryan Expwy

Kedzie

47th St.

51st St.

Garfield   Blvd.

59th St.

63rd St.

Halsted

State St.

Dr. Martin Luther King Jr. Dr.

Lake Shore Dr.

Marquette Rd.

Sheridan

Clark

Lake Michigan

Near North

Clybourn

Halsted

Lake Shore Dr.

La Salle

State

Downtown and South

N

0   2 miles
0   3 km

Category	Cost*
Very Expensive	over $40
Expensive	$25–$40
Moderate	$13–$25
Inexpensive	under $13

per person, excluding drinks, service, and sales tax (8½%)

Near North, River North, and Lincoln Park

American **The 95th.** Splendidly situated at the top of the third-tallest building in the world, The 95th commands a spectacular view of the city and beyond. Beaded-crystal chandeliers, lavish marble, mauve woodwork, and glass accents adorn its elegant dining room. Exquisite floral arrangements enhance the sense of luxury. Those who go to a restaurant primarily for the food will be heartened to learn that the cuisine, at this writing, has begun to rise to the level of the decor. The menu, changed seasonally, emphasizes fresh American regional meats, fish, and produce. A recent summer menu offered appetizers of California snails and wild mushrooms served with polenta and sautéed New York State foie gras on summer vegetables stewed with veal glaze and crème fraiche. The entrées emphasized seafood and poultry: Gulf shrimp and spinach linguine with tomato basil butter, roasted quail with ratatouille and rosemary butter; and one entrée each of beef, pork, veal, and lamb. Desserts are homemade daily. Remember that the lavish ambience and unparalleled view are included in the price of your meal. *John Hancock Bldg., 875 N. Michigan Ave., tel. 312/787–9596. Jacket required at dinner. Reservations; weekend reservations required. AE, DC, MC, V. Very Expensive.*

★ **Charlie Trotter's.** This tastefully renovated town house accommodates only 20 closely spaced tables, serving many fewer people than would like to eat here. The owner and chef Charlie Trotter prepares the newest of new American cuisine with hints of Asian flavors incorporated into classic European dishes. Menus have included appetizers such as red snapper carpaccio with Asian noodle salad and sesame mayonnaise, and foie gras ravioli with mango and lemongrass sauce. Entrées have included mahimahi with leek and sorrel sauce and mushroom ravioli, garlic-laced veal chop with wild mushrooms and eggplant tartlet, and lasagna of sea scallops with squid-ink pasta and saffron sauce. It's a good idea to make reservations well in advance. *816 W. Armitage Ave., tel. 312/248–6228. Jacket required. Reservations required. AE, DC, MC, V. No lunch. Closed Sun., Mon. Expensive–Very Expensive.*

Ditka's. Owned by the Chicago Bears' coach, Mike Ditka, this is one of the top-grossing restaurants in the U.S. If you're a sports fanatic, hanker for an excellent pork chop, and don't really care about much else, this is your place. The cavernous, dimly lit main room has booths and small tables; Ditka's packs in the fans whenever Bears games are televised. City Lights, the nightclub attached to the restaurant, usually provides a lively dance scene. The Chicago Sports Hall of Fame is next door. *223 W. Ontario, tel. 312/280–1790. AE, DC, MC, V. Reservations not required. Expensive.*

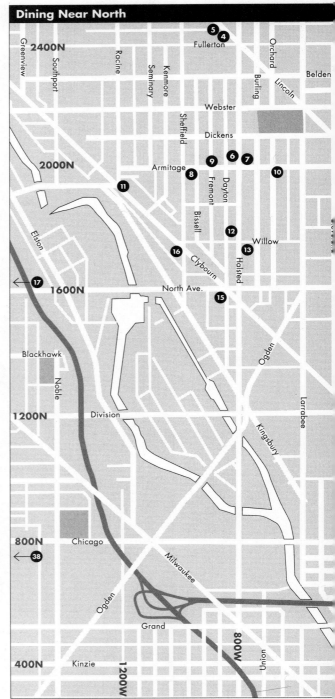

Dining Near North

★ **Gordon.** At Gordon the decor is rococo, with Oriental rugs, swag curtains alongside each table, and dark wood surrounding tables set with white cloths and centerpieces of fresh flowers. Consistently one of the most innovative contemporary restaurants in Chicago, Gordon's lighter new American cuisine features salsas and an extensive use of herbs in place of heavier cream-based sauces. The menus change often; representative offerings have included seared tuna with red tomato and chive vinaigrette; roasted sweetbreads with chanterelle mushrooms, prosciutto, and Chardonnay; and grilled beef tenderloin with Cabernet-braised mushrooms and marjoram. Half-size portions are available. On Friday and Saturday evening you can dance as well as dine. *500 N. Clark St., tel. 312/467-9780. Jackets required. Reservations required. AE, DC, MC, V. Closed holidays. Expensive.*

Hard Rock Cafe. Street signs, musical instruments, and posters adorn this branch of the London-based Hard Rock Cafe chain. Music blares over the din of 275 diners (or is it 1,000?). Hamburgers, lime-barbecued chicken, and Texas-style barbecued ribs are among the house specialties, but does anyone come to the Hard Rock Cafe for the food? *63 W. Ontario St., tel. 312/943-2252. Reservations accepted Mon.–Thurs. for lunch only. No reservations other times; the wait can be substantial. AE, MC, V. Closed some holidays. Moderate.*

Hillary's. This casual spot in hectic Water Tower Place lets you relax after heavy shopping and enjoy an attractive selection of salads, eggs, hamburgers, sandwiches, or—for something more substantial—several pastas, half a dozen chicken dishes, grilled fish, and grilled steak. *845 N. Michigan Ave., tel. 312/280-2710. Reservations advised for 6 or more. AE, DC, MC, V. Closed holidays. Moderate.*

Randall's Rib House. One of the classiest settings for the most expensive ribs in town, as well as popcorn shrimp; wings, shrimp, and catfish combo with barbecue sauce; southern fried chicken; catfish fillet. Of course there are numerous choices of ribs. Randall's is spacious and pleasant, though tiled floors make it noisy when crowded. There's an extensive beer list. *41 E. Superior St., tel. 312/280-2795. Reservations advised. DC, MC, V. No lunch Sat. Moderate.*

Rue St. Clair. This restaurant bills itself as an American bistro, a good characterization. French, Italian, and nouveau influences are evident. Pâté of the day rubs shoulders with gravlax and goat cheese on the appetizer menu; sandwiches include croque monsieur, eggs Benedict with hollandaise, Reuben, club, and hamburger. Salade Niçoise and shrimp-stuffed avocado with orange-cilantro mayonnaise share the salad menu with a garden salad of vegetables, greens, egg, and balsamic vinaigrette. Entrées are equally aclectic. Steak *pommes frites*, classic French bistro fare, shares its place with seafood crepes, baked eggplant Parmigiana, and grilled brook trout. A plat du jour ranges from pasta salad to ratatouille with shrimp to London broil. Toulouse-Lautrec posters and doors open on all sides create a casual atmosphere, enhanced by Jackie O'Shea at the piano and an outdoor summer dining room. *640 N. St. Clair St., tel. 312/787-6907. Lunch reservations advised. AE, DC, MC, V. Closed holidays. Moderate.*

P.J. Clarke's. A tile floor and a cappuccino machine in the front room set the tone at P.J. Clarke's. A lower-level dining room, with booth seating, is dimly lit; an upper-level dining room, with small tables, is brighter. A good selection of soups (gazpacho, beef barley, chili), salad offerings (spinach, Cobb, Niçoise, shrimp and pasta, Caesar), and hamburgers complements a menu of simply prepared entrées: grilled salmon, sautéed bay scallops with garlic and pasta, grilled veal chop with home fries, lemon butter chicken. Several Italian specialties are also available. The front bar is famous for its singles scene. *1204 N. State Pkwy., tel. 312/664-1650. Reservations advised. AE, DC, MC, V. No lunch weekdays. Inexpensive-Moderate.*

Robinson's No. 1 Ribs. This tiny restaurant's gray walls, blue ing than do most rib houses. Just about everything is barbecued or deep fried. Ribs (baby backs, tips) head the menu, followed by barbecued chicken, hot links, jumbo shrimp, pork and beef, cracklin' Louisiana catfish, and batter-dipped shrimp. Choose from side orders of natural cut fries, coleslaw, baked beans, and corn on the cob. A spinach salad and Robinson's No. 1 salad (a chef's salad) are offered for militant cholesterol watchers. *655 W. Armitage Ave., tel. 312/337-1399. AE, MC, V. Inexpensive-Moderate.*

Al's Italian Beef. This tiny spot on busy Ontario Street is probably the best in Chicago for those two local delicacies, "Italian beef" (thinly sliced, well-done beef, served on a bun with its juice and as many toppings—hot peppers, onions, ketchup, mustard—as you like), and the Chicago-style hot dog (hot dog with toppings in the same manner). You can get Italian sausage and meatball sandwiches here, too, as well as fries, sweet peppers, hot peppers, and chili. Eat at one of the tiny, cramped tables or carry the food away. *169 W. Ontario St., tel. 312/943-3222. No credit cards. Inexpensive.*

Billy Goat Tavern. A favorite hangout for reporters from the *Chicago Tribune*, this self-service bar and grill just across the street and up the stairs is the columnist Mike Royko's second office. Don't come here if you're watching your cholesterol level: The famed "chizboogers" are held together with grease. Do come for the atmosphere, a quick bite, and a cold one that won't set you back a day's pay. *430 N. Michigan Ave. (lower level), tel. 312/222-1525. No credit cards. Inexpensive.*

★ **Ed Debevic's.** When the successful Lettuce Entertain You restaurant group opened this imitation 1950s diner, many Chicagoans thought they had a loser on their hands. Instead, the group had correctly identified a nostalgia for good old home cooking. Half serious, half tongue-in-cheek, Ed's packs them in from morning till midnight. The signs are an important part of the decor: "If you don't like the way I do things—buy me out"; "If you're not served in 5 minutes—you'll get served in 8 or 9. Maybe 12 minutes. Relax." The menu features eight types of hamburger; a sandwich selection that includes tuna salad, chicken salad, chicken BLT, and Sloppy Joe; four chili preparations (plain, with macaroni and cheese, the same plus onion, and with onion and beans); five hot dog offerings; and a selection of "deluxe plates": meat loaf, pot roast, breaded pork loin, and chicken pot pie, all served with bread, butter, and choice of soup, slaw, or salad. Ask about the noodles du jour. Ed's has recently added more salads in a slight divergence from the dinner motif. The banana cream pie, coconut cream pie, and pecan pie are homemade. Unlike the real 1950s diner, Ed's has a selection of cocktails, wines, and Ed Debevic's Beer, Aged in its Own Bottle. *640 N. Wells St., tel. 312/664-1707. No reserva-*

*tions; the wait may be substantial. No credit cards. Closed
some holidays. Inexpensive.*

**American-
Continental**
Biggs. For dining in turn-of-the-century elegance, Biggs is the
place. Set in a Victorian mansion, the restaurant has seven intimate rooms, three with fireplaces, each with its own decor. A
turned-wood staircase leads you to the second floor, where individual rooms feature crystal chandeliers, Victorian carpeting, scrollwork ceilings, and parquet flooring. A succession of
chefs has attempted to update the menu while keeping the most
cherished of the old. At this writing the menu is eclectic, ranging from the traditional Individual Beef Wellington with Truffle Sauce to trendy items in the new Asian-American style,
such as grilled salmon Oriental with Napa cabbage and ginger.
The ambience makes Biggs special, regardless of its culinary
vagaries. *1150 N. Dearborn St., tel. 312/787–0900. Reservations advised. AE, CB, DC, MC, V. Closed lunch and holidays. Expensive.*

American Eclectic
Arnie's. Walk up a few stairs to a large lounge area with stained
glass and Tiffany lamps over the bar; move on to the large, sec-
tioned dining room outfitted lavishly in Art Deco style with
purple upholstery and stained-glass ceiling. One dining area
overlooks a garden. The appetizers at this well-known Chicago
restaurant draw on several cuisines, from smoked Norwegian
salmon to barbecued baby back ribs to sizzling chicken with
Thai peanut sauce and Mandarin spring salad to shrimp al
forno. Similarly, the soups include seafood gumbo and baked
onion soup Gruyere. Entrées are more conventionally American with an Italian accent: veal piccata, chicken Vesuvio, and
Sicilian veal chop share the menu with three steaks, sautéed
calves' liver, and sliced breast of duck with plum sauce. For
lighter, more casual dining, try Arnie's Cafe next door. *1030 N.
State St., tel. 312/266–4800. Jacket and tie required. Reservations advised. AE, DC, MC, V. Closed Mon.–Sat. lunch; holidays. Expensive.*

The Eccentric. Restaurateur Richard Melman has teamed with
talk-show star Oprah Winfrey to open this aptly named adventure in dining. The combination French café/Italian coffee-
house/English pub can seat 400 diners and is decorated with
the works of local artists. The food is surprisingly good, given
the novelty of the enterprise. Don't miss the excellent steaks
and chops, as well as Oprah's mashed potatoes with horserad-
ish. For dessert, try the butterscotch or bittersweet chocolate
pot de crème. And keep an eye out for Oprah. *159 West Erie, tel.
312/787–8390. No reservations. AE, CB, DC, MC, V. Closed
Sun. Moderate–Expensive.*

Metropolis 1800. Started as a tiny take-out food shop and winning wide acclaim, last year this restaurant moved to a large
new loftlike location. The owners dramatically expanded the
menu, and Metropolis 1800 blossomed into a very sophisticated
restaurant, successfully blending a casual atmosphere with
serious cooking. Offerings change daily. The emphasis is on
light, healthful, contemporary fare: fresh seafood, pastas, and
vegetarian dishes such as the seasonal vegetable pie. However,
those who wish to indulge themselves will find an occasional
hearty pâté or sinfully rich sauce. And save room for the
desserts—baked on the premises, they're killers. *1800 N.
Clybourn, tel. 312/642–6400. AE, MC, V. Moderate–Expensive.*

Montana Street Cafe. Although designed to look and feel like a classy neighborhood tavern, Montana Street Cafe has a more innovative and surprising menu than the average corner bar. Chef Barry Brooks' creations range from sandwiches such as a grilled ham and cheese filled with green onions and avocados on sourdough bread to light beer-batter chicken with red pepper jelly. Overall, the dishes are simple, and the flavors are true. *2464 N. Lincoln Ave., tel. 312/281-2407. Reservations advised. Closed lunch. AE, DC, MC, V. Moderate–Expensive.*

Chinese **Tang Dynasty.** Restaurants haven't fared well at this location—off the Michigan Avenue shopping district near Bloomingdale's—but this attractive Chinese eatery could buck the trend. Tang Dynasty may be the best-looking Chinese restaurant in the area. It also offers some of the best cooking. Alongside the usual pot stickers, wonton soup, and hacked chicken are many innovative dishes that change at the chef's whim. All are carefully prepared and professionally served. *100 E. Walton St., tel. 312/664-8688. Dress: casual. Reservations advised. AE, MC, V. Expensive.*

★ **House of Hunan.** The original Magnificent Mile Chinese restaurant, House of Hunan continues to please. The large, elegantly decorated dining area is appointed with porcelains and carvings. With offerings from the four principal Chinese culinary regions—Mandarin (from Beijing), Hunan, Szechuan, and Canton—the enormous menu offers a satisfying dinner to anyone who enjoys Chinese food. Spicy hot dishes are plentiful, but so are mild ones. Pot stickers (the best in town), scallop roll, satay beef, buns filled with minced pork and crabmeat, and stuffed crab claws are among the more than a dozen appetizers; cold dishes include drunken chicken, abalone salad, and jellyfish. Noodles, fish, shellfish, pork, duck, chicken, lamb, beef, vegetable, and mu shu (pancake-wrapped) specialties make up the remaining hundred or so preparations. The dishes are seasoned according to the customs of the region of origin. *535 N. Michigan Ave., tel. 312/329-9494. AE, DC, MC, V. Moderate–Expensive.*

Szechwan House. Oriental paintings adorn the walls here, carpeting softens the sound without covering the parquet floors, and the service is attentive. The menu is nicely balanced; highly seasoned and spicy hot dishes are plentiful, as one would expect from a Szechuan restaurant, yet there are plenty of choices for diners who prefer milder food. Try the pot stickers or the wonton to start; both dumplings are filled with meat, and the wonton come with spicy hot sesame sauce. The spicy snails, though tasty, are too small a portion for the price. The hot and sour soup combines spiciness and tartness in a way that is unusual but immediately pleasing. Cold noodle salad with shredded chicken, ham, and cucumbers, a classic Szechuan dish, is wonderfully refreshing on a hot summer day. Kung-pao chicken is another traditional preparation: The cubed chicken in a spicy sauce with peanuts and red peppers is wonderfully flavorful—but not for those who don't like hot food. Diners who are most comfortable with traditional Cantonese fare will prefer the sweet and sour chicken, deep-fried and served with green peppers and pineapple chunks, or shrimp with cashews, diced and sautéed in white wine sauce. The extensive menu boasts a dozen appetizers and noodle dishes, soups, shrimp preparations, chicken, duck, and beef. *600 N. Michigan Ave., tel. 312/642-3900. AE, DC, MC, V. Moderate–Expensive.*

European-Oriental   **Eurasia.** East meets West at Eurasia, where the cooking techniques and ingredients used in both Continental and Asian cultures are combined for a unique, if not always successful, experiment in dining. A typical dish here might be pieces of swordfish or tuna coated in Cajun spices and stir-fried, searing the outside but leaving the center rare. Good service and an attractive dining room make this an appealing choice for diners willing to take a culinary risk in a comfortable atmosphere. *200 E. Chestnut St., tel. 312/387-2742. Reservations advised on weekends. AE, CB, DC, MC, V. Expensive.*

Le Mikado. The chef's culinary flights of fancy usually succeed at Le Mikado, another of a growing number of restaurants where the tastes and ingredients of Eastern and Western cuisine merge in unique combinations. Try ravioli filled with Japanese eggplant or pheasant with Chinese cabbage. The two-level dining room offers privacy and refinement befitting the exceptional food. *21 W. Goethe St., tel. 312/280-5770. Reservations advised. AE, CB, MC, V. Expensive.*

French
★   **Ambria.** In the spacious atmosphere of a turn-of-the-century mansion, Ambria serves the most contemporary of French food and light cuisine. Gabino Sotelino, one of Chicago's best chefs, offers menus that change seasonally; a recent spring-summer menu offered terrine of salmon and striped bass with melon, tricolored ravioli of lobster and wild mushroom in lobster broth, sweetbread medallions breaded with pistachio and served with tomato basil sauce, and roast tenderloin of baby lamb with eggplant wrapped in crisp potato and served with couscous. The emphasis here is on using natural juices and vegetable reductions as accompaniments to the entrées, creating delectable food without excessive richness. The assortment of cheeses, sherbets, fruits, and pastries includes a hot soufflé. Ambria is a fine choice for those who want to dine graciously and well but not to excess. *2300 N. Lincoln Park West, tel. 312/472-5959. Dress: casual but neat. Reservations required. AE, DC, MC, V. Closed lunch; Sun.; holidays. Very Expensive.*

★   **La Tour.** One of Chicago's finest and most expensive restaurants, La Tour is a large room done in marble with tones of peach and green; one side looks out on the small Water Tower park, the other is more formal in atmosphere. Tuxedoed waiters serve you from an exquisite nouvelle French menu. Don't come here when you're slimming; you'd have to pass up the foie gras, apples, and potatoes in puff pastry; the raviolis of celery root with truffles and foie gras; and the veal medallions with cucumbers, morels, and cream. Come here for an elegant, grand splurge. La Tour is also one of the city's premier spots for power breakfasting. *Park Hyatt Hotel, 800 N. Michigan Ave., tel. 312/280-2230. Jacket required at dinner. Dinner reservations required. AE, DC, MC, V. Very Expensive.*

Le Perroquet. The image of this renowned restaurant has tarnished a bit since Jovan Trboyevic sold it to Jean-Pierre Nespoux and his brother Gerard; nonetheless, Le Perroquet continues to stand out as an oasis of civility in an otherwise chaotic city. The current kitchen staff blends nouvelle techniques, for which this restaurant gained its fame, with more classic French fare. For a set price of $48.50, diners can expect to sample some of the most carefully prepared, creatively conceived dinners available. The $21.50 fixed-price lunch affords diners the opportunity to enjoy the cuisine and atmosphere at comparatively low prices. Some may find the service stuffy or brusque, but the owners only intend to achieve the same sense of propriety found in the finest restaurants of France. Recommended dishes include the delectable mousses, fresh seafood dishes, and the famous floating island dessert. *70 E. Walton St., tel. 312/944–7990. Jacket and tie required. Reservations required. AE, DC, MC, V. Closed Sun. Very Expensive.*

Crickets. When you enter the dark, crowded dining room of Crickets, you find yourself in a world where toy airplanes, tanks, and cars hang from the ceiling together with industrial signs. Tables are close together; sharing conversations with those nearby is inevitable and can be part of the fun. This is a trendy spot with a middle-age and older crowd where many guests enjoy seeing others and being seen. The eclectic menu emphasizes traditional French preparations: pâté maison, baked oysters, ragout of snails, and mussels poulette share the appetizer menu with the more contemporary carpaccio (thinly sliced beef, marinated and served raw) and artichoke with balsamic-herb vinaigrette. Entrées include veal medallions with wild mushroom sauce, steak flambé au poivre, sweetbread medallions with terragon-truffle sauce, and tournedos of beef with Zinfandel shallot sauce. Soups, a selection of petite salads, and vegetable accompaniments are offered. The dessert menu includes Cricket's original cheesecake, chocolate mousse, creme caramel, rice pudding, ice cream, and fresh berries in season. *100 E. Chestnut St., tel. 312/280–2100. Jacket required. Reservations required. AE, DC, MC, V. Closed Sun. dinner; some holidays. Expensive–Very Expensive.*

★ **The Dining Room.** The Dining Room is done in a classic French style with walnut paneling, tapestry carpeting, and crystal chandeliers. The food is French with nouvelle accents; a specialty is foie gras salad. Daily specials complement the menu selections. Gracious service and fine food in a beautiful setting make this an outstanding restaurant. *Ritz-Carlton Hotel, 160 E. Pearson, tel. 312/227–5866. Jacket and tie required. Reservations required. AE, DC, MC, V. Closed lunch. Expensive–Very Expensive.*

Jackie's. This popular French restaurant features the cooking of famed, classically trained chef Jackie Etcheber. She puts together fascinating combinations of ingredients, such as sea scallops wrapped in phyllo dough with roe, tomatoes, lettuce, and caviar. In many restaurants, such exotic concoctions sound better than they taste, but Jackie's consistently delivers intense and satisfying flavors. If you have room for dessert, the restaurant is famous for its "chocolate bag," a dark chocolate shell filled with white mousse and raspberries. The servers are poised and proper, if occasionally stuffy. *2478 N. Lincoln Ave., tel. 312/880–0003. Reservations required. No denim. AE, DC, MC, V. Closed Sun., Mon. Expensive–Very Expensive.*

Bistro 110. Like any good bistro, this place can be noisy and chaotic at times, but third-generation restaurateur Doug Roth presides over the cacophony with élan. Bistro 110 has become a popular gathering place for the city's young executives. Besides the lively bar scene, the real drawing card here is the food from the wood-burning oven. From chicken to seafood, from mushrooms to the whole head of baked garlic placed before diners at the beginning of the meal to be spread on the crusty French bread, the kitchen consistently turns out excellent renditions of French classics, as well as contemporary Franco/American innovations. *110 E. Pearson St., tel. 312/266–3110.*

Reservations advised for lunch; for parties of 6 or more for dinner. AE, DC, MC, V. Expensive.

Cocorico. Named for the crowing sound made by French roosters, this simple, elegant restaurant is overrun with decorative roosters, from the banners outside to the centerpieces on the tables. Hearty Alsatian fare features country dishes such as *cassoulet* (meat-and-bean casserole), *bouillabaisse* (Mediterranean fish stew), and *choucroute* (sauerkraut with meat). The *escargots bourguignone*, prepared in their shells with garlic butter, are among the best in town. The atmosphere is relaxed and casual. Service can be erratic. *1960 N. Clybourn, tel. 312/248-0700. Reservations advised, required on weekends. AE, MC, V. Closed Mon.; Sun. dinner. Expensive.*

Mirador. Owned by Patrick and Amy Morton Kerr (daughter of famed Chicago restaurateur Arnie Morton), Mirador offers wonderfully flavorful French country cooking in a funky, intimate environment. The menu changes weekly, sometimes daily, sometimes by the minute, but diners won't go wrong with the chef's recommendations. Try the sweetbreads with greens if they're available, or the simple but compelling roast free-range chicken. A good, reasonably priced wine list complements the menu. After dinner, head upstairs to the blue room for a nightcap and great late-night people watching from the '40s-style overstuffed chairs. This is one of the best new restaurants on Chicago's dining scene. *1400 N. Wells St., tel. 312/951-6441. Reservations not required. AE, DC, MC, V. Closed lunch. Expensive.*

Toulouse. The muted colors, draperies, and mirrored walls of Toulouse, along with a bar and a pianist, create a pleasing, romantic ambience. The food, French with nouvelle and Oriental accents, uses contemporary ingredients such as radicchio, walnut vinaigrette, goat cheese, green peppercorns, and shiitake mushrooms to update classic preparations. The mushroom pâté with fresh herb cream sauce or the mussel soup with saffron would make a lovely start—unless you prefer the more substantial squab salad with marinated mushrooms, new potatoes, and walnut vinaigrette. Entrées include steamed stuffed breast of capon with ginger and leek sauce; red snapper, Oriental style, with sake ginger sauce; and sautéed veal steak with wild mushroom ravioli in chive cream sauce. A daily special is available, as is a daily low-sodium, low-cholesterol special. *51 W. Division St., tel. 312/944-2606. Jacket required. Reservations advised. AE, DC, MC, V. Closed lunch, Sun., holidays. Expensive.*

L'Escargot. This restaurant's two locations, on North Michigan and on North Halsted, are both simply decorated and comfortable. The French country cuisine emphasizes foods of the Loire region in summer and of Alsace in winter. The basic menu is extensive, with more than a dozen appetizers, including marinated mushrooms, spinach timbale, and homemade sausage in puff pastry with warm lentil salad. Several soups are offered. Entrées have included bay scallops on a bed of linguini with tomato and vermouth sauce, sautéed breast of chicken with wild mushroom sauce, fricassee of veal in Dijon mustard sauce, snails en casserole, and cassoulet. The daily specials that supplement the menu have featured sautéed bay scallops Provençal (with tomatoes, onions, and garlic), grilled tuna with ginger garlic sauce, and capon roulade stuffed with spinach and yellow beans. All entrées come with appetizer, house salad, and dessert. *L'Escargot on Michigan: Allerton Hotel, 701 N. Michi-*

gan Ave., tel. 312/337–1717. Reservations advised. AE, DC,
MC, V. Closed holidays. Moderate–Expensive. L'Escargot on
Halsted: 2925 N. Halsted Ave., tel. 312/525–5522. Reserva-
tions advised. AE, DC, MC, V. Closed lunch; Sun. Moderate–
Expensive.

Les Plumes. Ten years ago, North Halsted Street was just another declining urban neighborhood. Today it is in the forefront
of gentrification, with attractive new restaurants lining both
sides of the street from North Avenue to Belmont. The stylish
Les Plumes occupies the bottom floor of a town house on the
Halsted Street strip. A long, narrow front room done in wood
and shades of peach and dark green opens into a larger dining
room to the rear. Fish, seafood, poultry, and veal are the mainstays of a vouvelle French menu. Duck, sautéed medium-rare,
is served with Rouennaise sauce. Sautéed veal steak is accompanied by poached breast of chicken filled with chicken mousse
and topped with mushroom sauce. Gulf shrimp are served with
Belgian endive, avocado, mushrooms, snow peas, and lobster-
tarragon sauce. These dishes are not as low in fat as their
primary ingredients might suggest, but they are lovely
indulgences in a great culinary tradition. 2044 N. Halsted St.,
tel. 312/525–0121. Jacket required. Reservations required.
AE, MC, V. Closed lunch; Sun.; holidays. Moderate–Expensive.

★ **Un Grand Cafe.** This attractive Montmartre-style bistro is the
casual companion to the elegant Ambria at the same address.
Steak frites, cassoulet, and roast chicken are specialties on a
menu that reflects the simpler, earthier preparations of the
French bistro style while drawing on fresh American produce.
Though relaxed in ambience, the restaurant offers the same
outstanding quality of food and preparation as does its more
formal sibling. 2300 N. Lincoln Park West, tel. 312/348–8886.
No reservations; there may be a wait. AE, DC, MC, V. Closed
lunch; Sun. and holidays. Moderate.

Yvette. Yvette is the place when you want classic French cuisine in a comfortable setting at an affordable price. Appetizers
include scallop quenelles with pasta and chives, assorted pâtés
and sausages, ballotine of salmon with dill sauce, and sweetbreads with morel mushrooms. There's a warm salad of the
day, and soups are prepared daily. For an entrée, you might
have the veal medallions in wild mushroom sauce, salmon fumé
with Oriental-style vegetables, the seafood on fresh pasta (a
specialty), or the fish of the day. The informal Yvette's Cafe offers a lighter menu that emphasizes seafoods and salads. 1206
N. State Pkwy., tel. 312/280–1700. Reservations for 6 or more.
AE, DC, MC, V. No lunch in the dining room. Moderate.

Albert's Cafe and Patisserie. It's easy to overlook this charming
10-table spot that nestles inconspicuously in a town house behind the imposing mansion that houses Biggs Restaurant. A
cross between a bakery, a coffeehouse, and a white-tablecloth
restaurant, Albert's has an eclectic menu that includes steak,
seafood, and pasta dishes. The homemade pastries are beautiful to behold and sinful to eat, but they do go well with the excellent coffee. Prices are surprisingly low, given the quality
and the café's location in the Near North high-rent district. 52
West Elm St., tel. 312/751–0666. No credit cards. Closed Mon.
Inexpensive–Moderate.

German **The Golden Ox.** Dark wood, stained-glass windows, murals on
themes from German mythology, a hand-carved bar of golden

oak, cheerful waitresses in traditional costume, and strolling accordionists and zither players give this German restaurant— the last survivor in what was once a German neighborhood—an authentically ethnic flavor. White tablecloths laid with platters of pickles and relishes set the tone for leisurely, comfortable dining. The menu offers two dozen German specialties, including four veal preparations, two sausages, smoked pork loin, and several unusual items: roast goose with potato dumplings and red cabbage (Saturday and Sunday only), veal sweetbreads sautéed in butter with mushrooms, and hasenpfeffer (marinated rabbit in cream sauce, served with potato dumpling and red cabbage). This hearty, filling fare leaves you with a contented glow. *1578 N. Clybourn Ave., tel. 312/664–0780. Reservations advised on weekends. AE, DC, MC, V. Closed lunch Sun.; closed Sun. July and Aug. Moderate.*

Indian **Bukhara.** Specializing in the cuisine of northwestern India, Bukhara features an open kitchen where diners can watch their food prepared in clay ovens. Bread making is particularly theatrical, and the delicious product is likely to be an important part of your meal. Bukhara's food is spicy but not hot, and most dishes are intended to be eaten with the fingers or scooped up on pieces of bread. Plenty of hot towels are provided. Good choices for entrées include *sikandari raan* (leg of lamb marinated in rum and spices and roasted in a clay oven), *khyber tikka* (marinated chicken coated in egg yolk and grilled over charcoal), and the royal Kushan veal chop, seasoned with ginger and garlic. Unless you're extremely hungry, you may want to skip the appetizers, since main-dish portions are large and often quite rich. As in many Indian restaurants, desserts are very sweet and dense. *2 E. Ontario, tel. 312/943–0188. Reservations advised. AE, CB, DC, MC, V. Moderate–Expensive.*

Italian **Spiaggia.** Classy, pretty, and expensive, Spiaggia was designed to be the equivalent of The Four Seasons in New York, and in many ways it succeeds. However, prices are staggering for such dishes as crisp pizza with paper-thin crust topped with duck and goat cheese, delicately sauced ravioli filled with lobster meat, and grilled veal chop with rosemary. A meal at Spiaggia is worth the price for those on expense accounts. If you're not so fortunate, try Café Spiaggia next door, which offers many of the same dishes at lower prices. *One Magnificent Mile (Oak St. at Michigan Ave.), tel. 312/280–2750. Reservations advised. Jackets required; no denim. AE, CB, DC, MC, V. Closed Sun. lunch. Very Expensive.*

★ **Avanzare.** A handsome pair of marble, carpeted rooms, one raised a few steps above the other, is dominated by traditional accents of brass, leather banquettes, and a full-length mirrored bar between the rooms. Tables are topped with white butcher paper over cloth. The main room tends to be a bit noisy, the mezzanine less so. Avanzare offers a wide-ranging menu of pastas, unusual salads, and entrées. Try an appetizer of tuna carpaccio, paper-thin slices of raw tuna in soy sauce with avocado and sweet onions. A dozen carefully prepared pastas appear in the regular menu, but the best pasta offerings come from the list of daily specials. Among the entrées, try one of the unusual game dishes, a tempting seafood special, or the unsurpassed veal chop. Though expensive, Avanzare is consistently one of the best Italian restaurants on Chicago's Near North side. The freshness and quality of the ingredients shine through the preparations. *161 E. Huron St., tel. 312/337-8056. Reservations advised. AE, CB, DC, MC, V. Expensive.*

Bice. This is the ultimate see-and-be-seen Italian eatery; a strip of mirrored glass at eye level gives even diners with their backs to the room an opportunity to watch the goings-on. The food at Bice (pronounced Bee-chay) is quite good, especially the carefully prepared pastas with innovative sauces. Lapses in service seem de rigeur, but there's plenty of action to amuse you during the often interminable waits between courses. *158 E. Ontario St. tel. 312/664-1474. Reservations advised for inside dining room. Jacket and tie required. AE, DC, MC, V. Expensive.*

Fresco's. Most Italian restaurants are long on red sauce and short on theater—Fresco's is just the opposite. While a few dishes feature a very credible marinara, head for the more exotic offerings, such as black squid ink pasta with saffron and fresh seafood or meats and seafood from the grill. As for theater, chefs make fresh pastas and pizzas in the wood-burning oven daily from a showcase kitchen within sight of the dining room. And Fresco's also provides diners with sweeping views of the lake and the city. All is served in a classy environ by a careful, solicitous staff. *In the North Pier complex at 435 E. Illinois St., tel. 312/222-2526. AE, DC, MC, V. Reservations not required. Jacket and tie required. Expensive.*

Convito Italiano. A marble-top bar complements a dining room with fanciful murals and exposed brick, and the windows give an airy feel to the room at Convito Italiano. Flowers and a bottle of wine are set on each of the white-clothed tables. An assortment of homemade breads presented at the table makes a seductive start to a regional Italian meal. Among numerous dishes not readily found elsewhere are appetizers of veal, rolled and filled with *pancetta* (Italian bacon), spinach, and fontina cheese, seasoned with onion and sage, and served with pan juices; and eggplant stuffed with ricotta cheese and baked with tomato wine sauce and fontina cheese. The menu offers three unusual soups, a large selection of salads, and equally interesting pastas: A classic spaghetti with tomato-basil sauce is familiar but fresh; rigatoni in tomato-cream sauce with shrimp, bay scallops, and broccoli is less conventional. Entrées emphasize chicken and veal and include a veal chop stuffed with fontina cheese. A grilled steak with red onions and balsamic vinegar is also available. Pastas, breads, and pastries are all homemade. A casual lunch area has been added to the first floor, and in summer you can eat outside. The shop below has ingredients for your own Italian picnic and unusual kitchen and gift items. *11 E. Chestnut St., tel. 312/943-2984. Reservations advised. AE, MC, V. Closed Sun. lunch; holidays. Moderate-Expensive.*

Trattoria Gianni. This Lincoln Park establishment successfully re-creates the homey atmosphere and skillful cooking common in Italian trattorias, though at a higher price. Appetizers are a standout: choose among three antipasto plates—hot, cold, or vegetarian—or crunchy deep-fried squid, zucchini strips, or mussels. The vegetarian plate includes marinated eggplant and zucchini salads and an egg-and-vegetable frittata. Imaginative and usually well prepared pasta dishes include *rigatoni nocerina* (pasta tubes with cream, mushrooms, and sun-dried tomatoes), *farfalle contadina* (bow-tie macaroni with vegetables), and *gnocchi à la panna-pesto* (potato dumplings with cream-and-pesto sauce). Simple but satisfying entrées include grilled red snapper with herbs and olive oil, and the worthwhile charcoal-grilled cornish game hen. If you can, save room for desserts. *1711 N. Halsted Ave., tel. 312/266–1976. Reservations advised. MC, V. Closed weekend lunch and Mon. Moderate–Expensive.*

L'Angolo di Roma. Cotton tablecloths are covered with butcher paper and set with fresh flowers in the brightly lit dining rooms of L'Angolo di Roma. Cold appetizers on display allow diners to select in advance of ordering among carpaccio, sliced tomato and onion, radicchio salad, fennel salad, and endive with pea pods and tomato. Mussels marinara, baked Little Neck clams, and fried calamari are among the hot appetizers. Individual nine-inch pizzas—with prosciutto, artichoke, mushrooms, olive, and egg; four cheeses; or mussels and calamari in marinara sauce—are a specialty. Pastas and entrées change daily, but they might include *gnocchi* (potato dumplings) sautéed in tomato sauce with Parmigiana cheese, topped with mozzarella, and baked; rigatoni with tomato sauce, sausage, mushrooms, and broccoli; whole red snapper baked and served with olive oil, garlic, basil, and parsley; and chicken breast sautéed in Marsala wine with mushrooms and scallions. *2260 N. Clark St., tel. 312/935–8100. Reservations advised for 5 or more. MC, V. Closed holidays. Moderate.*

Scoozi! You'll recognize Scoozi! by the gigantic tomato over the front door. This is a huge, noisy, trendy place popular with the young professional crowd. Booths flank the walls of a multilevel dining room, and wood beams and ceiling decorations complement the country Italian food. A large selection of antipasti, pizza, and pasta is augmented by a small selection of entrées. Steamed clams in garlic and white wine, steamed mussels in tomato sauce, and *osso buco* (braised veal shanks in roasted vegetables) appear on a generally attractive menu that invites "grazing." Many offerings are available in small or large portions. *410 W. Huron St., tel. 312/943–5900. Reservations accepted for lunch, no reservations for dinner; the wait can be substantial. AE, DC, MC, V. Closed some holidays. Moderate.*

Sole Mio. Sole Mio is owned by the chefs Dennis Terczak and Jennifer Newbury. Its warm ambience is created by dark wood teamed with white walls, wood-framed mirrors, and photographs of the Italian countryside. The main dining room is flanked by three smaller rooms, one for nonsmokers. The food is inspired by the cuisine of Northern and regional Italy and enhanced by an imaginative contemporary approach. Try the *mozzarella casareccia alla Griglia* (homemade mozzarella cheese, grilled and served with spinach, grilled tomato, and balsamic vinaigrette). Pastas include *linguine alle sarde* (linguine with grilled fresh sardines, onion, fennel, garlic, tomato, herbs, and breadcrumbs) and *fettucine nere al calamari* (black-ink fettucine with squid in fresh tomato sauce). The individual 8-inch pizzas are outstanding, even the familiar pizza *margherita* with mozzarella, fresh tomato sauce, basil, and sausage. Entrées include the adventurous—*misto alla Griglia* is a mixed grill of lamb chop, quail, sausage, lentils, and escarole—and the tried and true veal scallops, center-cut veal chop, and grilled T-bone steak with peppercorns. A fresh ocean fish, freshwater fish, and shellfish are available daily, and there are homemade desserts and ices. *917 W. Armitage Ave., tel. 312/477–5858. No reservations (the wait is generally less than half an hour). AE, CB, DC, MC, V. Closed lunch and holidays. Moderate.*

Tucci Benucch. This cozy Italian country kitchen in the Avenue Atrium mall is a pleasant escape from the hustle and bustle of shopping outside its doors. Thin-crust pizzas and pasta dishes feature unusual toppings, such as smoked chicken, red peppers, and asiago cheese. Red sauces for spaghetti include julienned fresh basil. The grilled eggplant, red pepper, and onion sandwich is rich and crusty. Leave room for dessert, because the gelato is worth a try. *900 N. Michigan Ave., 5th floor, tel. 312/266–2500. No reservations. AE, DC, MC, V. Moderate.*

Tucci Milan. A cousin to Tucci Benucch, this contemporary restaurant in trendy River North produces some excellent renditions of Northern Italian pastas and grilled dishes. Bustling and noisy, the restaurant attracts a young, professional crowd with an active bar scene. The food is consistently good, but service is sometimes careless and hurried. *6 W. Hubbard St., tel. 312/222–0044. Reservations advised on weekends. Dress: casual but neat. AE, DC, MC, V. Moderate.*

Pizzeria Uno/Pizzeria Due. This is where Chicago deep-dish pizza got its start. Still run by original owner Ike Sewell, Uno has been remodeled to resemble its franchised cousins in other cities, but its pizzas retain their light crust and distinctive taste. Those not accustomed to pizza on a Chicago scale may want to skip the salad to save room. Beer and soft drinks can be ordered by the pitcher. You'll usually have a shorter wait for a table at Pizzeria Due (same ownership and menu, different decor and longer hours), a block away. Some say Uno's pizza is better, but the product at both establishments is among the best in town. *Uno: 29 E. Ohio St, tel. 312/321–1000. Due: 619 N. Wabash Ave., tel. 312/943–2400. No reservations, but phone-ahead orders are accepted weekdays only. AE, DC, MC, V. Inexpensive.*

Italian-American **Harry Caray's.** Housed in the handsome old ornamented brick building that for years was the Kinzie Steak House, Harry Caray's is one of the new breed of "celebrity" restaurant. The interior, completely redone, has a long wood bar, tile flooring, and high tables covered with checkered cloth. Baseball memorabilia decorates the walls, and souvenirs can be purchased from the souvenir stand. The food reflects Harry's own preferences: Steaks and chops share the bulk of the menu with traditional Italian preparations. Salads and cold platters are plentiful. This is a good spot for baseball fans who like to eat and don't take the dining experience too seriously. And, unlike the "name" owners of some celebrity restaurants, Harry really does stop by. Holy cow! *33 W. Kinzie St., tel. 312/465–9269. Lunch reservations advised. AE, CB, DC, MC, V. Moderate–Expensive.*

Japanese **Benkay.** In part because of a limited market, and in part because of the cost of buying and preparing the highest-quality ingredients in Japanese style, few Japanese restaurants in the country offer authentic Japanese high cuisine in an elegant setting. Benkay is one that does. Enter down a long, graceful stairway and pause a moment at the small pond at its base. For dining, choose among the serenely beautiful 50-seat main dining room served by tuxedoed waiters, the 20-seat sushi room, one of six traditional tatami rooms (foot wells make them as comfortable for Americans as for Japanese) served by kimono-clad waitresses, a teppan-yaki room (in which chefs do their work inconspicuously, so as not to intrude on diners' conversations), and two private Western-style dining rooms. The extensive menu is printed in English and Japanese. A full selection of appetizers, soups, *sashimi* (raw fish), *ni-mono* (steamed) dishes, *yaki-mono* (grilled) dishes, *age-mono* (fried) dishes, *sunomono* (vinegared) dishes, rices, noodles, and desserts is offered. The restaurant's specialty is its *Kaiseki* menu (three full-course dinners that include at least one item from each of the traditional Japanese styles of cooking). These dinners show the art as well as the refinement and elegance of classical Japanese dining. *Hotel Nikko, 320 N. Dearborn St., tel. 312/836–5490. Jacket and tie required at lunch and dinner. Reservations required. AE, DC, MC, V. Closed holidays. Very Expensive.*

Benihana of Tokyo. This darkly handsome restaurant specializes in the teppan-yaki, or grill-cooking, style of food preparation. Each of its dining rooms houses long ebony communal tables; in the center of each is a large grilling area. After soup and appetizer, the chef comes to your table to prepare your entrée. Meat or shellfish are sliced or cubed with lightning strokes of the knife, then tended with careful precision for the few minutes they need to cook. It is fascinating to watch the combination of skill and art, and that the perfectly fresh ingredients are—astonishingly, given the speed with which the morsels cook—prepared precisely to your order. Prices are in line with or a bit lower than those of other restaurants in the neighborhood and other Japanese restaurants. While the Japanese dining experience is somewhat Americanized at Benihana, the restaurant gives good value and does make one style of Japanese cuisine accessible to the American diner. *166 E. Superior St., tel. 312/664–9643. No reservations between 7:30 and 9 PM. AE, CB, DC, MC, V. Closed Sun. lunch; holidays. Moderate–Expensive.*

★ **Hatsuhana.** Hatsuhana has a long, angled sushi bar and wood tables set on purple carpeting; its white stucco walls are hung with Japanese lanterns. Sushi and sashimi lovers have long esteemed this restaurant as the best in Chicago for these Japanese vinegared rice and raw fish delicacies. The printed menu lists numerous appetizers (broiled spinach in sesame-soy sauce, fried bean curd with sauce, steamed egg custard with shrimp, fish, and vegetables) and only a few entrée selections. An extensive and unusual specials menu supplements the printed menu and has included steamed baby clams in sake, broiled king mackerel with soybean paste, boiled snails in sweet sauce, and chicken wings in special sauce. A small selection of moderately priced complete dinners is available. *160 E. Ontario St., tel. 312/280–8287. Reservations advised. AE, DC, MC, V. Closed Sat. lunch; Sun.; holidays. Moderate–Expensive.*

Honda. Owned and operated by a Tokyo restaurateur, Honda offers one of the most extensive Japanese menus in the city. Its sushi and sashimi are among the city's best, and it also features the country's first *kushi* bar, where morsel of meat, seafood, and vegetables are grilled or deep-fried. Diners have the option of sitting at the kushi bar or in one of Honda's several dining rooms. You can call a day in advance to reserve a traditional tatami room (foot wells under the low tables let you stretch your legs). The many authentic dishes include *chawan mushi* (steamed vegetables and fish in an egg custard). Sukiyaki is prepared at your table. Service can be uncoordinated, especially when large parties order a variety of entrées. *540 N. Wells,* *tel. 312/923–1010. Reservations not required. AE, CB, DC, MC, V. Closed Sat. lunch; Sun. Moderate–Expensive.*

Mexican **Topolobampo.** Located next door to Frontera Grill, Topolobampo shares more than just the same entrance with its sister restaurant. It has the same owners, the same kitchen, and the same dedication to quality. Everything that can be said for Frontera can be said at least as strongly about Topolobampo, which may be the best Mexican restaurant in the nation. More expensive than Frontera, Topolobampo offers a more stately atmosphere, accepts reservations, and most importantly affords the chef the opportunity to experiment with more expensive ingredients. The ever-changing menu features game, seasonal fruits and vegetables, and exotic preparations that almost always taste even better than they sound. Good service and an interesting wine list complete the scenario. *445 N. Clark St., tel. 312/661–1434. Reservations not required. AE, DC, MC, V. Closed Sun., Mon. Expensive.*

★ **Frontera Grill.** Chef/owner Rick Bayless and his wife, Deann, literally wrote the book on Mexican cuisine—*Authentic Mexican*—and that's what you'll find at this casual café, along with a tiled floor, bright colors, and Mexican folk art. Don't come for chips and salsa (available for unsophisticated gringos only on request). The Baylesses learned about regional Mexican cuisine by tramping across Mexico, hanging out in markets, eating in restaurants, and talking with the cooks. They serve a sampling of what they learned, and what a sampling it is—from charbroiled catfish, Yucatan style (with pickled red onions and *jicama* salad), to garlicky skewered tenderloin, Agauscalientes style (with poblano peppers, red onion, and bacon)! The menu changes frequently, and weekly specials are often the most tempting dishes. This place proves once and for all that Mexican cuisine is anything but limited and boring. *445 N. Clark St., tel. 312/661–1434. No reservations; expect a long wait. AE, DC, MC, V. Closed Sun. and Mon. Moderate.*

Hat Dance. Look for the Indian-style carvings in the imitation adobe exterior of the building to tell you that you've come to the right place. Inside, you'll find umbrellas hanging from the ceiling along with antique chandeliers, pillars sprouting into palm trees, women diving out of trees, animals in bas relief, and a great trompe l'oeil that gives the illusion of a marble wall. Hat Dance, whose culinary style and philosophy are far from the "authentic Mexican" of the Frontera Grill, is a creation of the Lettuce Entertain You group in partnership with the radio personality Steve Dahl. It is designed to appeal to trendy, upscale young professionals who enjoy crowds and noise as part of the dining experience. Appetizers include a selection of ceviches, sashimi, and tartares, as well as an assortment of quesos, quesadillas, carnitas, tacos, and guacamole. Entrées lean toward "nouveau" preparations. To the classic carne asada is added, for example, tuna asada: grilled tuna steak served rare, accompanied by chili-papaya relish. A chile relleno is stuffed with chicken, olives, raisins, and onions in a tomato-cinnamon broth. A good selection of desserts includes a vanilla-cinnamon pudding, a rice pudding, chocolate-coconut flan, and assorted pastries. *325 W. Huron St., tel. 312/649–0066. Reservations advised. AE, DC, MC, V. Closed weekend lunch. Moderate.*

Middle Eastern **Sayat Nova.** The cozy, even romantic, Sayat Nova has soft lighting and many tables in their own niches, separated by arched walls from other diners. All the Middle Eastern favorites are served here: Appetizers include cheese or spinach *beoreg* (in flaky pastry), *hummos* (chick-pea–sesame dip), *baba ghannouj* (eggplant-sesame dip), *raw kibbee* (Armenian steak tartare, made of lamb and bulghur wheat), and *plaki* (white beans in olive oil, onions, and spices). Entrées, which are preceded by a rich homemade vegetable soup and green salad, then stacks of fresh, hot pita pocket bread throughout your meal, include shish kebab, *sarma* (stuffed grape leaves), and *kufta* (ground meat balls stuffed with bulghur, nuts, and spices). The less adventurous may order the marinated sautéed chicken or the New York strip, and there is an attractive vegetarian combination dinner. A choice of two Middle Eastern desserts and sherbet rounds out your meal. The food is pleasingly prepared and subtly seasoned, the restaurant a great bargain in this neighborhood. *157 E. Ohio St., tel. 312/644–9159. AE, DC, MC, V. Closed Sun. lunch; July and holidays. Inexpensive–Moderate.*

Polish-American   **Busy Bee.** Busy Bee is one of the best of the many storefront Polish restaurants to be found throughout Chicago. Two large storefronts have been divided into one room with a large U-shaped counter and booths and a second that is carpeted and furnished with well-spaced, cloth-covered tables. What makes this and other restaurants of its type special is the generous quantities of pleasing, stick-to-the-ribs food at very low prices. *Pierogi* (dumplings stuffed with your choice of meat, potato and cheese, or potato and sauerkraut) are served with sour cream or applesauce. Homemade mushroom soup, barley soup, and *czarnina* (duck gravy soup) are among the daily specials. *Bigos* (hunter's stew), Polish sausages, boiled beef brisket, boiled short ribs, tripe stew, and roast duck are among the entrées. Plenty of standard American dishes are also available, satisfying finicky youngsters while parents enjoy ethnic specialties. Service can be somewhat slow. *1546 N. Damen Ave., tel. 312/772–4433. Reservations not required. No credit cards. Closed some holidays. Inexpensive.*

Seafood   **Catch Thirty Five.** A lot of money went into making this one of the most handsome restaurants in Chicago. Situated on one side of the lobby of the new Leo Burnett Building, this restaurant takes its name from its address and the 35 different types of fresh seafood featured daily. The chef (known simply as Eak) mixes Asian flavorings such as curry sauce with Latin influences such as cilantro sauce, to create innovative dishes with classic French overtones. The decor is also born of a Western and Eastern mixture, in this case West Coast and East Coast. A huge sculpture projecting a pattern of colored lights hangs over the piano bar, while to the right, the bird's-eye–maple-paneled dining room affords everyone a great view for people watching. At the time of this writing, the restaurant had yet to ignite with the trendy set to make people watching a prime sport here, but with intriguing dishes such as wok-steamed striped bass with black bean and ginger sauce, this seafood extravaganza will surely have a bright future. *35 W. Wacker, tel. 312/346–3500. AE, MC, V. Reservations not required. Dress: casual. Expensive.*

Chestnut Street Grill. Modeled after the famous Tadich Grill in San Francisco, this Water Tower Place establishment serves some of the best fresh seafood in the Chicago area. Menu offerings vary daily, as the catch is flown in fresh from the coasts and prepared in a variety of ways. Tile floors, dark wood, and white tablecloths give this restaurant a crisp air that makes it popular for business lunches. *845 N. Michigan Ave., tel. 312/280-2720. Reservations not required. AE, CB, DC, MC, V. Expensive.*

The Old Carolina Crab House. This waterside restaurant, with fishing tackle and pictures of fishermen covering the walls, is about as close as Chicago gets to that Southern-style "little crab house on the shore." When you want a break from shopping in the newly developed North Pier, stop in for a laid-back dinner of steamed crab and beer. The hush puppies and greens are the best in town. *In the North Pier complex at 435 E. Illinois St., tel. 312/321-8400. Reservations not required. Dress: casual. Moderate-Expensive.*

Shaw's Crab House and Blue Crab Lounge. Here is an East Coast-style oyster bar, in exposed brick and wood, with a wood bar adjoining the main restaurant, again in wood, softly lit, with models of fish on the walls. Preparations tend toward the simple and the classic. Appetizers include french-fried calamari, steamed blue mussels, and Maryland crab cakes. An oyster special of the day offers regional varieties that Midwesterners might not otherwise have a chance to sample. Crab, lobster, and shrimp offerings are standard on the menu; the fresh fish daily specials might include grilled Hawaiian tuna with purslane and tomato relish or a grilled Pacific king salmon with herb marinade. A few obligatory chicken and beef items are offered on the menu as well. *21 E. Hubbard St., tel. 312/527-2722. Reservations advised for lunch. AE, DC, MC, V. Closed weekend lunch; lounge closed Sun. Moderate-Expensive.*

JP's Eating Place at the Claridge and **JP's Eating Place North.** While both JP's provide for steak lovers with seared or blackened steak, *carne asada* (steak with sautéed mushroom and barbecued shrimp), and steak ranchero (tenderloin cubes sautéed with garlic, cilantro, shallots, mushroom, red peppers, onion, and tomato in wine sauce), and for fish haters with chicken salad, barbecued ribs, and several pastas; their focus is on gifts from the sea. Nachos share the appetizer menu with a ceviche of fresh swordfish, tuna, and salmon marinated in lemon and garlic and served with avocado salsa; breaded fried calamari; and mussels steamed in garlic and white wine. Entrées include two classic fish stews—bouillabaisse and California cioppino—and no fewer than two dozen fish and seafood varieties served sautéed, grilled, blackened, or marinated in teriyaki sauce, many accompanied by fresh salsas, according to your pleasure. Best of all, these restaurants know how to cook fish so that it retains its tenderness, moistness, and flavor. JP's North, the original restaurant, is a small room that has become a bit crowded as tables have been added to accommodate its growing clientele. The tables are covered with butcher paper over tablecloth, and crayons are provided so you can make notes about your order or work on a business problem. A tapestry is the focal point of the decor, complemented by carvings and other ethnic art. Service is cheerful, if sometimes harried. Jorge Perez opened JP's at the Claridge following the deserved success of the first JP's. It doubles as the Claridge's restaurant, offering breakfast and a slightly larger lunch and dinner menu in a more traditional setting than the original JP's. Green marble tables adorn the lounge area; the two dining rooms are done in neutral tones, and lighting—blue in one, rose in the other—provides the color. *J.P.'s at the Claridge: 1244 N. Dearborn Pkwy., tel.*

312/642–2088, J.P.'s North: 1800 N. Halsted St., tel. 312/664–1801. Reservations advised. AE, DC, MC, V. Closed Christmas. Moderate.

Spanish **Cafe Ba-Ba-Reeba!** Chicago's best-known exemplar of *tapas* cuisine (small edibles that once were used as covers for the glasses of sherry, wine, or beer that accompanied them), this large, open restaurant, with its prominent bar, is usually crowded with upscale young folk having a very good time. Choose among a large selection of cold and warm tapas, ranging from cannelloni stuffed with tuna, asparagus, and basil served with tomato basil sauce and white wine vinaigrette to veal with mushrooms, eggplant, and tomato with sherry sauce. A few soups and salads are available, as is a limited entrée menu that includes two *paellas* (meat and seafood or seafood only, baked in rice), a baked salmon with mustard topping and vegetable vinaigrette, sautéed pork tenderloin with caramel orange sauce, and two seafood casseroles. There are several desserts for those who have the room. *2024 N. Halsted St., tel. 312/935–5000. Limited reservations; the wait may be substantial. AE, DC, MC, V. Closed lunch; Sun.; holidays. Moderate.*

Steak **Eli's The Place for Steak.** Enter this Chicago institution
★ through the lounge, where you'll find a piano bar. This room, and the dining room beyond, are softly lit, done in club style, with lots of leather and warm wood. Eli's developed its outstanding reputation through an unflagging commitment to top-quality ingredients prepared precisely to customers' orders and generously served. A selection of complimentary appetizers appears at your table; one is a seductive chopped liver. Prime aged steaks are the specialty here, and you won't find better ones in Chicago. You'll also find a superb, thickly cut veal chop (order it medium-rare for maximum tenderness and succulence) and a splendid calves' liver. For dessert, order Eli's renowned cheesecake, now sold nationally in countless varieties. *215 E. Chicago Ave., tel. 312/642–1393. Reservations required. Jacket required. AE, DC, MC, V. Closed weekend lunch; holidays. Expensive.*

★ **Gene & Georgetti.** Would you give your right arm for a good, old-fashioned piece of prime aged beef or a plate of spaghetti with meat sauce and mushrooms? If so, Gene & Georgetti is for you. Here is one restaurant that hasn't fallen prey to trendiness and does what it has always done as it has always done it, to the immense relief of its customers. Service may be brusque. *500 N. Franklin St., tel. 312/527–3718. Reservations accepted for parties of 4 or more. AE, DC, MC, V. Closed Sun., some holidays. Moderate–Expensive.*

Thai **Pattaya.** Pale green walls and deep green carpeting with Thai paintings and flowers in Thai vases create an unusually pretty ethnic restaurant. In addition to *satay* (grilled, marinated pork on skewers, served with peanut sauce and pickled salad), the appetizers include fresh spring rolls and *peek gai tod* (chicken wings stuffed with ground pork and served with a spicy sauce). Try one of the six noodle entrées, along with the sausage-stuffed squid, steamed and deep fried and served with hot sweet and sour sauce. Banana cooked in coconut milk makes an unusual dessert. *114 W. Chicago Ave., tel. 312/944–3753. AE, DC, MC, V. Closed weekend lunch; holidays. Inexpensive–Moderate.*

Bangkok Cafe/Bangkok II. These sister restaurants, situated around the corner from each other, serve some of the best Thai dishes in the near north. Bangkok II is the larger and more attractive of the two, but both offer dependable versions of the more popular Thai dishes. Diners are served by friendly, helpful waiters who offer good advice on this light, healthful, and sometimes fiery cuisine. *Bangkok Cafe: 416 N. State St., tel. 312/744-1115. Closed weekends. Bangkok II: 9 W. Hubbard St., tel. 312/222-1178. Reservations not required. AE, CB, DC, MC, V. Closed holidays. Inexpensive.*

Ukrainian **Galans.** In the heart of Ukrainian Village, Galans has two dining rooms, one dark, classic, and simple, the other light and contemporary. White tablecloths are covered with butcher paper and paper napkins. Entertainment is provided, and guests in the mood can try out the dance floor between courses. Start with the *varenyky* (boiled dumplings filled with your choice of potato, meat, or sauerkraut) or the *kartoplyanyky* (oven-browned potato pancakes). Those who prefer soup will want to try the *vooshka* (with chicken or borsch dumplings). Entrées include the house specialty, *kovbassa* and *kapusta* (homemade smoked sausages with sauerkraut and potatoes). The sautéed walleye in mushroom sauce comes wrapped in a potato pancake; the broiled walleye is covered with spicy cabbage on a bed of rice. Truly hungry guests may want to try the "Kozak Feast": borsch, house salad, cabbage rolls, filled dumplings, Ukrainian sausage and sauerkraut, skewered beef and pork, potato pancake, coffee, and dessert. Desserts include European rolled pancakes filled with fruit preserves or cheese, hot apple strudel, cheesecake, and a torte of the day. *2212 W. Chicago Ave., tel. 312/292-1000. AE, MC, V. Closed Mon., holidays. Moderate.*

North

Afghani **The Helmand.** Green plants, wall hangings, Persian rugs, and ★ candles on linen tablecloths make The Helmand unusually inviting. As you would expect from Afghanistan's location, the cuisine is influenced by that of North India, yet Middle Eastern influences are obvious as well. The food is richly seasoned but not spicy hot, a pleasing cuisine for diners looking for something different and not ready for high adventure. The menu is divided into appetizers, soups, salads, entrées, and side dishes, but you'll find that some of the same dishes appear in several categories. That's because in Afghanistan people don't divide their meals as Americans do. You might prefer to do as Afganis do and order all your dishes at once. Be sure to try the *aushak* (Afghan ravioli filled with leeks, served on yogurt and topped with ground beef and mint) and the *mantwo* (pastry shell filled with onions and beef, served on yogurt and topped with carrots, yellow split peas, and beef sauce). The *koufta challow* (lamb and beef meatballs with raisins, turmeric, green pepper, green peas, and fresh tomato sauce, served with rice) is delicious. Vegetable lovers will enjoy an order of *sabzi* (literally, vegetable)—spinach sautéed with beef and spices); *bendi* (okra cooked to tenderness in a rich sauce); or *shornakhod* (a salad of potato, chickpeas, and scallions served with cilantro vinaigrette). This is satisfying food, graciously served. *3201 N. Halsted St., tel. 312/935-2447. Weekend reservations accepted. AE, DC, MC, V. Closed lunch; Sun. Moderate.*

Dining North

6400N

Devon

2400W

1600W

1200W

0 ___ 880 yards
0 ___ 800 meters

California

Peterson

Elmdale

Broadway

6000N

1

Maplewood

Lincoln

Virginia

North Channel

Clark St.

Ridge

Hollywood

Lake Michigan

Bryn Mawr

2

Balmoral

3

5200N

Foster

Argyle

4

6 Argyle **5** Argyle

Western

7

Lawrence

Damen

8

Sheridan

Clarendon

Sheridan Rd.

9

North Branch

Chicago River

4400N

Montrose

10

Berteau

Irving Park Rd.

Broadway

11

Kedzie

Lincoln

Ashland

Southport

Clark St.

3600N

California

Addison

12 **13** Halsted **14**

15

16 Roscoe

17

Elston

19

20 **18**

Belmont

22 **21**

JFK Expwy.

23

24 Wellington

2000W

25 **26** Diversey

Sheffield

800W

27

Sheridan Rd.

3200W

2800W

2800N

N

Angelina, **14**
Ann Sather, **22**
Arun's, **11**
The Bangkok, **13**
Casbah, **27**
Cozy Thai, **7**
Da Nicolá, **23**
Ethiopian Village, **15**
Gin Go Gae, **2**
Heidelberger Fass, **10**

The Helmand, **21**
Hue, **4**
Jimmy's Place, **17**
Le Cochonnet, **16**
Little Bucharest, **24**
Machu Picchu, **3**
Mama Desta's Red Sea, **20**
Matsuya, **12**
Mekong, **5**
Mont Blanc Cafe, **19**

Pasteur, **8**
Rio's Casa Iberia, **9**
Shilla, **1**
Tokyo Marina, **6**
Vaudeville, **16**
Yoshi's Cafe, **18**
Yugo Inn, **25**
Zum Deutschen Eck, **26**

Brazilian
★
Rio's Casa Iberia. Two long rooms are softly lit by oil lamps and furbished with white tablecloths, pink napkins, and rose-rimmed plates. The food spans three cuisines: Brazilian, Portuguese, and northern Spanish. Fresh seafood—mussels, clams, shrimp, squid—are plentiful in unusual preparations: clams are paired with smoked ham and sautéed with onions, tomato, green pepper, and parsley for one Brazilian appetizer; a Spanish entrée has fillet of sole cooked on a green garlic sauce and served with clams. The classic dishes associated with Brazil and Portugal are *feijoada* (a stew of black beans with pork, sausage, bacon, dry meat, and spices on rice) and *bacalhau* (grilled salt cod served with a Portuguese-style tomato sauce). There are several soups and two desserts, the traditional *flan* (caramel custard, served here with whipped cream) and *torta de laranja* (orange tart with orange liqueur sauce). *4611 N. Kedzie Ave., tel. 312/588–7800. AE, DC, MC, V. Closed lunch; Mon.; holidays. Moderate.*

Ethiopian
Ethiopian Village. Walking into this storefront, you are greeted immediately by the savory, spicy aromas of Ethiopian food. Soups and salads are available for starters, but the heart of the cuisine is the *wat* (a stew made of beef, chicken, or split peas cooked to tenderness with spices and berbere sauce, a blend of spices on the order of Mexican chili powder or Indian curry powder). These flavorful, messy dishes are eaten with *injera* (a kind of large, spongy pancake made from fermented batter, which functions both as serving medium and silverware). This is not food for the fastidious; those who roll up their sleeves and dig in will have a treat. *3462 N. Clark St., tel. 312/929–8300. AE, DC, MC, V. Closed weekend lunch. Inexpensive–Moderate.*

Mama Desta's Red Sea. Dramatically different from European cooking, the stewlike dishes at Mama Desta's are intriguing combinations of herbs and spices with complex aromas and interesting textures. The food here is flavorful, earthy, and simple. There's no silverware; diners use spongy, slightly sour flat-bread to scoop up the chef's creations. *3216 N. Clark, 312/935–7561. Reservations required for parties of 4 or more. AE, DC, MC, V. Closed Mon. lunch. Inexpensive.*

French
★
Jimmy's Place. Located in an unprepossessing light-industrial strip, Jimmy's Place serves consistently excellent contemporary French cuisine, with a Japanese accent supplied by the chef, Kevin Shikami. White tablecloths are adorned with fresh flowers, and music from grand opera plays softly. Choose from extensive daily specials, or order from a dinner menu that changes monthly and might include such appetizers as cold poached shrimp and avocado with saffron butter, grilled quail on a chartreuse of duck mousse, an assortment of house pâtés and terrines, and a fresh pasta. A fresh fish entrée is offered daily; other selections may include braised sweetbreads in applejack cream sauce with mushrooms and apples and grilled saddle of lamb on a bed of roasted peppers with white wine, shallot, and garlic sauce and sautéed goat cheese. Homemade pastries and desserts round out a splendid meal. *3420 N. Elston Ave., tel. 312/539–2999. Reservations required. CB, DC, MC, V. Closed Sat. lunch; Sun. Expensive–Very Expensive.*

Yoshi's Cafe. This tiny, simply decorated restaurant, with its crisp white linen tablecloths, is the establishment of Yoshi

Katsumura, one of the best chefs in Chicago. His menu tantalizes with such appetizers as pheasant pâté with duck liver mousse and lobster ravioli with champagne-caviar sauce; and such entrées as breast of chicken, sweetbreads, and shiitake mushrooms in filo purse with red pepper coulis. Yet the printed menu tells only half the story, for a daily menu more than doubles the offerings. Soft-shell crab tempura with tomato cilantro sauce is irresistible, as is a cream soup made with three types of mushrooms. The entrées emphasize fish and poultry: steamed woven fillets of fresh Dover sole and salmon on spinach pasta with lobster cream sauce, for example, and grilled quail and squab salad with radicchio and marinated shiitake and oyster mushrooms in warm red wine vinaigrette. Soups, a special salad, and desserts are prepared daily. These are elegant, original creations, skillfully prepared and exquisitely presented. *3257 N. Halsted St., tel. 312/248-6160. Reservations advised, required on weekends. AE, MC, V. Closed lunch; Mon.; holidays. Expensive–Very Expensive.*

Le Cochonnet. Tones of lemon-yellow and lavender light the arched ceilings and walls of Le Cochonnet, where etchings of pigs are hung. The fare is country-style French food, the kind ordinary folk eat. Appetizers recently included a pâté plate and a charcuterie plate (pâtés, sausages, and garnishes), oysters with spicy sausage, and fettucine with tomato and basil. Soups, salads, and egg dishes are available; entrées include chicken marengo (with tomatoes, mushrooms, and onions), loin of pork roasted with garlic and balsamic vinegar, and grilled salmon with chive beurre blanc. A three-course prix fixe dinner is available. Menus change frequently and reflect the season; game is featured in the winter. In warm weather, Le Cochonnet features an outdoor café. *3443 N. Sheffield Ave., tel. 312/525-8888. AE, DC, MC, V. Closed lunch; Mon.; most holidays. Moderate.*

Vaudeville. Connected to Le Cochonnet, this smaller, more casual café features soups, salads, sandwiches, pasta dishes, and simple country-French fare. Cream of carrot and other vegetable soups are delicately seasoned; included in the pasta offerings is a highly spiced linguine with sausage, sun-dried tomatoes, and mushrooms. Crusty fresh sourdough rolls are served with dinner. Desserts are inconsistent, but the flourless chocolate cake or the crème brûlée should satisfy anyone's sweet tooth. A nice selection of foreign beers complements the small wine list. The walls are decorated with posters from Broadway musicals, and original Broadway cast albums are played continuously. An outdoor patio is open during the summer. Service is genial but erratic. *3443 N. Sheffield, tel. 312/975-7800. AE, CB, DC, MC, V. Sat. and Sun. brunch. Closed Mon. Moderate.*

Mont Blanc Cafe & Patisserie. A tiny, airy café and bakery, Mont Blanc offers a small menu of elegant sandwiches, a salade Niçoise, and light entrées. The pastry alone is worth a trip. The shop's Japanese owner, trained as a pastry chef in France, opened the patisserie when he found restaurant owners in this country reluctant to hire a Japanese pastry chef. He has been so successful that Mont Blanc now supplies its baked goods to a number of Chicago's finest restaurants. If you have forgotten (or never knew) what real butter-cream icing tastes like, come here. *1114 W. Belmont Ave., tel. 312/525-7339. No credit cards. Closed weekday lunch; Mon. Inexpensive.*

German **Heidelberger Fass.** Although brighter than the typical beer hall, the Heidelberger Fass, with its stained glass, china, and menus in medieval German style, evokes the feeling of being on a street in Germany. The menu includes American favorites (turkey salad sandwich, poached or pan-fried trout, broiled filet mignon) and such German delights as liver dumplings, Kassler ribs (smoked pork loin, cooked to order), two types of sausage (veal and a veal/pork/beef combination), and sauerbraten. Specialties include the unusual venison schnitzel, in mushrooms with red wine sauce, and pheasant braised in its own gravy. The quality of the food can be uneven. *4300 N. Lincoln Ave., tel. 312/478–2486. Reservations advised. AE, CB, DC, MC, V. Closed Sun. lunch; Tues. Moderate.*

Zum Deutschen Eck. Here is a cozy German eatery where stained glass complements dark wood and costumed waitresses create a warm, comfortable atmosphere. The fare includes the typically German homemade *suelze* (head cheese), herring salad, potato pancakes, *Koenigsberger klops* (German meatballs), a *schlact platte* combination of bratwurst, knackwurst, and smoked pork loin, and *schnitzel à la jaeger* (cutlet sautéed in red wine with green pepper, onion, fresh mushroom, and red pepper sauce). Old favorites are also featured: sauerbraten, half roast duckling, Wiener schnitzel. Most entrées are served with whipped potato and sauerkraut; a few come with buttered noodles or spaetzle. *2914 N. Southport Ave., tel. 312/525–8389. Reservations advised. AE, CB, DC, MC, V. Closed mid–late Jan. Moderate.*

Italian **Da Nicola.** An old-world kind of restaurant, Da Nicola rises well above the usual American-style Italian food. Among the excellent pastas are ravioli filled with a puree of *porcini* mushrooms and a *rotolo di pasta* (a large sheet of pasta filled with spinach, ground meat, and cheeses, rolled, poached, then sliced and served). Portions are generous, but dollar-conscious diners will find Da Nicola a bit pricey compared to many Italian restaurants. *3114 N. Lincoln Ave., tel. 312/935–8000. Reservations required on weekends. AE, MC. No lunch. Closed Tues. Moderate.*

Angelina. The high-funk appeal of this restaurant attracts a loyal following among Chicago's hipsters and makes for some fascinating, offbeat people watching. Pastas, carefully prepared with fresh, quality ingredients, are the most reliable choices. The service can be erratic, and the wait may be long. Hang out in Joe's, a friendly neighborhood tavern next door, while waiting for a table. *3561 N. Broadway, tel. 312/935–5933. No reservations. MC, V. Closed lunch; holidays. Inexpensive– Moderate.*

Japanese **Matsuya.** This small storefront restaurant has a sushi bar, wood paneling, brown tile floor, and a wood floor-to-ceiling screen in front of the kitchen. Sushi and an extensive choice of appetizers dominate the menu: Deep-fried spicy chicken wings, steamed spinach with sesame, whitefish with white smelt roe, seafood and vegetables on skewers, and dumplings with sauce are just a few. Tempura and fish and meat teriyaki dishes and a few noodle dishes and bowl-of-rice dishes (with toppings of your choice) round out the menu. *3469 N. Clark St., tel. 312/248–2677. MC, V. Closed weekday lunch; holidays. Moderate.*

Tokyo Marina. Many Japanese restaurants strive for a gracious, refined atmosphere to complement the careful presentation of a small quantity of rather expensive food. Tokyo Marina is a refreshing contrast to this model, a welcome choice for Americans who want to try Japanese food but are put off by the excessive refinement, delicacy, and price of some establishments. Customers seat themselves at wood tables in this bright, 30-table restaurant and sushi bar. A large menu board covers one wall in the dining area, and Japanese paintings are on other walls. Conversations in Japanese and in English mingle in an amiable din. Servers scurry around, occasionally ordering each other about. Like the atmosphere, the food has a certain robustness. One-pot dishes brim with ingredients; try the nabe with crab, the better part of a whole, tender Dungeness crab braised in broth with assorted vegetables, tofu, and noodles—succulent, filling, and a bargain at the price. The several dozen entrées include preparations of fresh raw or cooked tuna, yellowtail, mackerel, red snapper, and lobster; "bowl" dishes of beef, chicken, pork, shrimp, or eel served on rice; wheat or buckwheat noodles with assorted ingredients in broth; and the familiar beef or chicken teriyaki, tempuras of all kinds, or sukiyaki. Portions are more generous than dainty. *5058 N. Clark St., tel. 312/878–2900. Reservations not required. MC, V. Inexpensive–Moderate.*

Korean **Shilla.** Exquisite tropical fish swim in a saltwater tank as you wait to be seated. To your right is the bar; ahead is a large dining room with sushi bar at the front, flanked by individual dining rooms accommodating intimate groups or larger parties. Americans may be steered to one of these rooms on the assumption that they will want mainly grilled foods prepared at their table. Grilled dishes are available in the main dining room, too, and those who prefer dining with other customers and hope to avoid the preparation process should ask for a table in the main room. The menu is enormous; in addition to grilled dishes, there are many noodle preparations, stewlike offerings, and stir-fries. Since the "appetizers" come in entrée-size portions (at entrée-size prices), you will want to exercise caution in the number of dishes you order. The Korean pancake is excellent, and the fried oysters are not to be missed. *Seng sun japtang* is the Korean equivalent of bouillabaisse. Entrées are served with an assortment of Korean relishes, including *kimchee*, the spicy pickled cabbage that accompanies every meal in Korea (ask for it hot if you like it that way). Shilla's food is authentic; the large number of Korean guests attests to that. *5930 N. Lincoln Ave., tel. 312/275–5930. Reservations advised. AE, MC, V. Moderate.*

★ **Gin Go Gae.** Two dining rooms, one casual, one more formally done with red carpeting and Oriental art, accommodate a large number of guests, many of them Korean. The food is plentiful and delicious; the servers are warm and attentive. Entrées come with *kimchee* (choose mild or spicy-hot) and an assortment of relishes that might make a meal in itself. Try the onion pancakes, here served with a sauce abundant with Oriental vegetables. The more adventurous diner will sample the noodles in cold broth. *5433 N. Lincoln Ave., tel. 312/334–3895. AE, MC, V. Inexpensive.*

Middle Eastern **Casbah.** There's nothing nouveau or trendy about the long-established Casbah. The deep dining room is done in red carpeting with Persian, Turkish, and Islamic trays and carpets hanging from the walls and ceiling. The menu presents a comprehensive selection of well-prepared Middle Eastern favorites. Appetizers include spinach or cheese in flaky pastry; grape leaves stuffed with rice, walnuts, and currants; *hummos* (chick-pea and sesame puree); *baba ghannouj;* and *Imam bayeldi* ("the Imam fainted"—presumably with delight—a braised eggplant with onions, tomatoes, and green peppers, served cold). Entrées are more unusual: *pastilla* (shredded cornish hen baked in almond sauce and wrapped in flaky pastry) and veal Mount Olive (sautéed tenderloin of veal with olives and onions in cream-brandy sauce) are two choices. The couscous—steamed grains of semolina served with a stew of vegetables or vegetables and chicken—is a welcome choice, even though its origins are more North African than Middle Eastern. There is a daily fish special, and three Middle Eastern desserts, including the favorite baklava, round out the menu. *514 W. Diversey Ave., tel. 312/935-7570. Reservations advised, required on weekends. AE, DC, MC, V. Closed lunch. Moderate.*

Peruvian **Machu Picchu.** Clean white walls complement beautiful Peruvian rugs; fresh flowers and red napkins adorn each table. The owner, Moses Asturrizaga, refers to the food as "nouveau Peruvian"; its spicy heat has been toned down in deference to American tastes, but all dishes can be ordered extra hot. Appetizers include *ceviche* and *escabeche* (chicken fillet marinated in onion sauce). For an entrée, you might have the duck in Amaretto sauce; in Peru it is served with sliced hot chilies, so that each bite of duck is accompanied by a jab of heat. The less adventurous diner may prefer the fish in tarragon sauce. The bread is heated before serving; the soups and desserts are limited. *5427 N. Clark St., tel. 312/769-0455. Reservations advised. AE, DC, MC, V. Closed lunch; Sun., Mon., holidays. Moderate-Expensive.*

Romanian **Little Bucharest.** A cozy, simple room adorned with stained-glass windows, Little Bucharest serves comforting foods Romanian style. The soups are hearty—chicken, oxtail, or veal meatball with dumplings and vegetables; a "European style" salad is the only other appetizer. Veal paprikash, *tocana à la Bucharest,* and beef goulash are prominent on the menu, which includes three veal roll preparations, several baked chicken entrées, four pork chop offerings, two sausage dishes, and the obligatory steak for the diner who will eat nothing else. An attractive entrée selection of stuffed vegetables (choose from eggplant, red peppers, green peppers, and cabbage) is available. Daily specials supplement the menu. *3001 N. Ashland Ave., tel. 312/929-8640. AE, MC, V. Closed Sun., Thanksgiving. Inexpensive.*

Serbian **Yugo Inn.** The hunter-green walls of the L-shaped dining room complement exposed brick and colorful table settings to create a cozy atmosphere. An atrium is decorated with Yugoslavian art. Come here only when you're hungry, for dinner begins with generous portions of complimentary appetizers and bread, and if you finish them off before your dinner comes, you'll find the bowls refilled. The menu offers several items that will look familiar to those who know Greek food, yet the preparations are a bit different. *Sarma* is cabbage leaves (not the grape leaves found in the Middle East) stuffed with rice and ground beef. *Musaka* is the classic preparation of eggplant and ground beef. The tripice, an unusual treat, is tripe simmered with garlic and sherry. Among several veal dishes you'll find a stuffed veal garnished with vegetables. The *cevapcici* (the classic Serbian sausage made of ground beef and veal) is served grilled. A small selection of desserts, for those who still have room, includes crepes, chocolate rum torte, and cheesecake. *2824 N. Ashland Ave., tel. 312/348–6444. Reservations advised. No credit cards. Closed lunch; holidays; week after Christmas. Inexpensive–Moderate.*

Swedish **Ann Sather.** Of this pair of Swedish restaurants, the North Clark Street house is the original, located in the heart of Andersonville, once a close-knit Swedish community. Today Asians and Middle Easterners have largely replaced the Swedes, though a few specialty stores remain. The large, light, airy Ann Sather restaurants emphasize in home-style food and service. Both are popular for weekend breakfasts. Specialties include homemade cinnamon rolls (served with every order), potato sausage, and chicken croquettes; a full sandwich menu is offered. A Swedish sampler lets you try duck breast with lingonberry glaze, a Swedish meatball, potato sausage, dumpling, and sauerkraut. Very reasonable entrée prices include an appetizer (Swedish fruit soup and pickled herring are among them), two side dishes (choose from Swedish brown beans, homemade applesauce, mashed or boiled potatoes, pickled beets, and more), and dessert: homemade fruit or cream pies, puddings, cakes, and ice creams. Daily specials augment the standard menu. *5207 N. Clark St., tel. 312/271–6677. 929 W. Belmont Ave., tel. 312/348–2378. MC, V. Closed holidays. Inexpensive.*

Thai **Arun's.** The owner and chef Arun Sampanvivat opened his orig-
★ inal storefront restaurant almost on a lark while doing doctoral studies in political science at the University of Chicago. While he knew he was a good cook, the success of his restaurant— many think it the best of Chicago's more than 80 Thai establishments—astonished him. Influenced by both Chinese and Indian cuisines, Thai food nevertheless has its own characteristics. Lemongrass, *kha* (a type of ginger), lime juice and leaves, and basil figure heavily in the cuisine, as do sauces based on coconut milk. Some dishes are spicy hot; let your server know if you prefer dishes mild or very hot. Appetizers include the familiar pork *satay* (marinated, grilled pork strips served with peanut sauce and cucumber) and egg rolls and the less familiar *yum wunsen* (glass noodles with cooked shrimp and ground pork, spiced with scallion, cilantro, chili peppers, and lime) and the seafood casserole in red curry (not to be confused with the flavor of Indian curry powder) on steamed Napa cabbage leaves. Soups include the classic *tom yum goong* (hot and sour shrimp soup in lime broth with chili peppers) and a chicken soup in coconut milk (flavored with kha, chili peppers, and lime). The *kai yang* is a deboned thigh of chicken spiced with garlic and coriander, grilled and served with sweet chili sauce. Shrimp or fish is a must; try the garlic prawns, the whole fried red snapper, or the squid in hot pepper sauce with garlic and chili peppers. The extensive basic menu is supplemented by daily specials. The two-level dining room has lots of natural wood, complemented by Thai art and a small art gallery—a far cry from the typical storefront ethnic restaurant. *4156 N. Kedzie Ave., tel. 312/539–1909. AE, DC, MC, V. Closed lunch; Mon., holidays. Moderate.*

The Bangkok. This comely and sophisticated little spot goes well beyond the typical storefront Thai restaurant to present some unusual and varied renditions of Thai cuisine. Although the Bangkok does serve hot and spicy dishes, many of the dishes depend on subtle flavorings rather than the one-note incendiary spicing found at some lesser Thai eateries. This restaurant is well worth sampling by serious food folks. *3542 N. Halsted St., tel. 312/327–2870. Reservations not required. Dress: casual. Weekend brunch buffet. AE, DC, MC, Moderate.*

Cozy Thai. One of the few storefront Thai restaurants in town to offer live Thai and American music on weekends, Cozy Thai is also one of the city's best. The chef spent several years at Arun's, another well-regarded establishment, not too far away. The atmosphere is sophisticated: Fresh flowers decorate each table, and the servers wear black and white. Dishes to try include *kai tod* (crisp fried chicken); spicy pad ped catfish; chicken wings stuffed with ground pork, garlic, bean thread, and black mushrooms; and pork satay. Attractive vegetable garnishes make classic Thai dishes look as good as they taste. *4834 N. Damen, tel. 312/334–7300. Reservations advised. AE, DC, MC, V. Closed weekend lunch. Moderate.*

Vietnamese **Hue.** The tiny storefront Hue restaurant, decorated with Vietnamese artifacts, promises "Vietnamese cooking with a French influence." One might note that many of the dishes have been influenced by Chinese cuisine as well. The food is carefully prepared and tasty, and dishes can be prepared mild or hot, low salt, and no MSG, according to your needs and preferences. *1138 W. Argyle St., tel. 312/275–4044. MC, V. Inexpensive–Moderate.*

★ **Mekong.** Mekong feels a bit crowded even on the rare occasion when it's empty. Many tables have been squeezed in, the aisles are narrow and winding, and ornate lamps overhang the tables. Now add the people: Masses of them jam the small waiting area on Saturday night, adding to the din of eaters chomping away, servers bustling to and fro, and dishes clattering in the partly open kitchen. Snacks are brought to the waiting multitudes to stave off hunger, but waits can seem long even so. Yet the food is worth the ordeal. Try the lemony Vietnamese-style barbecued beef (not at all like Texas barbecue), thinly sliced and served just at room temperature with salad; or have the whole crab in sauce; or try one of the many noodle preparations. *4953 N. Broadway, tel. 312/271–0206. AE, MC, V. Closed Mon. and Wed. Inexpensive–Moderate.*

Pasteur. Pasteur was opened just a few years ago by a family of Vietnamese refugees who arrived here with few resources, little English, and a need to earn money; their beginning was rocky, but they stuck with it and made it a success. The extensive menu includes appetizers of whole sautéed Dungeness crab, the classic shrimp paste wrapped around sugarcane, and the house specialty, a deep-fried shrimp cake served with fresh salad and special sauce. Noodle lovers will be delighted with the selection: three rice noodle soups, five egg noodle soups, five fried rice noodle dishes, five soft rice noodle dishes, and three fried egg noodle dishes. Shrimp, poultry, beef, pork, and fish selections are available. Many of the translated descriptions of the dishes sound like familiar Chinese preparations; the difference is in the seasoning and spicing. Vietnamese food relies on lemongrass and fish sauce—two ingredients not used in Chinese cuisine—to give dishes and dipping sauces their distinctive flavor. *4759 N. Sheridan Rd., tel. 312/271–6673. AE, MC, V. Closed Mon. lunch; some holidays. Inexpensive–Moderate.*

Downtown

American **Printer's Row.** The owner and chef, Michael Foley, opened this
★ stylish restaurant when the historic Printer's Row district was
just beginning to show signs of a renaissance after decades of
decay. Accordingly, his is now the established institution in
what has become a very attractive urban neighborhood of renovated loft buildings and gracious older apartment houses. The
lounge, to one side of the entryway, and the restaurant, to the
other, are done in warm woods and brown tones that contrast
pleasingly with the neutral walls and crisp white tablecloths.
The restaurant has consistently been one of the most interesting and satisfying in Chicago, largely because Foley constantly
refreshes his menu with new ideas and new approaches to cuisine. A current menu emphasizes game: braised pheasant with
black currants, grilled mallard duck with radicchio and endive,
cabbage, and venison sausage. There are several fish preparations and a ragout of sweetbreads with aromatic vegetables and
orzo pasta. Daily specials augment the menu; a "Simple Pleas-
ures" dish is low in sodium and fat. Cheese, a dessert menu, and
an excellent selection of fine ports, cognacs, and armagnacs are
available. This is one of Chicago's outstanding restaurants, and
it is substantially less expensive than many other restaurants
that offer a similar level of cuisine. *550 S. Dearborn St., tel. 312/
461–0780. Jacket advised. Reservations advised, required on
weekends. AE, DC, MC, V. Closed Sat. lunch; Sun. Expensive.*

Hinky Dink Kenna's. Basically a bar and burger joint, comfortable Hinky Dink Kenna's also offers pastas, seafood, salads,
and special entrées. This clublike restaurant, decorated in dark
wood and green leather, is a good spot to relax after a hard day
of shopping. Be sure to read about the restaurant's namesake
(an infamous turn-of-the-century Chicago political boss) on the
menu; and take in the photos of old Chicago that line the walls.
*Down Under at Marshall Field, Randolph and Wabash, tel.
312/781–3192. Reservations advised for lunch. AE, MC, V.
Closed Sun. Moderate.*

The Walnut Room. Wood archways and beams and Oriental
screens complement this carpeted, Victorian-style dining room
at Marshall Field. Long a haven for weary shoppers and business lunchers who seek a relaxing, unhurried spot, the Walnut
Room offers beef tenderloin tips Stroganoff, Field's own chick-
en pot pie, roast free-range chicken, scallop and vegetable fettucine, and a fresh fish of the day, broiled to order. The
extensive salad and sandwich selection includes Cobb salad,
Szechuan beef and noodle salad served in crisp potato basket,
several hamburger preparations, and a club sandwich. Among
the dessert possibilities are pudding, pie, cake, torte, and ice
cream sundaes. The traditional tea served at 3 PM boasts Field's
own Scotch scones with Devonshire clotted cream and jam. Complete bar service is available. *Marshall Field, 111 N. State St.,
tel. 312/781–1000. AE, MC, V. Closed dinner; Sun; holidays.
Moderate.*

Zincs. Two restaurants in one, Zincs has both a casual café,
done in marble and tile with a large bar area, and a more formal
dining room with parquet floors and floral curtains. The menu
is American with nouvelle and French accents, featuring such
appetizers as mussels stuffed and baked in a tomato herb butter; Vermont goat cheese wrapped in a flour tortilla with avoca-

Army & Lou's, **31**
The Berghoff, **10**
Chee King, **20**
Chon y Chano, **23**
Courtyards of Plaka, **15**
Crystal Palace, **1**
Edwardo's, **30**
Emperor's Choice, **22**
The Everest Room, **9**
Gennaro's, **14**
Harold's Chicken Shack, **26**
Healthy Food, **24**
Hinky Dink Kenna's, **3**
It's Greek to Me, **11**
Lou Mitchell's, **8**
New Rosebud, **13**
Nick's Fishmarket, **6**
Nuevo Leon, **17**
The Parthenon, **12**
Playa Azul, **18**
Printer's Row, **16**
Ribs'n'Bibs, **27**
Seven Treasures, **21**
Soul Queen, **33**
Tap & Growler, **7**
Taste of Jamaica, **32**
Ten-Tsuna, **28**
Three Happiness, **19**
TJ's, **29**
Trattoria # 10, **4**
University Gardens, **25**
The Walnut Room, **2**
Zincs, **5**

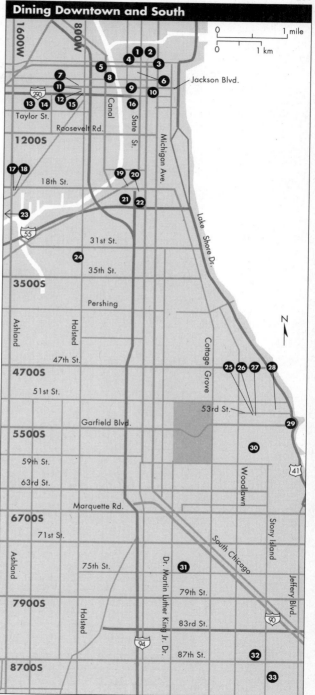

Dining Downtown and South

do, roasted peppers, and pine nuts; and a daily special pâté maison. The salad selection includes two Cobb salads and one of grilled duck breast with mixed greens and raspberry vinaigrette. Entrées are simple bistro style, with such dishes as salmon steak grilled and served with tomato béarnaise sauce and sautéed breast of chicken with cranberry-ginger sauce. The food is well prepared, the atmosphere relaxing. *555 W. Madison St., tel. 312/902-2900. No reservations in café. AE, DC, MC, V. No lunch weekends in dining room. Moderate.*

Tap & Growler. The first of the new breed of "brew pubs," Tap & Growler renews a local tradition that had ended with the closing of the last local brewery in 1977. In the late 1800s, when the building that houses this establishment was constructed, beer was made on the premises of small neighborhood pubs, hauled from the basement in pails called growlers, and served fresh to patrons. This large, bright, contemporary pub displays its brewery in a glassed-in area so that guests can watch the process as well as taste the results. The same approach extends to the exposed kitchen, and a long wood bar and marble flooring complete the setting. Tap & Growler brews four beers: a golden lager, a golden beer, an Irish ale, and a bitter. *901 W. Jackson St., tel. 312/829-4141. AE, DC, MC, V. Closed Sat. lunch; Sun. Inexpensive-Moderate.*

Crystal Palace. The Crystal Palace at Marshall Field is a replica of an old-time ice-cream parlor. Stained-glass windows help you forget the sales floor beyond as you indulge yourself in fantastic ice-cream confections: The Frango Grande is Field's own Frango mint soft-serve ice cream topped with Frango mint chocolate liqueur; Berries in a Blanket is a crepe filled with strawberry ice cream topped with whipped cream and fresh sliced strawberries. A chocolate corner offers six selections just for chocoholics. Quiche and a choice of four sandwiches on croissant are available for those who imagine they need something else, and there are coffees and phosphates. *Marshall Field, 111 N. State St., tel. 312/781-1000. AE, MC, V. Inexpensive.*

★ **Lou Mitchell's.** Be prepared to stand in line, and be assured that the wait is worth it. Management will give boxes of Milk Duds to the women and girls in your group, and when a spot is available for you, you're likely to be seated at a long communal table (smaller tables may require a longer wait). The waitresses have a rough and hearty style that gets everyone served promptly, if briskly. Fourteen omelets, made from eggs so fresh they remind you how eggs should taste, and cooked in lots of butter, are the centerpiece of a menu that includes pancakes, French toast, and Belgian waffles for breakfast; sandwiches, salads, and a few hot plates for lunch. People flock to Lou Mitchell's because the ingredients are top-quality, everything is fresh, and everything is homemade—the Greek bread, the raisin toast, the orange marmalade, the pies, the pound cake, and the pudding with cream. Portions are large, yet the food is so good that people routinely, and with only a little embarrassment, stuff themselves. Breakfast is served all day long. *565 W. Jackson Blvd., tel. 312/939-3111. No reservations. No credit cards. Closed dinner; Sun.; holidays. Inexpensive.*

French **The Everest Room.** The Everest Room, in the La Salle Street
★ Club in the heart of the financial district, is probably the best restaurant in Chicago at this writing. Come here for a superb dinner, graciously served, and expect to pay accordingly. Chef

Jean Joho has a personal approach that places dishes squarely in the classic French tradition yet appeals to contemporary tastes. Hors d'oeuvres include a ballotine of steamed quail with mushroom mousse and truffled salad vinaigrette, an herbed terrine of pheasant and partridge with truffled vinaigrette, and a crayfish cake with leek confit and tomato. Soups are prepared daily, as is a seasonal salad; another salad has garden vegetables and Illinois goat cheese sautéed in olive oil. Entrées change frequently; among recent offerings were fish fillet wrapped and roasted in potato with thyme; yellowfin tuna tournedos sautéed medium-rare with shallots and rice wine; and sautéed breast of squab with truffle coulis and Napa cabbage. An eight-course, fixed-price degustation menu is also available for a minimum of two diners. A fine wine list complements the menu. *440 S. La Salle St., tel. 312/663–8920. Jacket required. Reservations required. AE, DC, MC, V. Closed Mon. dinner; Sat. lunch; Sun., holidays. Very Expensive.*

German   **The Berghoff.** This Chicago institution has a splendid bar with Berghoff Beer on tap, oak paneling, a bustling beer hall ambience, and a huge dining room that is usually full. Because the Berghoff is a popular lunch spot with the business crowd, you can expect a wait of 15 minutes or so at midday. A menu of German classics (Wiener schnitzel, sauerbraten) is augmented by American favorites. The seeded rye bread is outstanding. The food and service (notwithstanding the formal dress of the very correct waiters) are a little too mass-produced for fine dining, and the brisk (some say brusque) efficiency with which orders are taken, food appears, and plates are whisked away does not conduce to lingering over coffee or conversation. Yet the food is competently prepared and occasionally excellent, and the portions are generous. *17 W. Adams St., tel. 312/427–3170. Reservations accepted for parties of 6 or more. AE, DC, MC, V. Moderate.*

Greek   **Courtyards of Plaka.** With its salmon-color walls, red-tile floors, aquamarine bar, white-clothed tables, and live music, Courtyards of Plaka is one of the most sophisticated Greek restaurants in Chicago. Friendly servers work hard to make sure everyone has a good time. Appetizers include the ubiquitous *saganaki* (fried cheese), *melizzanoszlata* (a purée of lightly spiced eggplant to be spread on Greek bread), and *taramosalata* (fish-roll salad). Also available, though it doesn't appear on the menu, is *skordalia* (garlic-flavored mashed potatoes). Entrées include all of the standard Greek offerings, plus a variety of creative dishes not found elsewhere. Given the dressed-up decor, careful preparation, and reasonable prices, Plaka offers the best value of all the Greektown restaurants. *340 S. Halsted St., tel. 312/263–0767. Reservations not required. AE, DC, MC, V. Moderate.*

It's Greek to Me. A pretty restaurant with wood floors and walls that are stucco below with murals of the sky and a town above, It's Greek to Me has some of the best Greek food you'll find in Chicago. Familiar appetizers of fish roe salad, flaming cheese, and cucumber with garlic in yogurt are supplemented with the more unusual squid or octopus in wine sauce, potato and garlic puree, and eggplant stuffed with onions and raisins in tomato sauce. You can have musaka and *pastitsio* (baked macaroni with meat and béchamel sauce) here, but you might prefer lamb stuffed with artichokes, pine nuts, feta cheese, peas, and tomatoes. A large selection of Greek pastries and desserts is available. Ingredients here are of unusually high quality. *306 S. Halsted St., tel. 312/977–0022. Reservations required. AE, DC, MC, V. Moderate.*

The Parthenon. The Parthenon pleases with well-seasoned, well-prepared classic Greek dishes. The large menu offers all your favorites: *saganaki* (flaming cheese), cheese pies in phyllo pastry, *taramosalata* (fish roe salad), yogurt and cucumber, and chilled octopus in wine sauce to start, followed by stuffed vine leaves, pastitsio, shish kebab, roast young pig, and Greek sausage. The specialty of the house is the lamb, barbecued, braised, roasted, or, best of all, lamb with artichokes in *avgolemono* (egg-lemon) sauce. The roomy, carpeted dining room, adorned with a mural of the Agora on one wall and photographs of Greece on others, is warm and comfortable. The wine selection is large. *314 S. Halsted St., tel. 312/726–2407. Reservations required for 5 or more. AE, DC, MC, V. Inexpensive–Moderate.*

Italian **Trattoria No. 10.** Quarry-tile floors; theatrical lighting; and a burnt-orange, red, and ocher color-scheme combine to give this former basement boiler room the charm and warmth of an outdoor café. One of the signature dishes at this eclectic Italian restaurant is ravioli with exotic fillings of lobster or mushrooms. The pastas are fresh, and the interesting antipasti include sea scallops with orange-fennel relish, and *rotolo di mozzarella* (homemade mozzarella cheese rolled around layers of pesto and prosciutto). The steaks, chops, and fish dishes are good but are not standouts on the menu. For dessert, try the *tirami su* (liquered-lady fingers topped with mascarpone mousse) or the triple-chocolate cannoli. *10 N. Dearborn, tel. 312/984–1718. Reservations advised. AE, MC, V. Closed weekend lunch; Sun. Expensive.*

New Rosebud Cafe. This extremely popular restaurant specializes in good old-fashioned, southern Italian cuisine. One of the best red sauces in town can be found here, and the roasted peppers, homemade sausage, and exquisitely prepared pastas are not to be missed. The wait for a table can stretch to an hour or more, despite confirmed reservations, but those with patience will find that the meal is well worth the wait. *1500 W. Taylor, tel. 312/942–1117. Reservations advised. AE, DC, MC, V. Closed weekend lunch; Sun. Moderate.*

Gennaro's. This unassuming bar and hearty southern-Italian restaurant is a Chicago classic. Customers must be buzzed in through a locked entrance to wait for a free table. Among the exceptional homemade pastas are egg noodles with butter and cheese, and stuffed eggplant served with spaghetti. The antipasto plate makes a good appetizer, as does the rich escarole soup. The homemade chocolate cannoli is a good bet for dessert. *1352 W. Taylor, tel. 312/243–1035. No reservations. No credit cards. Closed lunch; Mon.; Wed. Inexpensive.*

Seafood **Nick's Fishmarket.** This dark room, rich with leather and wood, adorned with sports paintings and fresh flowers on white linen tablecloths, has the feel of a traditional club. Doing business at dinner is facilitated by the presence of telephone jacks at each booth. Nick's is distinguished for its range of fresh fish and seafood. In addition to such standbys as sole, trout, and salmon, there are several preparations of fresh catfish, calamari, crab legs, scallops, frog legs, Hawaiian opakapaka, ahi, and abalone. Although the ingredients are fresh and top-quality, they are sometimes overcooked; ask for your fish underdone to insure moistness and tenderness. A porterhouse steak, a fillet, baby beef liver, and several pastas are available for diners who just won't eat fish. *1 First National Plaza, tel. 312/621–0200. Jacket and tie advised. Reservations advised. AE, DC, MC, V. Closed Sun.; holidays. Expensive.*

South

American **TJ's.** White linen tablecloths, banquettes looking out on a landscaped pool area, and a leisurely dining experience give TJ's a comfortable ambience. The unusual appetizers include sautéed wild mushrooms and fried calamari. While steaks and broiled entrées are available, you will do well to order one of the fish preparations in which the restaurant specializes—blackened redfish, for example, or salmon in phyllo pastry. A selection of reasonably priced wines is available. *5500 S. Lake Shore Dr., tel. 312/643–3600. Reservations advised. AE, MC, V. Closed some holidays. Moderate–Expensive.*

Harold's Chicken Shack. The name says it all: This cramped hole-in-the-wall carryout serves up perhaps the best fried chicken in the city, crisply coated on the outside and moist and tender within. Although the restaurant is part of a chain, Harold maintained control of all the branches and insisted that his techniques and recipes be followed everywhere. For an unusual snack treat, try the deep-fried gizzards in hot sauce (they can become an addiction). If you can wait that long, take your bag to the University of Chicago quadrangle or Promontory Point and have a picnic on the grass. *1364 E. 53rd St., tel. 312/667–9835. No credit cards. Inexpensive.*

Ribs 'n' Bibs. This is primarily a carryout-and-delivery establishment. Hickory-smoked here means just what it says; the mouth-watering aroma wafts over 53rd Street when the wind is right. Ribs cook slowly for hours, so they're lean and meaty, and the flavor goes right through. The sauce is unbeatable. Try the Ranch Owner's Smorgasbord when you're ready to sample the range of smoked delights: ribs, chicken, sausages, and onion rings come with it. All orders are served on bread, South Side style, with fries and cole slaw. *5300 S. Dorchester Ave., tel. 312/493–0400. No credit cards. Inexpensive.*

Caribbean **Taste of Jamaica.** If you've traveled in the Caribbean and eaten indigenous food there, one look at this menu will activate your salivary glands. There are no appetizers; instead, try one of the soups: pumpkin, pepper pot, manish water, conch, red peas, pigeon gungu peas, or tripe. Then move on to the curried goat, the ox tail and broad beans, the jerk chicken, or the brown-stewed fish. Nowhere else in Chicago can you find codfish and ackee or codfish and *callaloo* (that wonderful spinachlike vegetable). Entrées are served with rice, salad, and fried plantain. Side orders include rice and peas, yam, green banana dumpling, fried plantain, patties (meat pies), codfish fritters, jonny cake (chewy deep-fried-dough bread), and an astonishing variety of buns, flavored breads, and cakes (carrot, banana, dark wine rum fruit cake, coconut fruit drops). Soursop and other juices, fruit nectars, frosties, lemonade and limeade, and tamarind-passion fruit drink are available. *1448 E. 87th St., tel. 312/978–6300. BYOB. Reservations advised on Sun. No credit cards. Closed holidays. Inexpensive.*

Chinese **Emperor's Choice.** The husband and wife team who run this sophisticated but comfortable restaurant set out to demonstrate that Chinese seafood specialties can go well beyond shrimp with Chinese vegetables. They succeeded admirably; the seafood dishes are fresh and expertly prepared. *2238 S. Wentworth Ave., tel. 312/225–8800. Dress: casual. Reservations not required. AE, MC, V. Moderate.*

Chee King. This bright, spacious restaurant on one of Chinatown's side streets offers Cantonese and Szechuan cuisine, which means there's something here for everyone. The menu is large: a dozen appetizers (ranging from Cantonese barbecued pork to chilled jellyfish); as many soups (they come in three serving sizes); beef, chicken, pork, and noodle dishes; and a truly incredible selection of seafood and fish—prepared sweet and sour, steamed whole, in black bean and garlic sauce, with chili sauce, and in other ways. Chee King's is unusually well prepared and tasty food. *216 W. 22nd Pl., tel. 312/842–7777. AE, MC, V. Inexpensive.*

Seven Treasures. Those who love Chinese food will want to visit Seven Treasures. But not for the ambience; the cavernous room with its Formica-topped tables is pure 1950s cafeteria style. Reject the large menu filled with standard dishes for tourists and ask for the unprepossessing noodle menu. The dumplings with oyster sauce (plump, succulent mouthfuls of chopped shrimp, tree ear mushrooms, and other goodies enclosed in a noodle wrapper and steamed) would be an appetizer elsewhere; here all your dishes come at once. With the dumplings, try the noodles with shredded pork and onion (Peking style) soup: long, linguinelike strands of noodle mixed with bits of pork and vegetable in a richly flavored broth. Have an order of chow fun: wide rice noodles steamed and then fried so the outsides are crisp while the insides are soft, topped with beef, barbecued pork, or a meat of your choice mixed with Napa cabbage and other vegetables. Order chow mein, and you'll get tender, juicy morsels of chicken or beef with delicate braised Chinese cabbage in sauce, served over "two sides brown" noodles (a large pile of noodles lightly crisped on the outside while remaining soft and chewy within). Be sure to have a plate or two of Chinese fried bread, the long rolls that taste like unsweetened crullers. Even for a family with hungry teenagers in tow, it's hard to spend as much as $10 each, including tax, at Seven Treasures. Portions are large and the noodle dishes are filling, so order accordingly. *2312 S. Wentworth Ave., tel. 312/225–2668. BYOB. No credit cards. Inexpensive.*

Three Happiness. It's possible that folks eat lunch and dinner at Three Happiness, but those in the know go for the Sunday dim sum brunch, served from 10 AM to 2 PM. The restaurant opens at 10 AM, the crowd having begun to form at 9:30, and both floors of the spacious restaurant are full within minutes of opening. Try for a table near the door; that's closest to where the serving carts emerge from the kitchen. Servers wheel the carts around the dining room, stopping when you flag them down. Each cart is laden with six or so individual orders of dim sum: bite-size morsels of noodle dough wrapped around various fillings of pork or shrimp, then steamed or fried; deep-fried taro root stuffed with pork; rice cake filled with barbecued pork and steamed in banana leaf; and countless other varieties. Each cart carries different items, so be sure to investigate all of them. A few items are prepared to order at a grill in the dining room; walk around and see what they're making. Each order typically contains three individual dim sum; when you go with a group, you can mix and match. Servers tally your purchases on a "scorecard" at your table; you probably won't be able to keep track of what you've ordered or what it should cost, but don't worry, it's difficult to eat more than $8 worth before becoming stuffed. *2130 S. Wentworth Ave., tel. 312/791–1229. AE, DC, MC, V. Inexpensive.*

Italian-American **Edwardo's.** The pizzas of this chain regularly find a place on reviewers' lists of the city's best. The thin-crust pizzas are excellent, but the specialty of the house is the Chicago-style deluxe stuffed pizza, which comes plain or with additions to the basic mozzarella filling. Spinach lovers will delight in the fresh spinach filling; others may prefer the sausage. The sauce is outstanding for its intense flavor of fresh tomato. A limited selection of salads, pastas, and breads is also available. Edwardo's airy and comfortable setting has wood tables and chairs in the center of a room lined with booths. The divider between dining room and open kitchen is covered with pots of fresh basil, grown here year-round to insure the chefs an ample supply. Because all pizzas are cooked to order and take about 45 minutes to prepare, you may want to call your order in before you leave for Edwardo's. Takeout and delivery service are available. *1321 E. 57th St., tel. 312/241–7960. No reservations. BYOB. AE, MC, V. Inexpensive.*

Japanese **Ten-Tsuna.** Cloth napkins, wood tabletops, soft lighting, and a quietly attentive staff attired in traditional Japanese kimonos make this the restaurant to come to when you're ready to leave the clamor of your day behind. Take a table if you want a full-course meal, or choose the sushi bar for a lunch or dinner of the delicacies made of vinegared rice and raw fish. The sashimi is fresh and delicious; the *gyoza* (fried dumplings) are crispy outside and juicy within. The *nabeyaki udon* (noodles, vegetables, and egg in broth) delights the eye as well as the palate. Order the *shabu-shabu* if you prefer to have your waitress prepare your meal at tableside, quickly simmering vegetables, tofu, and noodles in broth. A good selection of Japanese beer and wine is available. *Harper Court, 5225 S. Harper Ave., tel. 312/ 493–4410. AE, CB, DC, MC, V. Closed weekend lunch. Moderate.*

Lithuanian-American **Healthy Food.** Think of the "healthy" in Healthy Food as referring to the size of the portions. This is honest home-style cooking: breakfasts lavish with eggs, sausage, or ham; Lithuanian light rye bread; and fried potatoes; almost all under $4 and many under $2; hearty sandwiches (pork chop, sausage, hamburger, hot beef with potatoes and salad); and filling dinners (Thuringer sausage, Salisbury steak, beef liver with onions, pot roast with tomato zucchini sauce). The Lithuanian specialties include *koldumai* (boiled meat dumplings served with bacon bits, butter, or sour cream), *kugelis* (baked potato pudding with sour cream), and *blynai* (pancakes with sour cream, with or without your choice of fruit filling). The setting is as simple and homey as the food: a large storefront with counter, booths, and plastic-covered tables. *3236 S. Halsted St., tel. 312/326– 2724. No credit cards or checks. Inexpensive.*

Mexican **Playa Azul.** You will find wonderful fresh oysters at both the original 18th Street location and the sister house on North Broadway. You will also find a full selection of fish and seafood soups, salads, and entrées, including abalone, octopus, shrimp, crab, clams, and lobster. Red snapper Veracruzaná (deep fried) or *al mojo de ajo* (in garlic sauce) are house specialties, both delectable. Grilled meat dishes and chiles rellenos are available for those who don't want fish, and there are Mexican beers. *1514 W. 18th St., tel. 312/421–2552. No reservations. No credit cards. Closed Sun. Inexpensive–Moderate.*

Chon y Chano. This clean, well-lighted place is the only United States outpost of a popular Mexico City chain, and it attracts diners from all over Chicago. Most of the menu is devoted to make-your-own tacos, with delicious and occasionally exotic fillings: grilled cactus, beef marrow, steak, barbecued pork, beans, and sausage, to name a few. You can watch the chef make the fresh corn tortillas that wrap the tacos. A house specialty, Aztec soup, consists of chunks of chicken breast in broth, with strips of tortilla and crumbled white cheese. A large toasted chile pepper is served on the side, and you can crumble as much of it into your soup as you wish. *3901 W. 26th St., tel. 312/522–0041. No reservations. MC, V. Inexpensive.*

Nuevo Leon. The simple storefront Nuevo Leon restaurant offers a pleasant atmosphere in which to enjoy familiar or less familiar dishes and come away satisfied. Appetizers include nachos, guacamole, quesos, and quesadillas with chili sauce. In addition to a large selection of enchiladas, tacos, tostadas, and tamales, you'll find such less familiar items as rich and flavorful *menudo* (tripe soup), several beef soups, pork stew, chicken in mole sauce, tongue in sauce, and chopped steak simmered with tomatoes, jalapeño peppers, and onion (a house specialty). Not all servers are fluent in English, but cheerful good will prevails. *1515 W. 18th St., tel. 312/421–1517. No credit cards. Inexpensive.*

Middle Eastern **University Gardens.** Once inside this dimly lit restaurant, you're transported immediately to the Middle East. Arabic music plays in the background, prayer rugs adorn the walls along with Arabic movie posters, and the Formica-top tables are placed close together. The service is genial but not always speedy. Use the pita-pocket bread, baked here daily, to dip in hummos or to surround felafel, lettuce, and tomato for a Middle Eastern sandwich. For dinner, choose a kebab plate, the lamb shank braised with Middle Eastern spices, or the spinach stew with meat. Ask for an order of pickled vegetables; they are quite unlike what Americans think of as "pickles." The tea is seasoned with sage, for a most unusual flavor. Finally, be sure to sample one of the pastries arrayed at the back. *1373 E. 53rd St., tel. 312/684–6600. BYOB. No credit cards. Inexpensive.*

Soul Food **Army & Lou's.** Under new ownership, Army & Lou's continues to provide soul-satisfying meals. Spreading across two storefronts, the spacious restaurant has wood-paneled walls, silk flowers on the tables, and carpeting that helps to mute the sound level. Start with the seafood or chicken gumbo. The menu offers an extensive selection of fish, five steaks, and prime lamb chops, but you didn't come here for them. On a Wednesday you can have the meaty oxtails in a rich jardiniere sauce with a hint of tomato; you can have the short ribs in the same sauce any day. Other daily specials include hocks or neck bones with white or red beans (hocks in greens are available daily). The fried chicken and ribs are outstanding. All orders are served with smothered cabbage and cornbread. Service is attentive, and the food comes to the table hot! There's a spacious parking lot adjacent to the restaurant. *420 E. 75th St., tel. 312/483–6550. AE, DC, MC, V. Closed Tues. and holidays. Moderate.*

Soul Queen. Come to Soul Queen for the food, not the ambience. Plentiful quantities of Southern-style entrées and down-home specials are available on a large buffet: channel catfish steaks served with Mississippi hush puppies, ham hock with fresh greens or peas and candied yams, and stewed chicken with homemade dumplings, greens, and deep-dish apple pie. *9031 S. Stony Island Ave., tel. 312/731–3366. No credit cards. Closed some holidays. Inexpensive.*

The Suburbs

French **Carlos.** Under the watchful eyes of owner Carlos Nieto (himself a Le Francais graduate), his wife, Deborah, and the new chef Gabriel Viti, Carlos continues to challenge Le Francais for the title of best French restaurant in the area. Expect food that tends more toward contemporary French cuisine than Le Francais, with an ever-changing menu that features the freshest and the best ingredients of the season. *429 Temple, Highland Park, tel. 708/432–0770. Reservations required. AE, DC, MC, V. Closed lunch and Tues. Very Expensive.*

Le Francais. A quiet revolution has taken place at Le Francais, long regarded as one of the top French restaurants in the country. Its founder, the famed wizard of haute cuisine Jean Banchet, sold the restaurant in 1989 to chef Roland Liccioni and his wife, Mary Beth. Fortunately, Le Francais has fared better than most restaurants that have gone through similar dramatic changes of command. The food still ranks among the best in the Midwest, and Chef Liccioni continues to prepare classic French food; meals can and should last for hours. The menu changes nightly to reflect the best ingredients available that day and the whim of the chef that night. *269 S. Milwaukee, Wheeling, tel. 708/541–7470. Reservations required. AE, DC, MC, V. Closed lunch and Mon. Very Expensive.*

7 Lodging

Chicago is a convention town, and while the opening of several new hotels in recent years has made many new rooms available, the accommodations situation can be tight when major events are scheduled. Prospective visitors should make their plans and book lodging well in advance of a visit. Early action is even more essential when the location and price of accommodations are important considerations.

Bed-and-Breakfasts An alternative to a hotel, particularly for those visiting such areas as Hyde Park or Lincoln Park, which are underserved by first-class hotels, is the bed-and-breakfast. This is a room in a private house or apartment, with the host providing breakfast as part of the tariff. Don't expect to save a great deal of money over the comparable level of accommodation at a hotel; B & Bs offer something different: the unique circumstances of your host's home, perhaps something of his or her company if you wish it, and a home-cooked meal. Here is the true personal service that many hotels tout but few can deliver, and the convenience of a lodging off the beaten track—where you want to be, rather than where the hotels are. **Bed and Breakfast Chicago** (Box 14088, Chicago 60614, tel. 312/951–0085) is the clearinghouse for more than 50 B & B establishments throughout the greater Chicago area.

Hotels Hotels are listed here according to their location (Downtown, South, Near North, and O'Hare Airport) and by price category within each location.

Business travelers may prefer Downtown hotels that are near the La Salle Street financial district, the exchanges, and the city's many large law firms. Downtown hotels are convenient to the Art Institute, Symphony Hall, the Civic Opera House, the Blackstone and Shubert theaters, the original Marshall Field (State Street) and Carson Pirie Scott department stores, and the Printer's Row redevelopment area. Visitors who are interested principally in shopping and fine dining may prefer the Near North hotels that cluster along Michigan Avenue's Magnificent Mile. But bear in mind that it is no more than three miles from the Chicago Hilton and Towers at the south end of the Downtown area to the Drake at the north end of the Near North; each of the attractions just mentioned is only a short walk or ride from any hotel in the area.

Because companies frequently schedule business conferences at the hotels and exposition centers in the O'Hare Airport area, several fine hotels have been built there in recent years. Business travelers can now fly to Chicago, attend three days of conferences, and return home without ever leaving the area of the airport; that is, without seeing the "real" city of Chicago. This may be efficient and cost effective, but it is sad nonetheless, for the charms of O'Hare are wanting when compared to the delights of the big city 20 miles to the southeast. Those who are not traveling on business, not visiting people in the northern suburbs or in Wisconsin, and not arriving on a late evening flight or departing on an early morning flight will probably want to pass up the airport hotels in favor of one Downtown or in the Near North.

Consider staying at the McCormick Center Hotel or the Hyde Park Hilton if you have business with the University of Chicago, the National Opinion Research Center, or one of the area's theological seminaries; otherwise, plan to spend a day in this unique neighborhood but lodge Downtown or in the Near North.

Our hotel price categories are based on the standard weekday rate for one room *(in general* the rate for double occupancy is about 10% more than for single occupancy). These are the "rack rates," the highest prices for which the rooms will be rented. Lower rates are often available, especially at the more expensive hotels; you may be eligible for them if you have the appropriate corporate, government, clerical, associational, age group, or other qualifications, and sometimes you can get a lower rate just by asking for one. If you have negotiating skills, don't hesitate to use them here.

Weekend and other special packages, when available, can be real bargains, particularly when there are two of you to share a room. You may even be able to take advantage of a weekend package for a portion of a longer stay. Note that, unlike standard rates, which are usually quoted on a *per room* basis, package rates are often quoted *per person, double occupancy.*

When you make your reservation, be sure to get a reservation number and keep it with you for reference. Notify the hotel if you anticipate arriving later than 5 PM; some hotels will guarantee your reservation to your credit card and have a room waiting for you even if you arrive at 2 AM. Should your plans change and you need to cancel your reservation, notify the hotel as soon as possible—and be sure to get a cancellation number.

The following price categories apply to the basic weekday rates (rack rates) for one room, whether single or double occupancy, and do not reflect special weekend or package rates or seasonal promotions. State and city taxes totaling 12.4% are added to all hotel bills.

Category	Cost*
Very Expensive	over $180
Expensive	$135–$180
Moderate	$90–$135
Inexpensive	under $90

All prices are for a standard double room, excluding 12.4% tax and service charges.

The following credit card abbreviations are used: AE, American Express; CB, Carte Blanche; DC, Diners Club; MC, MasterCard; V, Visa.

The most highly recommended hotels are indicated by a star ★ .

Downtown

Very Expensive **Chicago Hilton and Towers.** Built in 1927 at a cost of more than $30 million, the Chicago Hilton and Towers—then the Stevens Hotel—was conceived as the greatest hotel of all time. Today this massively handsome structure, conveniently located in Downtown South, is well on the way to recapturing that goal. Completely renovated in 1984–1986 at a cost of $185 million,

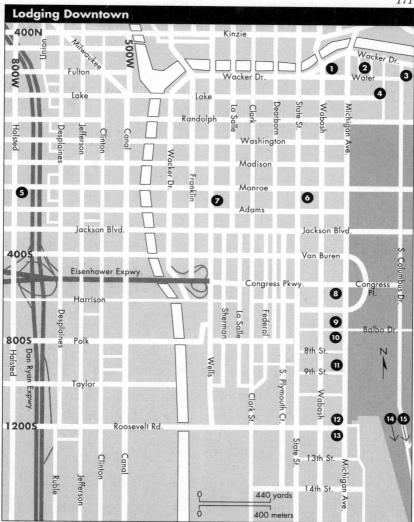

Lodging Downtown

Avenue Motel, **12**

The Blackstone, **9**

Chicago Hilton and Towers, **10**

Congress Hotel, **8**

Essex Inn, **11**

Executive House, **1**

The Fairmont, **4**

Hyatt Regency Chicago, **2**

HydePark Hilton, **15**

McCormick Center Hotel, **14**

The Midland, **7**

The Palmer House, **6**

Quality Inn Downtown, **5**

Swiss Grand Hotel, **3**

Travelodge, **13**

the hotel has achieved the seemingly impossible: a combination of decor, facilities, and service that delights just about everyone. Public areas are done in mauve and sea green, marble is used lavishly, and there are antiques and original artwork in the main lobby, the third-floor art gallery, the upper floor corridors, even the health club. The lobby shopping promenade has a jewelry store, a clothing boutique, a gift store, a florist, and a card shop. The splendid Grand Ballroom, reached by a magnificent curving two-sided stairway, just south of the Michigan Avenue entrance, was conceived as a room with no obstruction; accordingly, four enormous steel trusses replaced the 55 structural pillars that would otherwise have been required. The ballroom boasts huge crystal chandeliers imported from France, inset murals (hand-restored during the renovation), and gold leaf on its ornate wall carvings. Yet for all its grandeur, the Hilton and Towers is a very modern hotel, with smoke detectors, sprinklers, and enunciator alarms in every room. Bathrooms, outfitted in Italian marble with brass fixtures, have built-in hair dryers and a range of personal care products. Closets have full-length mirrors. The state-of-the-art health club features a 60-foot heated swimming pool, Universal progressive-resistance exercise equipment, two whirlpools, men's and women's saunas, attractive locker rooms with plentiful towels, and massage service. Business guests will appreciate the up-to-date office technology, which includes computer-generated graphics and presentation services, electronic mail and telex, tape duplication, work stations with word processors, access to major public databases, audiovisual equipment including overhead projectors, secretarial services, furnished private offices (which can be rented daily or hourly), transcription service, and photocopying. Guests who prefer the exclusiveness of a small European-style hotel will want to stay in the more expensive Towers, a hotel-within-a-hotel with its own registration desk and concierge. Its services and amenities include shoe shine, oversize bath sheets, two telephones in each room, a refrigerator and minibar, turndown service (with liqueur and chocolate-dipped strawberries), complimentary Continental breakfast and newspaper, a library with business periodicals, a VCR tape library, and a lounge with honor bar. Among the Hilton's restaurants are a fine small dining room and a lobby cafe; the live entertainment in the lobby lounge ranges from classical string ensembles to jazz piano. A family plan permits children to stay free in their parents' room. Weekend packages are terrific bargains. The hotel's only problem is that when large conventions are in residence, its food service facilities are overwhelmed. When that happens, try the 8th St. Deli just south of the hotel for breakfast and lunch. *720 S. Michigan Ave., Chicago 60605, tel. 312/922–4400 or 800/445–8667. 1,543 rooms. Facilities: pool, health club, 5 restaurants, cocktail lounge and tavern with live entertainment, 24-hour café, deli, valet and laundry service, 24-hour room service, free shopping and business-district bus shuttles. AE, CB, DC, MC, V.*

Executive House. The IBM Building is a stone's throw from Executive House; the rest of Downtown is within walking distance. A multimillion-dollar renovation completed in 1986 has vastly improved this hotel (and brought increased prices). The rooms are oversize, each with a variety of personal care products. Meeting and conference rooms and advanced audiovisual equipment are available. The top three floors comprise an executive club, which features a concierge, complimentary hors d'oeuvres and drinks, and many in-room amenities, including robes and TV in bathrooms. A restaurant and bar are in the hotel. Weekend packages are available. *71 E. Wacker Dr., Chicago 60601, tel. 312/346–7100 or 800/228–2828. 415 rooms, 60 suites. Facilities: restaurant, lounge, 3 concierge floors, 2 nonsmoking floors, 15 banquet rooms, valet laundry service. AE, CB, DC, MC, V.*

The Fairmont. One of Chicago's most attractive hotels, the Fairmont is a 45-story neoclassic structure of Spanish pink granite with copper roofs. Part of the Illinois Center complex, it offers fine views of the lake and Grant Park. Rooms are furnished in either contemporary or period styles; antiques and original artwork are part of the decor in the public areas. Clever design places every room no more than four doors from an elevator. The rooms are spacious, the beds are extra long, the marble bathrooms have oversize tubs. All rooms have color TV, a minibar, and an electric shoe polisher. The stunning art deco lounge has evening cabaret entertainment. Extensive meeting services, including conference and banquet spaces, exhibit space, teleconferencing facilities, closed-circuit TV, secretarial services, telex and fax, and notary public are available. Frequent corporate travelers receive special discounts and tie-ins to the American Airlines and Hertz frequent traveler programs. Weekend packages are offered. *200 N. Columbus Dr., Chicago 60601, tel. 312/565–8000 or 800/527–4727. 694 rooms, 66 suites. Facilities: cabaret lounge, 2 restaurants, lobby lounge serving high tea, guest memberships to nearby health club, valet and concierge service, 24-hour room service. AE, CB, DC, MC, V.*

Hyatt Regency Chicago. The Hyatt Regency Chicago in the Illinois Center complex, equidistant from the Magnificent Mile on Michigan Avenue and the Loop, is one of the city's premier convention hotels, with more than 2,000 rooms. Designed by A. Epstein & Sons, the west tower opened in 1974, the east tower in 1980, and a glass-enclosed skyway connects them. The main area is a four-story, half-acre, glass-enclosed atrium lobby with a central lagoon and loads of shrubbery and green plants; five restaurants and four lounges are located here. Scampi, the lobby restaurant, serves American and ethnic specialties 24 hours a day. A club floor (at higher rates) has its own concierge and private lounge with complimentary Continental breakfast and cocktails. All rooms have shampoo, bath crystals, showercap, shoe cloth, color TV, morning newspaper, and nightly turndown service. Special rates include a government rate and three weekend packages. Computerized "passports" speed checkin and checkout. *151 E. Wacker Dr., Chicago 60601, tel. 312/565–1234 or 800/233–1234. 2,033 rooms, 175 suites. Facilities: 10 restaurants, bar, comedy club, health club, concierge service, valet laundry service. AE, CB, DC, MC, V.*

Swiss Grand Hotel. The third luxury hotel to open in the Illinois Center complex (and the second in 1988), the 45-story Swiss Grand Hotel was designed by Harry Weese as a unique triangular structure of reinforced concrete with glass. The hotel aims to provide a quiet, European ambience rather than the hectic, bustling atmosphere of many large hotels. Intended primarily for business travelers, the Swiss Grand has oversize rooms, each equipped with a minibar refrigerator, a separate seating area, a writing desk, and a two-line telephone. Television monitors provide in-room communications, checkout, and

access to telex and fax. Marble bathrooms are outfitted with
toweling robes, telephones, and grooming items. Complimentary valet services include pressing, mending, and shoe shine;
newspapers are delivered each morning. If you are a frequent
visitor, you may leave soiled clothing behind in a valet garment
bag; it will be cleaned and ready for you on your return. Conference and meeting rooms with advanced audiovisual systems
are available, as are secretarial services, telex, and fax. Corporate rates are offered. A fitness center overlooking the lake has
a heated pool, exercise equipment, whirlpool and sauna, and
Swedish massage. *323 E. Wacker Dr., Chicago 60601, tel.
312/565–0565 or 800/654–7263. 625 rooms, 34 suites. Facilities:
health club, pool, 2 restaurants, lobby lounge, bar, pastry
shop, valet, concierge, business center with office equipment
access, 24-hour room service. AE, CB, DC, MC, V.*

Expensive   **The Midland.** An older hotel in the heart of the financial district, The Midland has been undergoing renovation since 1987.
The public areas are spacious and attractive. The Midland's
amenities include concierge, nonsmoking rooms, same day
laundry and dry cleaning (extra charge), phones in some bathrooms, and shoe cloth, shampoo, and mouthwash in all bathrooms. Conference rooms with photocopying service are
available. An elegant lobby is complemented by three restaurants. A two-tier pricing schedule reflects the difference between renovated and unrenovated rooms. *172 W. Adams St.,
Chicago 60603, tel. 312/332–1200 or 800/621–2360. 257 rooms,
54 suites. 2 restaurants, cocktail lounge with live entertainment, 12 conference rooms, fitness center, complimentary
newspaper, free shuttle service to downtown area, fax and photocopying available. AE, CB, DC, MC, V.*

The Palmer House. The Palmer House was built more than 100
years ago by the Chicago merchant Potter Palmer. Meant to be
opulent and luxurious, it accomplished its aim in its own time;
today it ranks with just a few other Chicago hotels in the elegance of its construction and its public areas. The street level,
with its marble floors and classic shops, is splendid, but you
must see the main lobby, up a flight of stairs, whether or not
you're staying here. The ceiling decorations consist of 21 paintings by Louis Rigal, the lobby furnishings reflect the fabrics
and textures of the Victorian period, including velvet, moiré
taffeta, and brocade, and there are crystal light fixtures and
custom-made carpeting. A decade-long renovation, nearly
complete, has modernized, upgraded, and refurbished the
guest rooms and improved the administrative and safety systems. A recently opened Executive Fitness Center offers pool,
whirlpool, steam room, sauna, aerobics, massage, and more
than 20 units of resistance exercise equipment. Other recent
additions include a conference center and a business center
with computers, modems, software, printers, secretarial and
photocopying services, and phone mail. Two rooms on each
floor are designed for disabled guests. A "towers" hotel-within-a-hotel offers additional amenities. Weekend packages are
available. *17 E. Monroe St., Chicago 60603, tel. 312/726–7500
or 800/445–8667. 1,600 rooms, 88 suites. Facilities: pool, fitness center, 7 restaurants, 2 lounges, live entertainment in lobby bar, business center with secretarial services, nonsmoking
floor, valet, concierge, and laundry services. AE, CB, DC,
MC, V.*

Moderate **The Blackstone.** Built in 1910, this once-grand establishment is badly in need of the renovation that is scheduled for this year, which will convert it to an all-suites hotel. Meanwhile, the hotel offers an excellent location, a concierge, same-day laundry and dry cleaning (extra charge), dining facilities, a discount rate on a nearby health facility, and conference rooms with secretarial services. In-room amenities are sparse, and there's no room service. Weekend packages lower the price. *636 S. Michigan Ave., Chicago 60605, tel. 312/427–4300 or 800/622–6330. 305 rooms. Facilities: restaurant, lounge, jazz club, live theater, business center across the street, 17 meeting rooms, ballroom, valet and concierge service. AE, CB, DC, MC, V.*

The Congress Hotel. A congeries of buildings and architectural styles, this hotel was apparently built in pieces. Some sections are in the grand old hotel tradition, others have no character or distinction whatever. Yet the location is excellent, and the restoration now in progress should improve the quality of the rooms and will add a health facility and better business and meeting space. *520 S. Michigan Ave., Chicago 60615, tel. 312/427–3800, 800/635–1666, or 800/223–5067 in Canada. 815 rooms. Facilities: 4 restaurants, 2 lounges with live entertainment, valet and concierge service. AE, CB, DC, MC, V.*

Essex Inn. Located just south of the "best" Downtown South area, the Essex Inn offers good value. Although not glamorous, the hotel is nicely situated opposite Grant Park, and its rooms are pleasantly decorated. Conference facilities are available, corporate rates are offered, and the weekend and "honeymoon" packages are excellent deals. The hotel houses the 8th Street Deli, a spacious casual restaurant that offers unusually pleasing New York-style food. *800 S. Michigan Ave., Chicago 60605, tel. 312/939–2800 or 800/621–6909. 255 rooms. Facilities: restaurant, lounge with live entertainment, outdoor heated pool, fax machine, game room, valet service, free shuttle bus to N. Michigan Ave. sightseeing. AE, CB, DC, MC, V.*

Quality Inn Downtown. Each successive owner has kept "Downtown" in the name of this large facility. Yet the hotel is more than half a mile west of what any Chicagoan (or any visitor) would consider "downtown." The disgruntlement of generations of clients who booked here unaware of its true location probably accounts for the hotel's marginal success. Nevertheless, if you're familiar with Quality Inns, you'll find that this one offers just what you'd expect: clean, pleasant surroundings and reliable service. Amenities include shampoo, lotion, and an in-room safe (modest extra charge). An outdoor pool is available in summer. Limited conference facilities and office space are available. The rates may be a bit high in relation to those charged by comparable establishments in better locations. Children stay free in their parents' room; additional adults are $10 each. *1 S. Halsted St., Chicago 60606, tel. 312/829–5000 or 800/228–5151. 406 rooms. Facilities: pool, restaurant, lounge with nightly live entertainment, 8 meeting rooms, valet and concierge service, free parking, free shuttle service to surrounding area. AE, CB, DC, MC, V.*

Inexpensive **Avenue Motel.** This no-frills has drab public spaces but a convenient location and pleasant rooms. Parking is included in the very modest price. Weekend packages reduce the rate even further. *1154 S. Michigan Ave., Chicago 60605, tel. 312/427–8200 or 800/621–4196. 75 rooms. Facilities: restaurant, lounge, valet, and concierge service. AE, CB, DC, MC, V.*

Travel Inn. The decor is in basic motel style, and the prices are basic motel, too. All rooms have color TV, direct-dial telephones, and a hot pot for making instant coffee or tea. Parking is included. The value is good, for the motel is a short walk from the Field Museum of Natural History, the Adler Planetarium, the Shedd Aquarium, and Soldier Field. *1240 S. Michigan Ave., Chicago 60605, tel. 312/427–4111 or 800/255–3050. 60 rooms. Facilities: discount use of nearby health club. AE, CB, DC, MC, V.*

South

Expensive **McCormick Center Hotel.** Located to the west of the original McCormick Place Convention Center exposition hall and across the street to the south of the new McCormick Place North building, this is a very convenient place to stay when you're attending a convention here. The Loop is only a couple of miles north, and the hotel provides free shuttle bus service. The hotel has that busy, purposeful ambience that convention guests tend to create. Rooms are attractively furnished following a recent $10 million renovation; each room contains a bar and a large selection of personal items. Nonsmoking rooms are available. The health club includes a domed heated pool, a Jacuzzi, Nautilus resistance exercise machines, sauna, steam room, and massage. Restaurants are available, though guests in search of a really good meal would do better elsewhere. A weekend package is offered. *23rd St. at Lake Shore, Chicago 60616, tel. 312/791–1900 or 800/621–6909. 650 rooms. Facilities: 3 restaurants, 1 lobby lounge with live entertainment, indoor pool, health club with sauna and steam room, valet and concierge service, free shuttle to local sightseeing. AE, CB, DC, MC, V.*

Moderate **Hyde Park Hilton.** Mauve and beige walls, marble-top coffee tables, brass pieces, and a maroon and beige geometric carpet decorate the entry of this modest hotel. Rooms are pleasantly done but hardly breathtaking. As Hyde Park and Kenwood's only first-class hotel, it can do less than it might and still attract business. A recent renovation converted part of the hotel into a conference center. *4900 S. Lake Shore Dr., Chicago 60615, tel. 312/288–5800 or 800/445–8667. 288 rooms. Facilities: restaurant, coffee shop, lounge, local health club admission free to guests, pool, valet and concierge service, conference room, free shuttle to downtown area. AE, CB, DC, MC, V.*

Near North

Very Expensive **The Barclay Chicago.** This intimate establishment one block east of the Magnificent Mile claims to be an all-suite hotel. Yet the "mini-suite" has only a "sitting area" with "sleeping alcove" and wet bar; the "executive parlour" has a "living room" with full kitchen and "sleeping alcove." You'll need the "one bedroom suite" if you really want a separate living room and bedroom. Nevertheless, the rooms are beautifully furnished and appointed, and there are only six to a floor. Service is gracious, and a multilingual concierge stands ready to serve you. Business meeting facilities and weekend packages are available. *166 E. Superior St., Chicago 60611, tel. 312/787–6000 or 800/621–8004. 120 suites. Facilities: 1 restaurant, 2 lounges, outdoor pools, concierge, valet service. AE, DC, MC, V.*
Chicago Marriott Downtown. This huge high rise is facing stiff

Lodging North

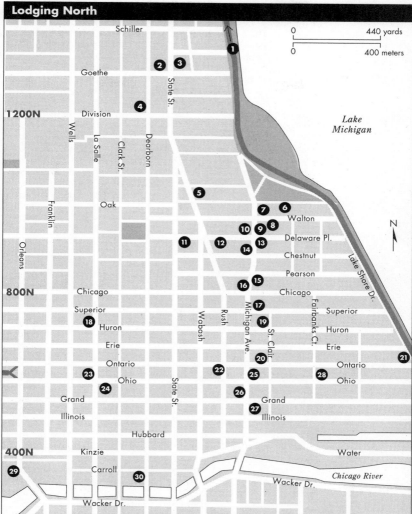

Ambassador West, **2**

Barclay Chicago, **17**

Chicago Marriott
Downtown, **26**

Claridge Hotel, **4**

Comfort Inn of
Lincoln Park, **1**

Days Inn of
Chicago, **21**

The Drake, **7**

Forum Hotel
Chicago, **27**

The Four Seasons, **10**

Holiday Inn Chicago
City Centre, **28**

Holiday Inn Mart
Plaza, **29**

Hotel Inter-
Continental, **27**

Hotel Nikko, **30**

Inn of Chicago, **25**

The Knickerbocker, **8**

La Salle Motor
Lodge, **18**

Le Meridien, **5**

Lenox House, **22**

Mayfair Regent, **6**

Ohio House, **23**

Omni Ambassador
East, **3**

Park Hyatt, **16**

The Raphael , **13**

The Richmont, **20**

Ritz-Carlton, **15**

River North Hotel, **24**

Sheraton, **19**

The Talbott, **11**

The Tremont, **14**

The Westin, **9**

The Whitehall, **12**

competition from a spate of new hotels in the immediate vicinity, and may expand in the next few years. The Marriott Downtown has two entrances, one on Michigan Avenue and one a block to the west on Rush Street. Enter from Michigan Avenue and step down to the lobby level. Shops are to your left and right, a huge lobby area with multistory ceiling faces you, and escalators sweep upward two and four stories, taking you to the bars, restaurants, and public areas above. *540 N. Michigan Ave., Chicago 60611, tel. 312/836–0100 or 800/228–9290. 1173 rooms, 39 suites. Facilities: 3 restaurants, 3 lounges, 4 non-smoking floors, indoor pool, health club, sauna, steam room, whirlpool, game room, concierge, valet parking, valet laundry, shops, parking across from hotel. AE, CB, DC, MC, V.*

The Four Seasons. Occupying 17 floors in the 900 N. Michigan building, this luxurious hostelry is one of the newest in Chicago. The hotel, which cost an estimated $300 million to build, decorate, and furnish, boasts a lavish traditional decor more suggestive of an English manor house than an urban skyscraper. Italian marble, handcrafted woodwork, custom-woven rugs, tasteful prints, and a subtle color scheme grace the rooms throughout, and the only wood-burning fireplace in a Chicago hotel is located in the elegant lobby. Guest-room amenities include three phones, remote-control color television, terry-cloth robes, hair dryers, bath supplies, and a complimentary morning newspaper. Traditional high tea is available in the Seasons Lounge. Bloomingdale's and a number of small shops and boutiques are conveniently located in the Avenue Atrium, a "vertical mall" below the hotel. *120 E. Delaware Place, tel. 312/280–8800 or 800/332–3442. 344 rooms, 121 suites, 16 apartments. Facilities: restaurant, 2 bars, pool, health spa with Jacuzzi and track, 24-hour room service, soundproof meeting rooms with audio-video facilities.*

Hotel Inter-Continental Chicago. This luxury property is a renovation of the 1929 Medinah Athletic Club, which underwent several incarnations as a hotel before being acquired by the Inter-Continental Hotels Corporation and completely overhauled in 1990. The Michigan Avenue location is within walking distance of most tourist destinations as well as the Loop and Near North business districts. Unlike most grand hotels, this one has a low-ceiling lobby done in dark green and dark wood, with an intimate bar to the left and a long lounge area to the right. Rooms are done in a 1920s neoclassical style, in beige and green; the furniture was designed specifically for the hotel. Bathrooms are roomy and nicely appointed. Amenities include hair dryers, robes, scales, and padded-silk hangers. The "executive" level has a spectacular skylit lounge area, with terrific views of several neighboring gothic-style skyscrapers. The showpiece of the Inter-Continental is its Italianate Junior Olympic–size swimming pool, fit for an Esther Williams water ballet with ornate gold and royal blue tiles, softly lit with orange lamps. It may be the only hotel pool in Chicago with a cocktail area. A fully equipped, more conventional-looking health club adjoins. Weekend and corporate rates are available. *505 N. Michigan Ave., Chicago, 60611, tel. 312/944–4100 or 800/332–4246. 338 rooms, 30 suites. Facilities: restaurant, bar, concierge, minibars in rooms, health club, 24-hour room service. AE, CB, DC, MC, V.*

★ **Hotel Nikko.** Hotel Nikko is one of Chicago's newest and most beautiful hotels. Enter through the oddly situated porte-cochere, set in from Dearborn Street, and you come to a 200-

year-old embroidered Oriental screen, one of many exquisite
pieces of Oriental art placed throughout the hotel. The low-rise
main lobby is outfitted in polished granite, Japanese ash, and
African mahogany; the south side of the lobby area is glassed-
in, giving views of a traditional Japanese garden and a riverfront park beyond. The rooms, furnished either in contemporary or traditional Japanese decor, offer marble baths
with plush robes, separate dressing area, minibars, and color
cable TV with remote control. Complimentary breakfast coffee
is brought to your room, and nightly turndown service includes
a Godiva chocolate. A concierge handles special requirements.
The three upper floors ("Nikko Floors") have their own check-
in and checkout, a special concierge, and complimentary breakfast and hors d'oeuvres. Two Japanese suites offer a *tatami*
sleeping room, large tub, and private rock gardens. The hotel
features an executive health club and cardio-fitness center with
sauna and massage. Business services include computers, telex
and fax, dictation equipment, secretarial and photocopying
services, a business library, and an executive lounge. Afternoon tea is served in a handsome lobby lounge; one restaurant
is American, one Japanese. The latter, Benkay, offers traditional Japanese *kaiseki* (haute cuisine) meals. Guests may
stroll the grounds and enjoy the landscaped rock gardens and
terraced promenades. *320 N. Dearborn St., Chicago 60610, tel.
312/744–1900 or 800/645–5687. 425 rooms, 26 suites. Facilities:
2 restaurants, lounge, fitness center, valet parking, concierge,
laundry, shoe shine, gift and sundry shop, parking. AE, CB,
DC, MC, V.*

The Knickerbocker. Located in the old Playboy Building,
theKnickerbocker has a clublike lobby with lots of wood and
marble and a concierge desk just beyond the entrance. This
pretty European-style hotel has just completed a large-scale
renovation.Weekend packages have sharply reduced prices.
*163 E. Walton Pl., Chicago 60611, tel. 312/751–8100 or
800/621–8140. 256 rooms, 40 suites. Facilities: restaurant,
lounge bar, valet laundry, concierge, valet parking. AE, CB,
DC, MC, V.*

Le Meridien. This sleek, post modern luxury mid–rise strives
to provide all the electronic creature-comforts of home: Each
room contains an entertainment center with a color television
and VCR, a compact disc player, and a stereo AM/FM receiver;
and three telephones equipped with call waiting, conference
calling, and speakerphone. Videotape rental and CD purchases
are available around the clock. The modern public areas and
some guest rooms are decorated with original photographs by
the late Robert Mapplethorpe. Guest rooms also feature duvet
bedcovers, stocked minibars, and full-length mirrors. Amenities include terry-cloth robes, nightly turndown service, hair
dryers, bath supplies, separate shower and tub, choice of morning newspaper, and car service to the Loop and Michigan Avenue. The business service center can provide fax and telex;
photocopying; personal computers; and secretarial, transla-
tion, and courier services. Children under 18 can stay in their
parent's room at no extra charge, and if more than one room is
needed to accommodate the family, the single-room rate applies to each room. *21 E. Bellevue Pl., tel. 312/266–2100 or
800/266–2101. 247 rooms, 35 suites, 6 penthouse suites. Facilities: restaurant, bar, café, 70% nonsmoking rooms, 24-hour
room service, laundry service, express checkin/checkout, valet*

parking, business services, conference rooms. AE, CB, DC, MC, V.

Omni Ambassador East. The Ambassador East, now an Omni hotel, has long been one of Chicago's fine hotels. The lobby has the old-fashioned elegance of crystal chandeliers, marble floors, and curving, hand-wrought banisters. Rooms are comfortably furnished in a 1920s style and are equipped with minibar, alarm clock radio, feather pillows, bathrobes, and personal care items. Turndown and shoe-shine service are offered. Meeting rooms are available. The hotel is the home of the famed Pump Room. Weekend packages are available. *1301 N. State Pkwy., Chicago 60610, tel. 312/787–7200 or 800/843–6664. 275 rooms, 52 suites. Facilities: restaurant, valet service, shoe shine, laundry, tobacco shop, valet parking, airport bus across the street. AE, CB, DC, MC, V.*

Park Hyatt. Renovation of the old Water Tower Hyatt hotel in 1980 brought into being the Park Hyatt, possibly Chicago's most expensive hotel. As lavishly opulent in a contemporary fashion as some of Chicago's grand old hotels are in their earlier style, the Park Hyatt offers a multilingual concierge and staff, with fine furniture, stereo system and bar, and multiple telephones in each room. La Tour is one of the finest restaurants in the city. The lobby lounge is one of Chicago's best, with overstuffed chairs and a pianist playing classical music, as well as some popular tunes. Although there's no health club, guests may request exercise bikes and rowing machines in their rooms. *800 N. Michigan Ave., Chicago 60611, tel. 312/280–2222 or 800/288–9000. 255 rooms, 43 suites. Facilities: restaurant, 2 lounges, concierge, valet service, parking in hotel. AE, CB, DC, MC, V.*

The Ritz-Carlton. Because the Ritz-Carlton Hotel occupies the floors above the Water Tower Place shops, you must ride an elevator to the 12th floor to reach the registration area (while your baggage is handled on the ground floor). The lobby is very grand: A great skylighted fountain is enhanced by bronze sculptures, and lavish plantings line the far wall, which is a floor-to-ceiling window. Tucked away in one corner of the area, the Greenhouse is a lobby lounge where lunch and afternoon tea are served. Farther on, The Dining Room is one of Chicago's finest restaurants, and The Bar is highly regarded among the club-going crowd for its live music and dancing. Rooms are decorated with fine furniture; the amenities include three telephones (one in the bathroom), color TV with remote control and five cable channels, AM/FM clock radio, minibar, bathrobes, hair dryers, lighted makeup mirrors, and more. The concierge and staff assist with special requirements. On the floor below the registration floor, a health club maintains a swimming pool, whirlpool, and men's and women's athletic departments with exercise equipment, steam rooms, sauna, massage, and locker facilities. *160 E. Pearson St. (in Water Tower Pl.), Chicago 60611, tel. 312/266–1000 or 800/332–3442. 433 rooms, 55 suites. Facilities: 3 restaurants, bar, indoor pool, health club, sauna, valet, laundry, concierge, gift shop, valet parking and garage next door. AE, CB, DC, MC, V.*

The Westin Hotel. At the north end of Michigan Avenue's Magnificent Mile, The Westin offers more than 700 rooms, including those of the Plaza Tower. Public areas and rooms are attractive and contemporary; amenities include express and video checkout. A concierge is available. The Executive Level offers additional luxuries: a welcome gift, a lounge with honor bar, complimentary hors d'oeuvres, and Continental breakfast. The Westin's meeting rooms have full audiovisual facilities. A health club is on the premises. Children stay free in existing beds in their parents' room. Weekend packages are available. The hotel's restaurants are undistinguished, but the Lion Bar & Grill is unusually attractive. *909 N. Michigan Ave., Chicago 60611, tel. 312/943–7200 or 800/228–3000. 747 rooms, including 45 suites. Facilities: 3 restaurants, bar, 2 nonsmoking floors, health club and sauna, laundry, in-house parking, 24-hour room service. AE, CB, DC, MC, V.*

Expensive **The Ambassador West.** North State Parkway is one of Chicago's better kept secrets: The extension of bustling State Street in the Loop, it becomes a street of handsome old turn-of-the-century residences north of Rush Street. Equidistant between the Magnificent Mile and Lincoln Park, this is the site of the small, European-style Ambassador West, whose oak-paneled lobby is filled with art treasures. The hotel has recently completed renovating its exterior and upgrading the amenities in guest rooms. Included in the tariff are complimentary Continental breakfast, cocktails, and daily newspaper; nightly turndown service; complimentary shoe shine; and honor bar. Business-meeting rooms and related services are offered. Weekend packages are available. *1300 N. State Pkwy., Chicago 60610, tel. 312/787–7900 or 800/621–8090. 217 rooms, 41 suites. Facilities: restaurant, two nonsmoking floors, valet laundry, concierge, parking at hotel, airport transportation. AE, CB, DC, MC, V.*

★ **The Drake.** The Drake is perhaps the grandest of Chicago's traditional hotels. Designed and built by Ben Marshall after the style of Italian palaces of the Renaissance, the hotel opened in 1920 and was listed in the National Register of Historic Places in 1981. Situated at a bend in the Lake Michigan shoreline, the Drake offers splendid lake views from rooms on two sides. Guests enter the Drake from either Walton Street or Oak Street: The hotel spans the entire city block on Michigan Avenue. The Drake's street-level arcade is an attractive enclosed shopping mall with boutiques offering men's and women's clothing and accessories, a drug store, a travel agent, a fine confectionery, a florist, and a china and jewelry shop. The main lobby, reached by climbing a short flight of stairs at the Walton Street side, is lavishly carpeted, decorated with original art, chandeliered, accented in oak throughout, and furnished with wing and club chairs, couches, and coffee tables in conversational arrangements that invite the visitor to linger and enjoy a refreshment. In the middle of the lobby, a splendid marble fountain is surrounded by cherubs riding dolphins who spray water into an 18th-century French bronze urn at the fountain's center. The lobby alone is worth a visit, even if you aren't staying here. The Drake's 535 rooms include singles, doubles, and suites, many custom decorated, all fully renovated in a $20 million restoration completed in 1983. All rooms are equipped with two telephones, alarm clock, remote-control TV, and optional in-house movies and cable TV. Amenities include fresh fruit and flowers, afternoon ice delivery, bed turndown, pillow chocolate, and morning newspaper delivery. For business travelers, the Vista Executive Floor at the top of the hotel offers valet service, lounge, conference center, and complimentary breakfast and cocktails. Businesswomen can request one of the hotel's 34 Executive Business Women's Suites, whose foldaway beds permit easy conversion from bedroom into conference room. All guests are encouraged to use the services of the concierge in obtaining dinner reservations and theater tickets. The Oak Terrace dining room serves breakfast, lunch, and dinner, offering well-prepared traditional American food in a pleasant setting. English tea is served in the Palm Court lobby daily 3–5:30. The Cape Cod Room was for many years Chicago's premier seafood restaurant; the room, with its nautical motifs, is still handsome, but the food and the service have earned increasingly negative reviews from Chicago residents and restaurant critics. (Many other restaurants are located within easy walking distance of the hotel.) The Drake offers various reduced-rate plans and packages. *140 E. Walton Pl., Chicago 60611, tel. 312/787–2200 or 800/445–8667. 535 rooms, 65 suites. Facilities: 3 restaurants, 2 lounges, laundry and valet service, shoe shine, secretarial service, notary public, TELEX/cable facilities, interpreters, wheelchairs, shopping arcade, valet parking, 24-hour room service. AE, CB, DC, MC, V.*

Forum Hotel Chicago. Adjoining this more plush Hotel Inter-Continental, this mid-priced high-rise business hotel is run by the same company. This 1960s vintage building was completely renovated in 1990; both the guest rooms and the public areas are done in grays and other cool neutrals. The furniture is modern and nondescript, but the spacious bathrooms include full-length mirrors, the rooms have large desks, and more expensive rooms have views of Lake Michigan. Forum guests may use the Inter-Continental's health club, including the spectacular rococo swimming pool, for a $5 fee. Weekend and corporate rates are available. *525 N. Michigan Ave., Chicago, 60611, tel. 312/944–0055 or 800/332–4246. 517 rooms, 6 suites. Facilities: 2 restaurants, minibars in rooms, 24-hour room service, concierge. AE, CB, DC, MC, V.*

Holiday Inn Chicago City Centre. This bustling, modern hotel catering to business travelers as well as individuals offers attractive and tasteful rooms. Children under 18 sleep free in their parents' room, and free parking is offered for guests' cars. The McClurg Court sports facility is connected to the hotel; guests may use the facilities. A restaurant and lounges are available. Weekend packages are offered. *300 E. Ohio St., Chicago 60611, tel. 312/787–6100 or 800/465–4329. 500 rooms. Facilities: restaurant, 2 bars, nonsmoking rooms, indoor pool, sauna, valet, concierge, gift shop, parking in hotel. AE, CB, DC, MC, V.*

Holiday Inn Mart Plaza. Situated atop the Apparel Center and next door to the Merchandise Mart, this hotel principally serves the business traveler. Conventions and business meetings are facilitated by complete audiovisual equipment. Rooms are equipped with color TV, plush carpeting, and spacious bathrooms. The hotel has no health facility, but it does have a heated indoor swimming pool. The restaurants in the hotel are undistinguished, but more interesting places are just blocks away. While fine for attending meetings or doing business downtown, the Mart Plaza may be too busy, too impersonal, and (at regular rates) too expensive to please most individual travelers. *350 N. Orleans St., Chicago 60654, tel. 312/836–5000 or 800/465–4329. 525 rooms, 14 suites. Facilities: 2 restaurants, bar, indoor pool, exercise room, game room, valet laundry, shops, parking lot, transport to airport. AE, CB, DC, MC, V.*

The Mayfair Regent. Situated on the lakefront and small by contemporary standards, the 19-story Mayfair Regent emphasizes the elegance, privacy, and personal attention found in fine European hotels. Tea and fresh fruit are served on your arrival. Rooms are equipped with minibar, color TV with remote control, and telephones at bedside, bathside, and desk. There are toweling robes, makeup and shaving mirrors, scales, and toiletries. You'll find an umbrella in case it rains. Shoes left outside your door at night appear shined the next morning. Afternoon tea is offered in the Mayfair Lounge daily 3–5. Limousines, theater tickets, and other needs can be arranged through the concierge. Meeting rooms have audiovisual equipment. Weekend packages are available. The hotel restaurants are the Ciel Bleu (wags note that the "blue sky" refers to the location of the prices rather than the quality of the food) and the Palm, a steak and lobster house known as much for its brusque service as for its oversize lobster. But don't worry; fine restaurants abound in the area. *181 E. Lake Shore Dr., Chicago 60611, tel. 312/787–8500 or 800/545–4000. 201 rooms, 30 suites. Facilities: restaurant, lounge, nonsmoking floor, beauty salon, valet service, concierge, valet parking. AE, CB, DC, MC, V.*

Sheraton Plaza. Another inhabitant of the elegant side streets east of Michigan Avenue's Magnificent Mile, the Sheraton occupies the floors above 14 in a 40-story building. All guest rooms were refurbished in 1987; the renovation, at a cost of $3 million, brought new furniture, wall, window, and bathroom treatments, and an upgraded safety system. Room decor is homelike rather than formal or grand. Each room has color TV with cable, a bar, shower massage, and retractable clothesline. A concierge will help with special requests. A family plan permits children under 18 to stay free in their parents' room using existing bedding. There are weekday and weekend packages and special rates for frequent guests, travel agents, airline employees, retired people, clergy, government, and AAA members. *160 E. Huron St., Chicago 60611, tel. 312/787–2900 or 800/325–3535. 334 rooms, 100 suites. Facilities: 70 nonsmoking rooms, outdoor rooftop pool, restaurant, valet laundry, lounge, gift shop, concierge, 24-hour room service. AE, CB, DC, MC, V.*

The Talbott. This hotel, the Delaware Towers (25 E. Delaware Pl.), and The Elms (18 E. Elm St.) are members of the Gold Coast Group; their accommodations and facilities are similar. Small European-style hotels, they offer suite accommodations, all with kitchen and bar, in attractively renovated older buildings. Nightly turndown service and complimentary morning coffee and newspaper are among the amenities. Personal care items are provided; hair dryers are available on request. There are weekend packages and special rates for stays of one month or more. *20 E. Delaware Pl., Chicago 60611, tel. 312/943–0161 or 800/621–8506. 138 suites. Facilities: transport to airport. AE, CB, DC, MC, V.*

The Tremont. Situated in a handsome old building of 1923, the Tremont was renovated in 1985. Extensive use of wood and brass make the lobby reminiscent of a men's club. The Tremont offers a concierge, a multilingual staff, and turndown service with cognac and mints. Like its sister hotel, the Whitehall, the Tremont seems to have changed little over the years, which is probably just what its established clientele values. The hotel's restaurant is the unique Cricket's, and there is a lounge on the premises. *100 E. Chestnut St., Chicago 60611, tel. 312/751–*

1900 or 800/621–8133. 123 rooms, 8 suites. Facilities: restaurant, lounge, concierge, valet, parking, laundry, 24-hour room service. AE, CB, DC, MC, V.

The Whitehall. Muted and formal in style, the Whitehall is one of Chicago's older, fine small hotels. As with its sister, the Tremont, one feels that time may have passed it by. In recent years its vaunted service has been less than flawless, and its Whitehall Club restaurant has seen ups and downs. The location, just west of Michigan Avenue and the John Hancock Center, is unbeatable for shoppers and others headed for the Near North. Business meeting facilities are available. *105 E. Delaware Pl., Chicago 60611, tel. 312/944–6300 or 800/621–8295. 227 rooms, 16 suites. Facilities: restaurant, lounge, valet, concierge, valet parking, laundry. AE, CB, DC, MC, V.*

Moderate **Claridge Hotel.** Nestled among Victorian houses on a tree-lined
★ Near North street, this building of 1930s vintage was fully renovated in 1987. With 173 rooms on 13 floors, the hotel is intimate rather than bustling. The simply but tastefully furnished rooms have remote-control TV and minibar. Complimentary Continental breakfast is served, and a newspaper is provided. A concierge is on duty. Two floors are designated for nonsmokers; three parlor board rooms can accommodate small business meetings. The hotel restaurant is JP's, an outstanding, moderately priced seafood restaurant. *1244 N. Dearborn Pkwy., Chicago 60610, tel. 312/787–4980 or 800/245–1258. 173 rooms, 3 suites. Facilities: restaurant, piano bar, access to nearby health club, valet parking, concierge and limousine service. AE, CB, DC, MC, V.*

Days Inn of Chicago. The location is great, but the rooms here are on the small side, and the furnishings are merely adequate. The hotel has an outdoor pool and sun deck for warm weather use, a coffee shop, a revolving rooftop restaurant, and two lounges. Meeting rooms are available for the business traveler; corporate rates can be arranged. While nothing is wrong here, the rates seem steep in relation to what you get and to what's available elsewhere. *644 N. Lake Shore Dr., Chicago 60611, tel. 312/943–9200 or 800/325–2525. 580 rooms, 6 suites. Facilities: 2 restaurants, 2 lounges, outdoor pool, access to McClury Sports Complex, valet laundry, parking in hotel. AE, DC, MC, V.*

Inn of Chicago. This hotel, opened some 60 years ago, recently became a Best Western property. After a three-year, $15 million renovation, Inn of Chicago is attractive and tasteful. Each room has color TV. Handicapped-equipped rooms are available, and the entrance is handicapped accessible. A restaurant remains open 24 hours. The hotel is not lavish, but neither are its prices, which are quite reasonable given its great location just east of Michigan Avenue. The top floor, once the Chicago Press Club, has been turned into business suites. Facilities for business travelers include screens, monitors, VCRs, projectors, and computers. Weekend packages are a good deal. *162 E. Ohio St., Chicago 60611, tel. 312/787–3100 or 800/528–1234. 358 rooms, 26 suites. Facilities: restaurant, lounge, valet laundry, access to health club. AE, CB, DC, MC, V.*

Lenox House. Lenox House is conveniently located to North Michigan Avenue and is not too far from downtown. An "all-suite" hotel, Lenox House has "executive studio suites" furnished in living-room style: Beds fold out from a wall closet. The one-bedroom suite offers separate living and bedroom space. All accommodations come with wet-bar kitchen. Weekend packages are a bargain, and long-term corporate rates are offered. *616 N. Rush St., Chicago 60611, tel. 312/337–1000 or 800/445–3669. 330 suites. Facilities: restaurant, bar, concierge. AE, DC, V.*

★ **The Raphael.** On one of the nicest Near North streets, east of Michigan Avenue and next to the John Hancock Center, the Raphael offers the same intimacy, the same European-style multilingual service, the same tastefully furnished and appointed rooms with color TV and refrigerator that other hotels provide—at half the price. True, there are no galleries of fine art or state-of-the-art business equipment. But for those who want the experience of a fine hotel at the price of a chain hotel, the Raphael is the place to come. Weekend packages reduce the rates even further. *201 E. Delaware Pl., Chicago 60611, tel. 312/943–5000 or 800/821–5343. 175 rooms. Facilities: restaurant, lounge. AE, DC, MC, V.*

★ **The Richmont.** One of a new breed of hotel, the Richmont is an intimate establishment in recently renovated quarters. Charming rather than luxurious, comfortably rather than elegantly appointed, hotels such as this one offer a lot at relatively reasonable prices. Continental breakfast and hors d'oeuvres at cocktail time are included in the tariff. Weekend packages are a bargain. The delightful Rue St. Clair restaurant is on the premises. *162 E. Ontario St., Chicago 60611, tel. 312/787–3580 or 800/621–8055. 193 rooms, 13 suites. Facilities: restaurant, piano bar, access to Grand Ohio Health Club, valet service, valet parking, transport to airport. AE, CB, DC, MC, V.*

River North Hotel. In keeping with what's happening in the rest of the River North neighborhood, this Best Western hotel was recently renovated and is now strikingly done in tones of mauve and gray. Rooms are equipped with remote-control cable TV and refrigerator; shampoo, conditioner, and face lotion are provided. The health facility has a pool, a sundeck, a small selection of resistance weights, and a sauna. Suites equipped with exercise machines and slant boards are available. The hotel provides fax services, typing, and photocopying on request. *125 W. Ohio St., Chicago 60610, tel. 312/467–0800 or 800/528–1234. 149 rooms, 24 suites. Facilities: restaurant, lounge, indoor pool, health club, valet, concierge, free parking. AE, CB, DC, MC, V.*

Inexpensive **Comfort Inn of Lincoln Park.** A bit out of the way when your business or pleasure is Downtown or on the Magnificent Mile, this Comfort Inn is nonetheless pleasantly situated in a vintage building at the northern edge of the Lincoln Park neighborhood. As at all Comfort Inns, you can expect a complimentary Continental breakfast, color TV, and attractively clean rooms. Nothing fancy here, but neither is the price. Corporate and government rates are available. *601 W. Diversey Ave., Chicago 60614, tel. 312/348–2810 or 800/228–5150. 74 rooms. Facilities: free parking. AE, CB, DC, MC, V.*

La Salle Motor Lodge. The rooms of this unusually nice establishment have been recently renovated, and the pleasant furnishings include color TV. The La Salle Cafe on the premises provides room service. Don't expect amenities here; what you will get is more than the minimum accommodation and a good location, five blocks west of the Magnificent Mile, at close to a minimum price. *720 N. La Salle St., Chicago 60610, tel. 312/664–8100. 71 rooms, 4 suites. Facilities: restaurant, free parking. AE, DC, MC, V.*

Ohio House. Strictly motel modern in style, the well-located Ohio House motel has color TV in every room. Amenities are about what you'd expect from a quality motel, and so is the price. *600 N. La Salle St., Chicago 60610, tel. 312/943–6000. 50 rooms, 1 suite. Facilities: coffee shop, free parking. AE, DC, MC, V.*

O'Hare Airport

Expensive **Embassy Suites Hotel.** Part of the new wave of hotel construction at O'Hare, the 11-story Embassy Suites has 300 suites, each with living room and bedroom, two TVs, three telephones, a wet bar, and a refrigerator. The living room comes with a queen-size sofa bed, a work table, and a conference area. The decor is attractive and comfortable. Complimentary full breakfast and a cocktail reception are included in the tariff. Meeting and conference facilities are available; business equipment includes fax machines and computers. *6501 N. Mannheim Rd., Rosemont 60018, tel. 708/699–6300 or 800/362–2779. 300 suites. Facilities: restaurant, bar, indoor pool, sundeck, health club, valet parking, laundry. AE, CB, DC, MC, V.*

Hotel Sofitel. One of the newer luxury hotels, the Sofitel offers public areas richly appointed with marble, wood, glass, and Oriental rugs. Murals of French scenery and fresh flowers enhance the decor. The rooms, furnished in contemporary style, feature full-length mirrors, oak furniture, and floral arrangements. Amenities include turndown service with a fresh rose and a French chocolate truffle. The concierge is available around the clock. A French restaurant and brasserie and a French bakery are on the premises. Facilities for business meetings are available, as are support services. There are rooms equipped for disabled guests and nonsmokers. Corporate rates and weekend packages offer substantial reductions. *5550 N. River Rd., Rosemont 60018, tel. 708/678–4488 or 800/223–5959. 305 rooms, 16 suites. Facilities: restaurant, bar, bakery, indoor pool, health club, sauna, massage, nonsmoking rooms, concierge, room service, valet parking, free airport shuttle. AE, CB, DC, MC, V.*

Hyatt Regency O'Hare. You'll recognize the Hyatt Regency O'Hare by the four gold mirror-paned towers visible from miles away. Inside, a central atrium soars eight stories to the glass roof, and glass-enclosed elevators glide up and down. Leafy vines hang from the ceiling and walkways facing the atrium, but even the lavish use of plants doesn't overcome the stark, massive look of the poured concrete interior. Rooms equipped for the disabled are available. The health club offers a dome-enclosed swimming pool, weights, exercise bikes, Jacuzzi, and sauna. Two club floors have concierge service and a private lounge with honor bar. Business services include secretarial help, word processing, and photocopying. Northwest or Delta frequent fliers should ask about the hotel's tie-in with these programs. *9300 W. Bryn Mawr Ave., Rosemont 60018, tel. 708/696–1234 or 800/223–1234. 1,100 rooms, 52 suites. Facilities: 2 restaurants, café, lounge, indoor pool, health club, concierge, 24-hour room service, nonsmoking rooms, executive services, free parking, free airport shuttle. AE, CB, DC, MC, V.*

Radisson Suite Hotel O'Hare Airport. A newcomer on the O'Hare hotel scene, the Radisson Suite Hotel capitalizes on the growing demand for suite rather than room accommodations. The low-rise hotel's 296 two-room suites are furnished in comfortable, homelike style, complete with color schemes that don't match. The use of light woods gives a casual ambience. Living rooms are equipped with wet bar, refrigerator, microwave, sofa bed, arm chair, and dining table with four chairs; each suite has two TVs and two telephones. Room rates include American-style breakfast and a two-hour free cocktail hour in the evening—amenities usually available only in expensive "club" accommodations, if at all. Each suite opens onto a balcony overlooking an interior courtyard. Health facilities include a pool, resistance weights, whirlpool, and sauna. Conference facilities are available. A weekend package includes a complimentary bottle of champagne on arrival. Radisson has travel partnerships with Continental, Northwest, and Piedmont airlines. *5500 N. River Rd., Rosemont 60018, tel. 708/678-4000 or 800/333-3333. 296 suites. Facilities: restaurant, bar, health club, indoor pool, parking on premises, free airport van. AE, DC, MC, V.*

The Westin O'Hare. The long, low-rise modern concrete strucshrubbery adorn the front of the building. A glassed-in front lobby has wood paneling and an arched white ceiling, and a lobby lounge is here. Rooms are pleasantly decorated if nondescript: Each has a guest bar and refrigerator, color TV with cable, and a second TV in the bathroom. The health club includes a small pool, Jacuzzi, sauna, 2 racquetball courts, and a sundeck. An executive club offers additional amenities: concierge, separate check in and express check out, lounge, complimentary Continental breakfast and newspaper, and complimentary cocktails. The Business Center provides office and meeting space, copying and secretarial services, computers, and telex and fax. The hotel's restaurant and café both offer dinner and theater packages in combination with the Westin's Rose Theatre. *6100 N. River Rd., Rosemont 60018, tel. 708/698-6000 or 800/228-3000. 527 rooms. Facilities: 2 restaurants, café, indoor pool, health club, sauna, whirlpool, 24-hour room service, concierge, secretarial services, telex and fax, 135 nonsmoking rooms, parking, free airport shuttle. AE, CB, DC, MC, V.*

Moderate **Holiday Inn O'Hare.** While this older concrete structure looks worn outside, it is pleasant within. The recently refurbished lobby has a marble front desk and a small seating area with skylight above. Beyond it, an indoor atrium is lined with shops and restaurants. On the lower atrium level, an attractive area decorated lavishly with plants and shrubs is the setting for umbrella-topped tables, couches, and a bar. A large health facility provides resistance weights, exercise bikes, sauna, and whirlpool. A putting green, an electronic game room, and a game area (ping-pong and badminton) are part of the complex. Several large meeting and conference rooms are available, and support services can be provided. A new executive floor features a private lounge, complimentary Continental breakfast and hors d'oeuvres at cocktail time, and built-in hair dryers and toweling robes in bathrooms. Business facilities include conference rooms, audiovisual equipment, closed-circuit TV, and teleconferencing. Weekend packages are available. *5440 N. River Rd., Rosemont 60018, tel. 708/671-6350 or 800/465-4329. 507 rooms. Facilities: restaurant, cafe, lounge, indoor/outdoor* *pool, health club, sauna, nonsmoking floor, free airport shuttle. AE, CB, DC, MC, V.*

Howard Johnson O'Hare Plaza Hotel. This concrete structure is sparsely landscaped, its decor minimal. Yet the hotel is clean and conveniently located to public transportation (the el stop is across the street). The staff seem inexperienced but pleasant and helpful. A club floor offers free Continental breakfast and other amenities. Handicapped-equipped rooms are available, as are several small meeting rooms. Business support services can be provided. Weekend packages are offered. *5615 N. Cumberland Rd., Chicago 60631, tel. 312/693–5800. 245 rooms. Facilities: restaurant, bar, outdoor pool, valet laundry, nonsmoking rooms, parking, free airport shuttle. AE, CB, DC, MC, V.*

O'Hare Hilton. This hotel is directly opposite the airport terminal area and is connected to it via walkways. Shops line the promenade (lower) level between the hotel and the airport. The Hilton's 10 floors have 885 rooms, all of which may be filled when bad weather forces large-scale flight delays. The ready availability of customers probably accounts for this hotel's relative lack of amenities, compared to other airport hotels in the same price range. Rooms are clean but could use redecoration; public areas do little to delight the eye: The effect is a bit worn and dreary. Rooms equipped for the disabled are available. Business services are limited to secretarial help that can be booked with an agency located in the hotel promenade; the concierge may help with additional requirements. Two undistinguished restaurants, a coffee shop, and three lounges may provide some solace to the weary traveler. TWA, American Airlines, and United Airlines frequent fliers get points when they stay here. Weekend packages are available. *Box 66414, O'Hare International Airport, Chicago 60666, tel. 312/686–8000 or 800/445–8667. 885 rooms. Facilities: 2 restaurants, cafe, 3 lounges, concierge, nonsmoking rooms, shops. AE, CB, DC, MC, V.*

Sheraton International at O'Hare. The bright, low-ceiling lobby has brass accents, plants, and several comfortable couches. Two restaurants and a lounge are just off the lobby. While the surroundings are a bit drab, the hotel's "European courtyard" is pleasant in summer; the spacious outdoor area includes a large patio, gardens, a heated pool, and a children's playground. The hotel has a concierge. Amenities include a telephone in each bathroom. At this writing, guest rooms are being refurbished. Weekend packages and handicapped-equipped rooms are offered. American Airlines frequent fliers get points when they stay here. *6810 N. Mannheim Rd., Rosemont 60118, tel. 708/297–1234 or 800/325–3535. 463 rooms. Facilities: 2 restaurants, lounge, heated pool, concierge, room service, nonsmoking rooms, free airport shuttle. AE, CB, DC, MC, V.*

Inexpensive **Comfort Inn.** Those who are familiar with Comfort Inns will know what to expect here. The three-story modern concrete building is brand new, the rooms sparkling clean. While the accommodations are not lavish, neither are the prices, and you'll get more amenities than you'd expect. Exercise equipment includes a weight machine, bicycles, and a whirlpool. A 24-hour restaurant is on the corner. Continental breakfast is included. Meeting rooms and valet service are available. *2175 E. Touhy Ave., Des Plaines 60118, tel. 708/635–1300 or 800/228–5150. 150 rooms, 16 suites. Facilities: restaurant, cafe, bar, health* *club, whirlpool, free airport transportation. AE, CB, DC, MC, V.*

Sixpence Inn. The Sixpence Inn's motto is "the best of the budgets," and it's not far off the mark. Don't look for amenities here; while the rooms have telephones and color TV, there is no restaurant or lounge (a Denny's is across the street), no shuttle service to the airport. But for a very low rate you'll get a clean, pleasant place to spend the night, and you won't pay for frills you may not need or want. *9480 W. Lawrence Ave., Schiller Park 60176, tel. 708/671–4282. 143 rooms. Facilities: restaurant nearby. AE, MC, V.*

8 The Arts and Nightlife

The Arts

Chicago is a splendid city for the arts. In addition to dozens of classical music organizations, including a world-class symphony orchestra and opera company, there are hundreds of clubs featuring jazz, rock, folk, and country music; some 50 theaters; an outstanding dance company; and movie theaters that show everything from first-run features to avant-garde films.

Music

The Chicago Symphony is internationally renowned, and Chicago's Lyric Opera may be the best opera company in America today. Season subscribers take virtually all the tickets to these performances, but subscribers who can't use their tickets sometimes return them to the box office. If you go to the opera house or Symphony Hall a half hour before performance time, you may find someone with an extra ticket to sell.

Orchestras   **Chicago Symphony** (220 S. Michigan Ave., tel. 312/435–8122). The season at Symphony Hall extends from September through May. Daniel Barenboim is scheduled to take over the baton from Sir Georg Solti in the 1991–1992 season. In the summer you can see and hear the Chicago Symphony at Ravinia Park in suburban Highland Park, under the direction of James Levine. It's a trip of about 25 miles from Chicago, accessible by train. The park is lovely, and lawn seats are always available even when (rarely) those in the Shed and the smaller Murray Theatre are sold out. Performances usually feature one or more notable soloists. For program, ticket, and travel information, tel. 312/728–4642.

Grant Park Symphony Orchestra (tel. 312/294–2420). Sponsored by the Chicago Park District, the Grant Park Symphony gives free concerts during the summer at the James C. Petrillo Bandshell in Grant Park, between Michigan Avenue and Columbus Drive at about Adams Street (enter from Monroe Street and follow the crowd). Performances usually are on Wednesday, Friday, Saturday, and Sunday evenings. The weekly *Reader* or a daily newspaper will have details of programs and performance times.

The **Orchestra of Illinois** (tel. 312/341–1975) performs at various locations around the state.

Concert Halls   **Auditorium Theatre** (70 E. Congress Pkwy., tel. 312/922–2110). Subscription concerts and recital series are given throughout the year.

Orchestra Hall (220 S. Michigan Ave., tel. 312/435–8122). A variety of concerts and recitals are programmed during the year.

Mandel Hall (57th St. at University Ave., tel. 312/702–8068). Guest orchestras and performers are scheduled on a regular basis at this hall on the University of Chicago campus.

Smaller halls in the Loop/Near North area include **Fullerton Hall** in the Art Institute (Michigan Ave. at Adams St., tel. 312/472–5964), the **Newberry Library** (60 W. Walton Ave., tel. 312/943–9090), and the **Three Arts Club** (1300 N. Dearborn Pkwy., tel. 312/944–6250).

Choral and   The **Chicago Children's Choir** (tel. 312/324–8300) is one of the
Chamber Groups   country's premier children's choral groups, with members drawn from a broad spectrum of racial, ethnic, and economic groups. Performances are given each year during the Christ-

mas season and in early June; other concerts are scheduled periodically.

City Musick (tel. 312/642–1766) has received critical acclaim for its performance of Baroque works on period instruments. It has an outstanding small chorus.

Music of the Baroque (tel. 312/663–1900), the granddaddy of independent ensembles in Chicago, is a nationally known, highly polished professional chorus and orchestra concentrating on the works—particularly the choral works—of the Baroque period. It schedules two concert series, with performances at various locations each year.

The **William Ferris Chorale** (tel. 312/922–2070), a distinguished choral ensemble that focuses on 20th-century music, gives concerts throughout the year.

Two other small choral groups that do outstanding work are the **Oriana Singers** (tel. 312/907–3290) and **Basically Bach** (tel. 312/334–2800).

Opera **Chamber Opera Chicago** (500 N. Orleans St., tel. 312/822–0770). A relatively new troupe, the Chamber Opera performs major works in English.

Chicago Opera Theatre (2936 N. Southport Ave., tel. 312/663–0048). The Chicago Opera specializes in English-language productions of smaller works suited to the intimate setting of the comfortable church auditorium in which it performs. Its 1990 productions include Delibes' *Lakmé* and Rodgers and Hammerstein's *Carousel*.

Lyric Opera of Chicago (20 N. Wacker Dr., tel. 312/332–2244). The season at the Civic Opera House runs from September through January; the tickets are difficult to come by.

Light Opera **The Light Opera Works** (tel. 312/869–6300). Gilbert and Sullivan operettas and other light operas are performed during a June–December season.

Theater

While road-show productions of Broadway hits do come to Chicago, the true vigor of its theater scene springs from the multitude of small ensembles that have made a home here. They range from the critically acclaimed Steppenwolf and the Goodman Theatre to fringe groups that specialize in experimental work. Visitors can get a full listing of current Chicago theater attractions from **Curtain Call** (tel. 312/977–1755).

Many smaller companies perform in tiny or make-shift theaters, where admission prices are moderate to quite inexpensive. You can save money on seats at **Hot Tix** (24 S. State St.), where unsold tickets are available at half price (plus a small service charge) on the day of performance; you can't learn what's available until that day, and you have to pay cash. The Hot Tix booth is open Monday noon–6, Tuesday–Friday 10–6, and Saturday 10–5; tickets for Sunday performances are sold on Saturday.

Theater groups from throughout the world perform at the annual International Theatre Festival, held every other year in the spring. In 1990 the big draws were Kenneth Branagh's productions of *King Lear* and *A Midsummer Night's Dream*.

Commercial Theater Most of the houses listed here are hired by independent producers for commercial (and sometimes nonprofit) productions; they have no resident producer or company.

Apollo Theater Center (2540 N. Lincoln, tel. 312/935–6100). This modern space is located in one of Lincoln Park's few strip malls.

Auditorium Theater (70 E. Congress Pkwy., tel. 312/922–2110). Acoustics and sight lines are excellent in this Louis Sullivan architectural masterpiece. In 1990, the smash musical *Phantom of the Opera* played here to packed houses.

Blackstone Theater (60 E. Balbo, tel. 312/341–8455). This grand and ornate space is now owned by DePaul University and used for productions by its theater school.

Briar St. Theater (3133 N. Halsted St., tel. 312/348–4000). Local productions of hit Broadway plays often find their way to this modest space in Lakeview.

Candlelight Dinner Playhouse (5620 S. Harlem Ave., Summit, tel. 708/496–3000). Just over the city line in Summit, the Candlelight usually offers superb productions of classic Broadway musicals. The food is edible, and the dinner/theater package is a good deal, or you can just go for the show. The Forum, a smaller theater, is next door.

Chicago Theater (175 N. State St., tel. 312/236–4300). This former movie palace and vaudeville house was gaudily but lovingly restored in 1986, but it has floundered since then under various management companies and spends most of its time empty and dark.

Halsted Theater Center (2700 N. Halsted, tel. 312/348–0110). This new complex has two small theater spaces, with an adjacent parking lot.

Mayfair Theater (Blackstone Hotel, 636 S. Michigan Ave., tel. 312/786–9120). The audience-participation mystery *Shear Madness* has been playing here for the last eight years and shows no signs of closing.

Organic Theater (3319 N. Clark St., tel. 312/327–5588). Once a theater company in its own right, the Organic is now largely just another performance space.

Royal George Theater Center (1641 N. Halsted St., tel. 312/988–9000). A new building, the Royal George has one large, gracious theater, one smaller studio theater, a cabaret space, and a restaurant.

Shubert Theater (22 W. Monroe St., tel. 312/977–1700). A grand 19th-century-style theater, the Shubert is one of the few remaining remnants of the Loop's once-thriving theater district.

Wellington Theater (750 W. Wellington St., tel. 312/975–7171). The former Ivanhoe Theater (explaining the exterior's medieval half-timbered look) was refurbished and reopened in 1989.

Performing Groups Chicago's reputation as a theatrical powerhouse was born from its dozens of small not-for-profit theater companies that produce everything from Shakespeare to Stephen Sondheim. The groups listed below do consistently interesting work, and some have gained national attention. Some, such as Steppenwolf and the Remains Theater Company, are ensemble troupes; others, notably the Goodman, the Court, and the Body Politic, are production companies that use different casts for each show. Keep an open mind when you're choosing a show to see; even a group you've never heard of may be harboring one or two underpaid geniuses. *The Reader* carries complete theater listings and reviews of the more avant-garde shows.

Body Politic/Victory Gardens (2257–61 N. Lincoln Ave., tel. 312/871–3000). These two venerable institutions have traditionally offered polished productions of both modern American plays and works of Shakespeare and Shaw. The Body Politic, however, recently underwent a change of artistic directors and may shift its focus.

City Lit Theater Company (Live Bait Theater, 3912 N. Clark St., tel. 312/271–1100). This imaginative troupe presents original scripts based on novels and other literary works. The hit of its 1989–1990 season was *The Good Times Are Killing Me*, an adaptation of cartoonist Lynda Barry's novel about growing up amid racial tension.

Court Theater (5535 S. Ellis Ave., tel. 312/753–4472). On the University of Chicago campus, the Court revives classic plays with varying success.

Goodman Theater (200 S. Columbus Dr., tel. 312/443–3800). One of the oldest and best theaters in Chicago, the Goodman is known for its polished performances of contemporary works starring well-known actors. Now situated behind the Art Institute, it's due to move into two former movie palaces in the north Loop. At press time no date had been set for the transfer.

Interplay (Pilsen East Center for the Arts, 1935 S. Halsted, tel. 312/243–6240). This small theater stands in a developing artists' neighborhood, which is still far from gentrification, southwest of the Loop.

Next Theater Company (Noyes Cultural Arts Center, 927 Noyes, Evanston, tel. 708/475–1875). Founded by an Evanston woman who thought it would be fun to produce plays (and evidently was right), the Next specializes in rarely performed scripts.

Pegasus Players (1145 Wilson Ave., tel. 312/271–2638). Pegasus tackles interesting and difficult works, usually producing at least one Stephen Sondheim musical each season. The spacious theater is at the city's Truman College.

Remains Theater (1800 N. Clybourn, tel. 312/335–9800). Remains specializes in original scripts by American writers, featuring gritty acting in the Steppenwolf tradition. Cofounder William Petersen turns up in the movies now and then.

Steppenwolf (tel. 312/472–4141). The nationally known Steppenwolf company brings a dark, brooding, Method-acting style to its consistently successful productions. Illustrious alumni include John Malkovich, Joan Allen, and Laurie Metcalf. Its Broadway production of John Steinbeck's *The Grapes of Wrath* won a Tony award in 1990 for best play. The company is moving to a new and larger theater at 1650 N. Halsted in late spring 1991 and using the Apollo Theater (*see* above) for its productions during the first few months of the year.

The Theatre Building (1225 W. Belmont Ave., tel. 312/327–
5252). This rehabbed warehouse provides a permanent home
for half a dozen small companies of local renown, including the
Absolute Theatre Company, American Blues Theatre, Com-
mons Theatre, Immediate Theatre Company, New Tuners
Theatre, and Touchstone Theatre.

Wisdom Bridge Theater (1559 W. Howard, tel. 312/743–6000).
Wisdom Bridge's innovative productions are too varied to pi-
geonhole, but usually worth seeing.

Dance

Though there are fewer organized dance troupes in Chicago
than one might expect to find in a city so renowned for music
and theater, there are several companies that perform regularly.

Ballet Chicago (222 S. Riverside Plaza, tel. 312/993–7575) is the
city's only resident classical ballet troupe, successor to the
now-defunct Chicago City Ballet. The new company formed in
1988 under the artistic direction of Daniel Duell, formerly of
the New York City Ballet, and has received critical acclaim for
its work. The group is currently planning to conduct a spring
season only.

Chicago's most notable success story in dance is the **Hubbard
St. Dance Company** (tel. 312/902–1500), whose contemporary,
jazzy vitality has made it extremely popular. Three other companies worth seeing are the **Chicago Repertory Dance Ensemble** (1016 N. Dearborn St., tel. 312/440–9494), the **Joseph
Holmes Dance Theater** (1935 S. Halsted Ave., tel. 312/942–
0065), and the **Muntu Dance Theater** (Catherine Dunham Theater, 6800 S. Wentworth Ave., tel. 312/285–1721).

Film

Many cinemas on the near north side offer first-run Hollywood
movies on multiple screens, including **Chestnut Station** (830 N.
Clark St., tel. 312/337–7301), **Water Tower Theater** (845 N.
Michigan Ave., tel. 312/649–5790), **900 N. Michigan Theater**
(tel. 312/787–1988), and **McClurg Court** (330 E. Ohio St., tel.
312/642–0723).

The **Esquire** (58 E. Oak St., tel. 312/280–0101), an Art Deco
landmark, recently underwent a renovation that preserved its
facade but divided it into four theaters.

A north-side first-run movie house of some historical interest is
the **Biograph Theatre** (2433 N. Lincoln Ave., tel. 312/348–
4123); gangster John Dillinger was shot in front of the
Biograph by FBI agents in 1934. If you ask around, you may be
able to find a local who can show the bullet marks in the side of
the building.

The most convenient first-run movie theater for those staying
in the south Loop is the recently built **Burnham Plaza** (826 S.
Wabash Ave., tel. 312/922–1090).

For something a bit different, try **The Fine Arts Theatre** (410 S.
Michigan Ave., tel. 312/939–3700), whose four screens show independent, foreign, and avant-garde films.

The Film Center of the Art Institute (Columbus Dr. at Jackson
Blvd., tel. 312/443–3737) specializes in unusual current films
and revivals of rare classics. The program here changes almost

daily, and filmmakers sometimes give lectures at the Film Center.

Facets Multimedia (1517 W. Fullerton, tel. 312/281–4114) presents a variety of rare and exotic films; call and see whether a particular day's fare appeals to you. The basement has a videotape-rental library.

The Music Box Theatre (3733 N. Southport Ave., tel. 312/871–6604) is a small and lovingly restored 1920s movie palace. Programs at this richly decorated theater change nightly, except for special runs; the theatre shows a mix of classics and outstanding recent films, emphasizing independent filmmakers. The theater organ is played during intermission at special events and as an accompaniment to silent films. If you love old theaters and old movies, don't miss a trip to the Music Box.

Nightlife

Chicago comes alive at night, with something for everyone, from loud and loose to sophisticated and sedate. *The Reader* (available Thursday and Friday in Lincoln Park and Hyde Park) is your best guide to the entertainment scene. The *Chicago Tribune* and the *Chicago Sun-Times* on Friday are good sources of information on current shows and starting times. Shows usually begin at 9 PM; cover charges generally range from $3 to $7, depending on the day of the week; Friday and Saturday nights are the most expensive.

If you want to find "Rush Street," the famous Chicago bar scene, don't bother looking on Rush Street itself. Most of the nightlife is now located on Division Street between Clark and State streets, having been pushed north by office- and apartment development. Among the better-known singles bars are **Mother's** (26 W. Division St.), featured in the motion picture . . . *About Last Night;* **P.S. Chicago** (8 W. Division St.); and **Butch McGuire's** (20 W. Division St.). If you are in the mood for dancing, try **Eddie Rocket's** (9 W. Division St.). This area is particularly festive on warm weekend nights, when the street adopts a carnival-like atmosphere.

You can find a similar atmosphere in the establishments at the North Pier development (455 E. Illinois St.), notably the **Baja Beach Club** and **Dick's Last Resort**. North Pier is the center of a growing nightlife scene just north of the Loop and east of Michigan Avenue.

The list of blues and jazz clubs includes several South Side locations, and visitors to Chicago should be cautious about transportation here late at night, since some of these neighborhoods are dangerous. Drive your own car or a previously reserved cab or limo, and avoid public transportation. Some clubs provide guarded parking lots or can arrange cab service for visitors.

Parking in North Side neighborhoods, particularly Lincoln Park and Lakeview, can be scarce on weekends. If you're visiting nightspots in these areas, consider leaving your car behind and taking cabs or public transportation.

Music

Blues In the years following World War II, Chicago-style blues grew into its own musical form. Blues flourished here in the 1950s, then faded in the 1960s with the advent of rock and roll. Today

Chicago blues is coming back, although more strongly on the trendy North Side than on the South Side where it all began.

Biddy Mulligan's (7644 N. Sheridan Rd., tel. 312/761–6532). The neighborhood ambience attracts a nice mix of customers. The music has expanded beyond blues, yet blues is still the focus. Expect this place to be amiably crowded. Cover charge on weekends. Music starts at 10 PM weekends.

B.L.U.E.S. (2519 N. Halsted St., tel. 312/528–1012). The best of Chicago's own musicians play here and attract a large, friendly crowd.

Blue Chicago (937 N. State St., tel. 312/642–6261). This large room has a good sound system and attracts a cosmopolitan, heterogeneous crowd. Minimum.

B.L.U.E.S. Etcetera (1124 W. Belmont Ave., tel. 312/525–8989). A spacious and comfortable change from overcrowded spots.

Buddy Guy's Legends (754 S. Wabash Ave., tel. 312/427–0333). One of Chicago's own blues legends is part-owner of this converted double storefront in the south Loop. It's spacious, with good sound, good sight lines, and weekday sets that start at 8:30 PM. Cover charge varies.

Kingston Mines (2548 N. Halsted St., tel. 312/477–4646). One of the North Side's oldest spots, the Mines attracts large numbers of blues lovers and cruising singles, the first because of its continuous live weekend entertainment on two stages, the second because of its late closing (4 AM Friday, 5 AM Saturday).

Lilly's (2513 N. Lincoln Ave., tel. 312/525–2422). Lilly's is tiny, warm, and friendly.

New Checkerboard Lounge (423 E. 43rd St., tel. 312/624–3240). Although the neighborhood is rough, this remains one of the great old South Side clubs. The music by name performers is usually worth the trip.

Rosa's Lounge (3420 W. Armitage St., tel. 312/342–0452). Expect good music, at this homey spot in a Hispanic and Polish neighborhood. No cover Monday.

Wise Fools Pub (2270 N. Lincoln Ave., tel. 312/929–1510). The intimate room is an old-time Lincoln Park spot that books name performers. Minimum Saturday.

Jazz **Andy's** (11 E. Hubbard St., tel. 312/642–6805). Once just a big old friendly neighborhood bar in the shadow of the IBM Building, Andy's has become one of Chicago's best spots for serious jazz. The jazz at noon is a boon for music lovers who aren't night owls. No cover at noon.

The Bar at the Ritz-Carlton Hotel (160 E. Pearson St., tel. 312/266–1000). Those who prefer sophisticated jazz in a sophisticated setting will enjoy this place.

The Bulls (1916 N. Lincoln Park West, tel. 312/337–3000). The Bulls, a small club, showcases the best of local groups.

The Cotton Club (1710 S. Michigan Ave., tel. 312/341–9787). This spot is a favorite of upscale young black professionals.

George's (230 W. Kinzie St., tel. 312/644–2290). Once one of the city's best Northern Italian restaurants, George's food has declined while the music remains outstanding, the acoustics excellent. Minimum.

Get Me High Lounge (1758 N. Honore St., tel. 312/252–4090). This place is fun and friendly in a weird sort of way.

Gold Star Sardine Bar (680 N. Lake Shore Dr., tel. 312/664–4215). Housed in a splendid renovated building that once was the Chicago Furniture Mart, this tiny spot books top names that attract a trendy clientele. Minimum.

The Green Mill (4802 N. Broadway, tel. 312/878–5552). This Chicago institution, off the beaten track in untrendy Uptown, has been around for most of this century and has been skillfully renovated to look as if it hasn't been redecorated since it opened. The entertainment ranges from good to outstanding, and the club can get crowded on weekends. On Sunday evenings, the Uptown Poetry Slam, a competitive poetry reading, takes center stage.

Jazz Showcase (636 S. Michigan Ave., tel. 312/427–4300). Nationally known acts perform in the once elegant but decaying setting of the Blackstone Hotel.

Milt Trenier's Lounge (610 Fairbanks Ct., tel. 312/266–6226). Cabaret acts are augmented by Milt himself, who plays with his jazz quintet on weekends.

Moosehead Bar & Grill (163 W. Harrison St., tel. 312/922–3276). One of Chicago's newer spots, Moosehead is located near the Dan Ryan Expressway at the north end of the Printer's Row district. The large, attractive room can be crowded and noisy, particularly with after-work revelers (music starts at 5:30, Monday–Friday).

The Other Place (7600 S. King Dr., tel. 312/874–5476). Here is one of the great South Side places for jazz, although the upscale, mostly black clientele doesn't always seem to be listening to the music. No cover; drink prices are higher during gigs by big-name performers.

Oz (2917 N. Sheffield Ave., tel. 312/975–8100). An intimate, crowded neighborhood bar, Oz features quality local performers Thursday–Saturday.

Pops for Champagne (2934 N. Sheffield Ave., tel. 312/472–1000). Despite the incongruous name, this is a good spot for serious jazz fans. Pops sports a popular champagne bar.

Rock   **Avalon Niteclub** (959 W. Belmont Ave., tel. 312/472–3020). The building's been around for a long time, the acts are up and coming.

Batteries Not Included (2201 N. Clybourn Ave., tel. 312/348–9529). This small place catering to a young, chummy crowd doesn't book big names, but there's lots of youthful talent.

Cabaret Metro (3730 N. Clark St., tel. 312/549–0203). The Metro presents a wide range of artists, from the nationally known to the cream of the local crop, and a wide range of rock styles. People come for a specific show, so the crowd will vary according to the attraction. There's dancing in the Smart Bar, downstairs.

Club Dreamerz (1516 N. Milwaukee Ave., tel. 312/252–1155). Rising young local talent is presented here.

Club Stodola (5553 W. Belmont, tel. 312/545–8166). Local bands play at this somewhat punk spot far west on the North Side.

Cubby Bear (1059 W. Addison St., tel. 312/327–1662). A variety of acts play this scruffy but roomy venue across the street from Wrigley Field. The music usually starts around 10 PM. During baseball season, the Cubby Bear opens in the afternoon to give Cub fans another place to drown their sorrows.

Lounge Ax (2438 N. Lincoln Ave., tel. 312/525–6620). A mix of local rock, folk, country, and reggae acts is presented here nightly.

The Wild Hare (3530 N. Clark St., tel. 312/327–0800). Local groups perform reggae; a Caribbean decor adds to the atmosphere.

Folk and Ethnic **Abbey Pub** (3420 W. Grace, tel. 312/478–4408). Irish music by Irish performers is the fare at this neighborhood establishment.

Deni's Den (2941 N. Clark St., tel. 312/348–8888). This large, attractive spot features Greek performers. Until 4 AM Friday, 5 AM Saturday.

Earl's Pub (2470 N. Lincoln Ave., tel. 312/929–0660). Famed in another incarnation as the Earl of Old Town, Earl still provides outstanding American folk music.

Kitty O'Shea's (720 S. Michigan Ave., tel. 312/922–4400). This handsome room in the Chicago Hilton and Towers recreates an Irish pub, complete with Irish music and food by Irish chefs.

Miomir's Serbian Club (2255 W. Lawrence Ave., tel. 312/784–2111). Come to this club restaurant not for the food but for the music (nightly) and a rousing good time. Full floor shows on weekends.

No Exit (6970 N. Glenwood Ave., tel. 312/743–3355). Folk, jazz, and poetry readings are offered in a comfortable coffeehouse setting reminiscent of the late 1960s. Backgammon and chess sets are available.

Old Town School of Folk Music (909 W. Armitage Ave., tel. 312/525–7793). Chicago's only folk music school, Old Town offers outstanding folk performances.

Tania's (2659 N. Milwaukee Ave., tel. 312/235–7120). This Cuban restaurant becomes a nightclub with salsa bands on weekends. No cover or minimum; no jeans.

Country There isn't much country music in Chicago, but you might try one of these places:

Carol's Pub (4659 N. Clark St., tel. 312/334–2402).
Emerald Point Lounge (3432 W. Irving Park Rd., tel. 312/588–9335).
Lakeview Lounge (5110 N. Broadway, tel. 312/769–0994).
Qamar's Two (3551 N. Elston Ave., tel. 312/539–1121).

Eclectic Clubs in this category don't limit themselves to a single type of music. If you have a strong preference for the kind of music you're going to hear, you will want to call ahead to learn what's playing.

At the Tracks (325 N. Jefferson St., tel. 312/332–1124). An upstairs location affords a fantastic view of the maze of railroad tracks coming into the city from the west. The music is usually excellent, the food pretty good.

Fitzgerald's (6615 W. Roosevelt Rd., Berwyn, tel. 708/788–2118). Though a bit out of the way, Fitzgerald's draws crowds from all over the city and suburbs with a mix of folk, jazz, and blues and a homey summer-cabin ambience.

Park West (322 W. Armitage Ave., tel. 312/929–5959). Shows here tend to be name acts glossily performed; expect high cover and drink prices. The hall itself is large, with good sight lines and acoustics. Jacket required; no jeans.

The Roxy (1505 W. Fullerton Ave., tel. 312/472–8100). A warm, friendly place, the Roxy's decor includes plenty of Hollywood artifacts.

Dance Clubs

Asi Es Colombia (3910 N. Lincoln Ave., tel. 312/348–7444). Good salsa bands attract good dancers. Jacket required.

Cabaret Metro (3730 N. Clark St., tel. 312/549–0203). Dance here to outstanding rock music.

Eddie Rockets (9 W. Division St., tel. 312/787–4881). Dance till dawn with a young singles crowd. Open until 4 AM Friday, 5 AM Saturday.

Esoteria (2247 N. Lincoln Ave., tel. 312/549–4110). The hot new Esoteria is high tech, high camp, and crowded.

Excalibur (1632 N. Dearborn St., tel. 312/266–1944). This River North brownstone hides a super-disco with multiple dance floors and bars, a game room, and a restaurant. Popular with young adults, it attracts a large suburban crowd on weekends. Open Fri. till 2 AM, Sat. till 3 AM. No cover.

Exit (1653 N. Wells St., tel. 312/440–0535). Noisy and punk, Exit is open until 4 AM Friday, 5 AM Saturday.

Gordon (500 N. Clark St., tel. 312/467–9780). Principally a fine restaurant, Gordon has a very good jazz combo that plays after 9 PM Saturday for dancing.

Jukebox Saturday Night (2251 N. Lincoln Ave., tel. 312/525–5000). Recognizable by the red 1950s Chevy jutting from the facade, Jukebox promises plenty of dancing to golden oldies. Open until 2 AM Friday, 3 AM Saturday.

Medusa's (3257 N. Sheffield Ave., tel. 312/935–3635). This popular, punked-out juice bar is set up in an anonymous, industrial-looking building in Lakeview. Progressive rock videos compete with live heavy-metal bands on weekends in the club's three dance rooms. No alcohol is served. Open Fri. and Sat. 7–10:30 PM for all ages, till 2 AM for those over 17.

Moscow at Night (3058 W. Peterson Ave., tel. 312/338–6600). A noisy, good-spirited restaurant, Moscow has a Russian band playing both vocal music and eclectic dance music.

Neo (2350 N. Clark St., tel. 312/528–2622). Neo is loud but not way out. Open until 4 AM Friday, 5 AM Saturday.

Riviera Night Club (4746 N. Racine Ave., tel. 312/769–6300). Laser beams and name bands are the attractions at this cavernous former movie palace. Open until 4 AM Friday, 5 AM Saturday.

Piano Bars

Close-Up Piano Bar (537 S. Dearborn St., tel. 312/663–0439). The Close-Up is a jazz piano bar. A trio plays on Fridays and Saturdays.

Four Seasons (120 E. Delaware, tel. 312/280–8800). Enjoy drinks or dessert to the sounds of jazz piano.

The Salon at the Park Hyatt (800 N. Michigan Ave., tel. 312/280–2222). The Salon is an intimate, elegant spot.

Sports Bars

Ditka's/City Lights (223 W. Ontario St., tel. 312/280–1790). Coach Iron Mike's restaurant and nightclub.

Sluggers (3540 N. Clark St., tel. 312/248–0055). Across from Wrigley Field, this roomy, comfortable bar is packed after Cub games, and the players themselves make occasional personal appearances. Check out the fast- and slow-pitch batting cages on the second floor.

Brew Pubs

Beer brewed on the premises is the attraction at these new spots, and each offers its own distinctive product. All serve food, but only Sieben's is good enough to recommend.

Goose Island Brewery (1800 N. Clybourn Ave., tel. 312/915–0071).

Sieben's River North (436 W. Ontario St., tel. 312/787–7313).

Tap & Growler (901 W. Jackson Blvd., tel. 312/829–4141).

Comedy Clubs

Improvisation has long had a home and a successful following in Chicago; stand-up comedy has fared less well. Up-and-coming local talent has brightened the scene in recent years.

Catch a Rising Star (Hyatt Regency Chicago, 151 E. Wacker Dr., tel. 312/565–4242). The spacious club offers top-name acts. Cover charge, minimum weekends.

Comedy Cottage (9751 W. Higgins Rd., Rosemont, tel. 708/696–4077). This is the convenient place to go for those staying near the airport. A long-established club, Comedy Cottage has nurtured some of today's stars and retains its high quality.

Funny Firm (318 W. Grand St., tel. 312/321–9500). Chicago's newest comedy club books both local and national stand-up talent.

Improvisations (504 N. Wells St., tel. 312/782–6387). When you tire of the comedy here, you can munch dim sum in the attached restaurant. Cover charge and minimum.

Improvisation Institute (2939 W. Belmont Ave., tel. 312/588–2668). The resident improv group is very good.

Last Laff (6350 N. River Rd., Rosemont, tel. 708/823–5233). Another good spot near the airport, this club features mainly local talent.

Second City (1616 N. Wells St., tel. 312/337–3992). An institution for more than 20 years, Second City has spawned some of the hottest comedians around. Yet in recent years the once bitingly funny, loony improvisation has given way to a less imaginative and more raunchy style.

Zanies (1548 N. Wells St., tel. 312/337–4027). Perhaps Chicago's best stand-up comedy spot, Zanies books outstanding national talent. Reservations recommended.

Index

Personal Itinerary

Departure *Date*

Time

Transportation

Arrival *Date*   *Time*

Departure *Date*   *Time*

Transportation

Accommodations

Arrival *Date*   *Time*

Departure *Date*   *Time*

Transportation

Accommodations

Arrival *Date*   *Time*

Departure *Date*   *Time*

Transportation

Accommodations

Personal Itinerary

Arrival *Date*   *Time*

Departure *Date*   *Time*

Transportation

Accommodations

Arrival *Date*   *Time*

Departure *Date*   *Time*

Transportation

Accommodations

Arrival *Date*   *Time*

Departure *Date*   *Time*

Transportation

Accommodations

Arrival *Date*   *Time*

Departure *Date*   *Time*

Transportation

Accommodations

Personal Itinerary

Arrival *Date*   *Time*

Departure *Date*   *Time*

Transportation

Accommodations

Arrival *Date*   *Time*

Departure *Date*   *Time*

Transportation

Accommodations

Arrival *Date*   *Time*

Departure *Date*   *Time*

Transportation

Accommodations

Arrival *Date*   *Time*

Departure *Date*   *Time*

Transportation

Accommodations

Personal Itinerary

Arrival *Date*   *Time*

Departure *Date*   *Time*

Transportation

Accommodations

Arrival *Date*   *Time*

Departure *Date*   *Time*

Transportation

Accommodations

Arrival *Date*   *Time*

Departure *Date*   *Time*

Transportation

Accommodations

Arrival *Date*   *Time*

Departure *Date*   *Time*

Transportation

Accommodations

Addresses

Name _____

Address _____

Telephone _____

Name _____

Address _____

Telephone _____

Name _____

Address _____

Telephone _____

Name _____

Address _____

Telephone _____

Name _____

Address _____

Telephone _____

Name _____

Address _____

Telephone _____

Name _____

Address _____

Telephone _____

Name _____

Address _____

Telephone _____

Name _____

Address _____

Telephone _____

Name _____

Address _____

Telephone _____

Name _____

Address _____

Telephone _____

Name _____

Address _____

Telephone _____

Name _____

Address _____

Telephone _____

Name _____

Address _____

Telephone _____

Name _____

Address _____

Telephone _____

Addresses

Name	*Name*
Address	*Address*
Telephone	*Telephone*
Name	*Name*
Address	*Address*
Telephone	*Telephone*
Name	*Name*
Address	*Address*
Telephone	*Telephone*
Name	*Name*
Address	*Address*
Telephone	*Telephone*
Name	*Name*
Address	*Address*
Telephone	*Telephone*
Name	*Name*
Address	*Address*
Telephone	*Telephone*
Name	*Name*
Address	*Address*
Telephone	*Telephone*
Name	*Name*
Address	*Address*
Telephone	*Telephone*

Fodor's Travel Guides

U.S. Guides

Alaska	Florida	Pacific North Coast	USA
Arizona	Hawaii	Philadelphia & the	The Upper Great
Boston	Las Vegas	Pennsylvania	Lakes Region
California	Los Angeles	Dutch Country	Vacations in
Cape Cod	Maui	Puerto Rico	New York State
The Carolinas & the	Miami & the	(Pocket Guide)	Vacations on the
Georgia Coast	Keys	The Rockies	Jersey Shore
The Chesapeake	New England	San Diego	Virgin Islands
Region	New Mexico	San Francisco	Virginia & Maryland
Chicago	New Orleans	San Francisco	Waikiki
Colorado	New York City	(Pocket Guide)	Washington, D.C.
Disney World & the	New York City	The South	
Orlando Area	(Pocket Guide)	Texas	

Foreign Guides

Acapulco	Central America	Kenya, Tanzania,	Saint Martin/
Amsterdam	China	Seychelles	Sint Maarten
Australia	Eastern Europe	Korea	Scandinavia
Austria	Egypt	Lisbon	Scandinavian Cities
The Bahamas	Europe	London	Scotland
The Bahamas	Europe's Great Cities	London Companion	Singapore
(Pocket Guide)	France	London	South America
Baja & the Pacific	Germany	(Pocket Guide)	South Pacific
Coast Resorts	Great Britain	Madrid & Barcelona	Southeast Asia
Barbados	Greece	Mexico	Soviet Union
Belgium &	The Himalayan	Mexico City	Spain
Luxembourg	Countries	Montreal &	Sweden
Bermuda	Holland	Quebec City	Switzerland
Brazil	Hong Kong	Morocco	Sydney
Budget Europe	India	Munich	Thailand
Canada	Ireland	New Zealand	Tokyo
Canada's Atlantic	Israel	Paris	Toronto
Provinces	Italy	Paris (Pocket Guide)	Turkey
Cancun, Cozumel,	Italy 's Great Cities	Portugal	Vienna & the
Yucatan Peninsula	Jamaica	Rio de Janeiro	Danube Valley
Caribbean	Japan	Rome	Yugoslavia

Wall Street Journal Guides to Business Travel

Europe	International Cities	The Pacific Rim	USA & Canada

Special-Interest Guides

Cruises and Ports	Fodor's Flashmaps	Shopping in Europe	Smart Shopper's
of Call	New York	Skiing in North	Guide to London
Healthy Escapes	Fodor's Flashmaps	America	Sunday in New York
	Washington, D.C.		Touring Europe